The
FOUNDATIONS
of
MINDFULNESS

Also by Eric Harrison

BOOKS

Teach Yourself to Meditate (1993)
Meditation and Health (1999)
The Naked Buddha (1999)
Do You Want to Meditate? (2001)
The 5-Minute Meditator (2005)
The Art of Awareness (2007)

CD RECORDINGS

How to Meditate, Part 1 (2012)
How to Meditate, Part 2 (2012)
Short, Active Meditations (2012)

The
FOUNDATIONS
of
MINDFULNESS

*How to Cultivate
Attention, Good Judgment,
and Tranquility*

ERIC HARRISON

THE EXPERIMENT

NEW YORK

The Experiment, LLC | 220 East 23rd Street, Suite 301 | New York, NY 10010-4674
theexperimentpublishing.com

This book contains the opinions and ideas of its author. It is intended to provide helpful and informative material on the subjects addressed in the book. It is sold with the understanding that the author and publisher are not engaged in rendering medical, health, or any other kind of personal professional services in the book. The author and publisher specifically disclaim all responsibility for any liability, loss, or risk—personal or otherwise—that is incurred as a consequence, directly or indirectly, of the use and application of any of the contents of this book.

Many of the designations used by manufacturers and sellers to distinguish their products are claimed as trademarks. Where those designations appear in this book and The Experiment was aware of a trademark claim, the designations have been capitalized.

The Experiment's books are available at special discounts when purchased in bulk for premiums and sales promotions as well as for fund-raising or educational use. For details, contact us at info@theexperimentpublishing.com.

Library of Congress Cataloging-in-Publication Data

Names: Harrison, Eric, author.
Title: The foundations of mindfulness : how to cultivate attention, good judgment, and tranquility / Eric Harrison.
Description: New York : Experiment, [2017] | Includes bibliographical references and index.
Identifiers: LCCN 2016051345 | ISBN 9781615192564 (hardcover)
Subjects: LCSH: Meditation--Buddhism. | Satipatthana (Buddhism) | Buddhism--Doctrines. | Attention--Religious aspects. | Emotions.
Classification: LCC BQ5612 .H3697 2017 | DDC 158.1/2--dc23
LC record available at https://lccn.loc.gov/2016051345

ISBN 978-1-61519-256-4
Ebook ISBN 978-1-61519-257-1

Cover and interior design by Sarah Smith
Cover illustration *Study of Cumulus Clouds* by John Constable copyright © Rochdale Art Gallery, Lancashire, UK/Bridgeman Images

Manufactured in the United States of America
Distributed by Workman Publishing Company, Inc.
Distributed simultaneously in Canada by Thomas Allen & Son Ltd.

First printing April 2017
10 9 8 7 6 5 4 3 2 1

CONTENTS

INTRODUCTION

Meditation is a simple skill. Having a teacher can help, but meditators often figure it out for themselves. I taught myself to meditate when I was still a teenager, but in 1975 I stumbled on a remarkable twenty-five-hundred-year-old text. This was the *Satipatthana Sutta*, usually translated as *The Foundations of Mindfulness*. The word *sati* means "attention" or "mindfulness," and the word *sutta* means "text." From now on, I'll refer to this text simply as the *Sutta*.[1]

This text is the Buddha's original, do-it-yourself, "how to meditate and be mindful" manual. If a Buddhist knows any original text it is likely to be the *Sutta*. It consists of thirteen groups of exercises and provides the authority for the popular ten-day Burmese-style "Vipassana" retreats. Vipassana, in turn, is the direct inspiration for the use of mindfulness in psychology.

The *Sutta* is only a few pages long. Its great virtue for modern purposes is that it is more about mindfulness practice than Buddhist dogma. The translation I read in 1975 came from the Victorian era, so I converted its outmoded language into modern English, and memorized it. It gave a clear shape to my existing meditation practice and mapped out possibilities I'd never imagined. The *Sutta* has been my touchstone ever since.

Soon afterward I attended my first ten-day Vipassana retreat, led by a young and enthusiastic former monk, Christopher Titmuss. (He is still teaching, and I owe him my thanks.) Memorably, on the third day of that retreat, at 10:30 in the morning, it came to me, with absolute certainty, that my life would revolve around meditation—and so it turned out. Over the next decade I spent a total of eighteen months doing Vipassana, Tibetan, Zen, and yoga retreats.

In 1987 I opened the Perth Meditation Centre and was soon teaching a thousand people each year. From the start, the *Sutta* helped me avoid several pitfalls. For example, most people assume that to meditate we have to sit still with our eyes closed. However, the Buddha said that this is just the starting point. In fact, he regarded sitting meditation as nothing more than the *first* part of the *first* of the four "foundations" of mindfulness.

The Buddha did not identify "mindfulness" with a formal sit-down meditation, as we tend to do nowadays. He viewed mindfulness as a quality of discriminating attention that should be cultivated all day long. In the *Sutta*, he explains how to meditate while sitting, walking, standing, and lying down. He saw this capacity for continual self-observation as essential for tranquility, clear understanding, and good judgment on the inner path. Over my years of teaching, I developed a repertoire of what I call "spot meditations" based on this versatile approach. The *Sutta* was the inspiration for what became the forty-two exercises in my 2005 book, *The 5-Minute Meditator.*

Teaching meditation became my full-time career, and I've written seven books on the subject, but I never had any appetite for Buddhism itself. I dislike the monastic, world-denying values of traditional Buddhism, and its reliance on karma and reincarnation to explain suffering. Conversely, I found popular Buddhism too sentimental and shallow to take seriously. As a meditation teacher, I made it clear that my values were *not* Buddhist, *not* yogic, and *not* New Age. I couldn't abandon my Western lineage even if I tried. My spiritual heroes are Socrates, Aristotle, the natural philosophers of the Enlightenment, and their scientific descendants. When students ask me what I believe in, I usually say that I am a "critical thinker."

Fortunately, in the *Sutta* it is remarkably easy to distinguish meditation practice from Buddhist dogma. Buddhism is not meditation. Meditation is not Buddhism. No one has to buy the Buddhist package, or any part of it, to meditate. We can easily extract the Buddha's superb mind-training techniques from the *Sutta*, and use them for our own purposes. When I opened the Perth Meditation Centre, I was committed to teaching only what I genuinely believed in. So I extracted from the *Sutta* what I found practical for my students and myself and diplomatically neglected the rest.

For most of my peers, however, the relationship between meditation and Buddhism remained problematic. In 1994 I attended a four-day conference of 150 Western meditation teachers in San Francisco, hosted by Jack Kornfield. Most of us were noncelibate, unaffiliated teachers who had studied in Buddhist settings. We discussed the vexed question of how we could conscientiously integrate the Asian monastic tradition with the demands and values of Western civilization. The simple answer seems to be: You can't. They are antagonistic.

En route to the conference, I shared the bus with a molecular biologist from the University of Massachusetts named Jon Kabat-Zinn. His book *Wherever You Go, There You Are* became a bestseller that year and is a landmark in the Modern Mindfulness movement. We had an exciting conversation about the aforementioned difficulties, and his parting words to me were: "Don't give up on meditation just because the Buddhists are crazy!"

Over the following years I pursued my own studies in science and psychology and hoped for the time when meditation could be regarded as scientifically sound. Two more big conferences and a decade later, I despaired that this would ever happen in my lifetime. My peers valued Buddhism much more than I did and were more likely to identify with it. As a meditation teacher who was trying to be as rational and non-mystical as possible, I felt very isolated.

Then, around 2005, the situation started to change. The most telling sign was a change of name. As a teacher, I get phone calls every week from prospective students. Many callers used to say, "My psychologist [or doctor] has told me to learn meditation." Now they were saying, "My psychologist has told me to learn *mindfulness*." The technique hadn't changed, but "meditation" had mysteriously morphed into "mindfulness." How did this happen?

The explanation starts with the *Sutta*. Early last century in Burma, there was a revival of meditation practice which drew its methodology directly from the *Sutta*. As a *lay*, not monastic, movement it had no precedent in Buddhist history.

Its leader, the charismatic politician U Ba Khin, established the International Meditation Centre (IMC) in 1952 and authorized laymen *and* -women *and* Westerners as teachers. This secular movement was reinforced by the great reformer monk Mahasi Sayadaw, who was also an enthusiastic teacher of laypeople.

IMC established the model of ten-day Vipassana retreats that have since swept the world. The retreats were known for being "just meditation, not Buddhism," and it wasn't long before many Westerners (including me) were leading meditation retreats for purposes far removed from the original Buddhist goals.

One of these new purposes was pain management. In 1979 Jon Kabat-Zinn faithfully adapted the format of the ten-day Vipassana retreat into an eight-week wellness program at the University of Massachusetts Medical School. He called the new therapy "mindfulness-based stress reduction" (MBSR). Originally designed for people in chronic pain, it was soon adapted for broader psychological use. Other therapies had independently promoted mindfulness, but MBSR, as a single-method discipline, quickly became the market leader.

Mindfulness seemed to work. The research followed. Educators, athletes, the self-help industry, corporate trainers, and even the military took it up. The wave of interest became a tsunami. In the popular press, "mindfulness" as a label more or less came to trump "meditation." So was this just a fashion-driven change of name or is there a genuine difference?

When I ask my students why they want to learn to meditate, they typically say something like "I'm too anxious. I can't stop thinking and I have trouble sleeping." Basic meditation practice can be ideal for them. This involves two skills. The first is learning to relax quickly and consciously. The second is learning to pay attention, and so control runaway thought. Meditation is a perfect way to learn relaxation and attention at the same time. Focusing on the body relaxes it, and the act of focusing weakens our habitual thoughts and calms the mind.

As sit-down practices, mindfulness and meditation are identical. No beginner could make any distinction between them. Same rootstock. Same benefits. Same skills: relaxation and attention. Very few people and very few therapies go beyond this point, and perhaps they don't need to. The benefits of this alone can be life changing. So does it matter that popular writers now call this technique "mindfulness" rather than "meditation"?

It does. "Mindfulness" and "meditation" are not naked, stand-alone concepts. "Meditation" comes from monastic traditions based on withdrawal from the world. It is related to Buddhism, yoga, and New Age spirituality, and it is usually explained in spiritual terms. Anyone who attends a course or reads a book about meditation will likely encounter spirituality as an embedded value of meditation practice within minutes. The implication is that anyone who is seriously interested in meditation will need to explore that spiritual hinterland.

"Mindfulness," by contrast, is more clearly related to psychology, scientific research, and rational thought. Mindfulness practice is more about Stoic acceptance than monastic withdrawal. It is about coping better with life's complexities, changing what you can and adjusting to what you can't. It is not about trying to escape from the world. "Mindfulness," in other words, can embrace the whole field of self-observation, self-improvement, and our messy ordinary lives in a way that "meditation" (as "time out") never could.

Fortunately, psychologists have now extracted these practices from the grip of Eastern spirituality. We can be grateful to Kabat-Zinn and the other early writers who managed to import meditation into the mainstream of Western culture. Equally important is the fact that people are discussing "mindfulness" in a serious way. The concept of mindfulness has finally been met with a critical, analytic language and an ongoing debate that "meditation" for the most part has lacked.

And yet, thirty-eight years after Jon Kabat-Zinn launched his seminal mindfulness program at the University of Massachusetts, no consensus has yet materialized about what mindfulness actually is. Buddhists, psychologists, and popular writers all have differing views of it. Ignorance of the past and half-truths are endemic. Poor-quality research and extravagant promotional claims muddy the waters.

If you feel confused by all this, realize you are not alone. In 2012 the researchers David Vago and David Silbersweig summed up what they called "the major problem in the field right now": "There remains no single 'correct' or 'authoritative' definition of mindfulness and the concept is often trivialized and conflated with many common interpretations."[2] Mindfulness is popular for the simple reason that it works, but it still lacks scientific credibility. Why is this?

Aristotle, who established more scientific disciplines than any other person in history, said that a science has to start with a clear axiomatic definition free of ambiguities.

Unfortunately, "mindfulness" as we now use it has no core meaning that could form the basis of a scientific discipline. It is a conglomeration of disparate meanings. It is variously used to describe a meditation practice (Vipassana); a cognitive function (attention); a psychotherapy (mindfulness-based cognitive therapy); an ideal state of mind (nonjudgmental acceptance); a way of life (as with the countercultural imperative made famous by Ram Dass: "Be here now"); and the essence of Buddhism itself. Throughout this book, and to distinguish it from the Buddha's quite different use of the term, I will refer to this protean bundle as "Modern Mindfulness." For ease of use I will define Modern Mindfulness as "a state of nonjudgmental acceptance."

Strange to say, "to be mindful" in common usage is *not* a confusing term. It has been doing good service in the English language since the fourteenth century. "To be mindful" means "to pay attention to what you are doing to avoid mistakes or improve performance." This straightforward meaning is also compatible with the way the Buddha uses the term.

Since there is no dispute that the *Satipatthana Sutta* is the source of Vipassana, of mindfulness-based stress reduction, and of the various permutations of Modern Mindfulness, it would seem useful to go back to those "foundations of mindfulness" and see what the Buddha originally said.

Unfortunately, it is not easy to just dip into the *Satipatthana Sutta*. The standard English translation is almost indecipherable to a newcomer. It is clogged with long and numerous liturgical refrains, jargon words, and the Victorian oratory of its first translator. It is hard to hack a way through all this to the lean and muscular training discipline at its core. So nearly everyone who tries to read the *Sutta* soon gives up or, at best, scavenges a few ideas.

That first translator was T. W. Rhys Davids, a Victorian administrator in Ceylon. He and his extended team worked from 1881 to 1925 to translate the vast corpus of early Buddhist texts from the original Pali language. Without him, that work might still be untranslated. Because his pioneering efforts were so magisterial and comprehensive, no one has attempted a genuinely new translation since. The Pali Text Society (PTS) that he founded is the unchallenged custodian of that work in English, and their latest edition of the *Sutta*, with Bhikkhu Bodhi as its editor, was published by Wisdom Books in 1995.

I imagine that Bodhi and I agree fairly well on matters of interpretation, but our translations are vastly different. His translation fills eleven large pages. Mine takes four smaller ones. His version omits a few of the thirteen liturgical refrains. I omit nearly all of them. His version describes at length certain archaic practices (such as meditating on corpses) that I pass over in a sentence. Without excluding anything, I give priority to the practical application of the Buddha's mind-training methods for rational twenty-first-century Westerners like myself. I have tried to highlight the clear lines of the discipline and avoid getting tangled in detail. (Throughout this book, when I quote the *Satipatthana Sutta*, I will be quoting from my version, included here as chapter 12.)

In the *Satipatthana Sutta*, the Buddha builds a systematic four-stage training program on the concept of attention (*sati*) in a way that would certainly have impressed Aristotle. The language is plain and direct. The terms are clearly defined. The methodology and goals are obvious. If the *Sutta* were better known, it would at least give a coherent and logical alternative to the modern versions of mindfulness.

So what exactly is mindfulness, according to the Buddha? In 1881 Rhys Davids, for his own reasons, chose to translate the *Sutta*'s crucial term *sati* as "mindfulness." In fact, *sati* means "attention" in exactly the way a modern cognitive psychologist would understand that word. To be more precise, *sati* means the kind of purposeful attention that can discriminate good and bad, right or wrong, useful and useless in any situation.

In the *Satipatthana Sutta*, the word *sati* is inseparable from two other terms that help to define it. It is often linked to a word (*sampajjana*) that literally means "accurate understanding" but in practice is used in the sense of "evaluation" or "good judgment." A clear perception of a sensation, thought, or emotion lets us evaluate it in the context of our larger goals.

Furthermore, *sati* is linked to a word (*atapi*) that means "strong intention." This implies purpose and goal-directed behavior. For example, the Buddha's monks weren't just sitting around being peaceful, living in the present, and waiting for insight. They were striving "ardently" to cut off all their attachments to the world and become enlightened.

The four sections of the *Sutta* are: Mindfulness of the Body; Mindfulness of Emotion; Mindfulness of States of Mind; and Mindfulness of Thought. These are the four "foundations" or "training disciplines" or "contemplations" or "objects of attention" that make up the *Sutta*, and all four are necessary. As the Buddha said, "The systematic four-stage training of attention is the only way to Enlightenment."

This book loosely follows this fourfold structure. The first ten chapters correspond to the large "mindfulness of the body" section that opens the *Sutta*. These chapters cover very thoroughly, and with some side trips, what we recognize as standard meditation practice. Done well, this body-based meditation leads to profound states of tranquility, pleasure, mental control, and a degree of philosophic detachment. For readers who regard mindfulness and meditation as being more or less identical, and who have little interest in the full application of mindfulness, these chapters will be quite sufficient.

The rest of this book is the graduate level. In chapters 11–15, I offer my own version of the *Sutta*. I give a full analysis of the Buddha's key term *sati* according to the traditional commentaries, and I explain how the *Sutta* works as a training manual. In chapters 16–22, I explain the training disciplines relating to the other three foundations of the *Sutta*: namely, mindfulness of emotion, of states of mind, and of thought. The last four chapters discuss the modern applications of mindfulness.

The title of this book, *The Foundations of Mindfulness*, happens to be the common translation of the title of the *Satipatthana Sutta*. This entire book is my commentary on this text. I will also use the word "foundation" in another way. I describe how the *Sutta*, despite its antiquity, can still be an excellent foundation for a systematic mind-training discipline based on meditation. It has certainly been the foundation for my own practice since 1975. It has also served as the foundational manual for my career as a meditation teacher since 1987.

The Buddha was a clear-minded, systematic philosopher, but we should be willing to acknowledge that his values are often at odds with ours. Not everything about traditional Buddhism is automatically benign or unquestionably wise. I believe it shows him far more respect as a human being to present his doctrines accurately, rather than airbrush them for broader appeal.

The Buddha was a real man. We know what he said. There is no mystery about what he taught. We have tens of thousands of words attributed to him, collected in the colossal body of original Pali-language texts known as the Pali Canon. Those texts suggest that he was not at all as sympathetic as the Buddha of the modern imagination. He hardly ever mentioned compassion. That is more of a Tibetan theme. Above all, he was an ascetic who regarded all sensual pleasures and worldly pursuits as antagonistic to inner peace.

Many of us will feel that we have a reasonably coherent idea of Buddhism, but this is more of a modern construction than we realize. We can think of it as Western Buddhism. It is typically a mixture of various forms of Buddhism along with whatever Christian, Stoic, liberal, New Age, psychological, and spiritual values seem compatible with it. This is vastly different from original Buddhism. When I talk about Buddhism, however, I will refer *only* to what the historical Buddha originally taught. This means that any beliefs and opinions that I attribute to the historical Buddha can be readily corroborated by the Pali Canon.

DISCRIMINATING ATTENTION OR NONJUDGMENTAL ACCEPTANCE?

Although this book is a commentary on the *Sutta*, I still need to address one huge contradiction in the field. The Buddha understood mindfulness (*sati*) as the function of discriminating attention. The very purpose of attention is to refine our capacity for accurate judgment and decision-making in all matters, big and small. So how did "mindfulness" become so widely used in a sense that is virtually the opposite: a state of nonjudgmental acceptance? How did this everyday cognitive function turn into an ideal meditative state of mind?

The journey that *sati* takes from the Buddha to Modern Mindfulness is quite direct, but it mutates each step of the way. *Sati* means "attention." This is basically a verb or an action. When Rhys Davids chose instead to translate it as "mindfulness," he converted it into a noun and a "thing." This means that "mindfulness" could then be used as a label for the ten-day Vipassana retreats based on the *Sutta*.

When Kabat-Zinn developed his MBSR program from the ten-day Vipassana retreat format, it was natural for him to call it "mindfulness-based stress reduction." However, when he defined mindfulness itself, he changed its meaning yet again. Kabat-Zinn was a dedicated Zen practitioner long before he encountered Vipassana. So he used the word "mindfulness" to describe not "attention" but the ideal Zen state of mind. This is usually called *sunyata*, or "emptiness."

Since he couldn't use spiritual terms for his secular program, he alluded to it through adjectives instead. He defined mindfulness as "a state of nonjudgmental acceptance" along with a passive "openness" to present moment experience. This is a remarkably accurate, workable description of *sunyata*, or "emptiness." In fact, nearly everything Kabat-Zinn says about mindfulness throughout all his books reflects his strong identification with Zen.

To summarize, *sati* as "attention" refers to an ordinary cognitive function. We automatically or consciously pay attention to things all day long. Modern Mindfulness, on the other hand, refers to an ideal state of mind ("emptiness") which is really only attainable in meditation. There is room for both interpretations in the mindfulness field, but it would help to recognize that they refer to fundamentally different things.

While writing this book, I have kept several prospective readers in mind. Although this is not intended as a self-help book, it does contain some spin-off exercises that a novice meditator can try out immediately. I've also considered the keen meditator who is confused by the mindfulness literature; the young psychologist who wishes she could make more sense of it all; the researchers who are struggling to define the phenomena; and the Western Buddhist who has not yet tackled the *Sutta*. I hope I can offer something of value to each of you.

I could not have written this book without the help of many others. I am indebted to the psychiatrists and psychologists who have generously shared their knowledge and resources with me. I would particularly like to thank Mark Craigie, Kate James, and Jane Genovese. My thanks are also due to my friend, colleague, and researcher Paul Majewski, who has shaped this book in more ways than he can imagine.

Perth, Australia
November 2016

SOME USEFUL TERMS

Three Definitions of Mindfulness

Vernacular English: to pay attention to what you are doing to avoid mistakes and improve performance; to be mindful of one's actions and their consequences.

Sati: attention, or the conscious perception and evaluation of something. The *Sutta* invites us to systematically observe our body sensations, emotions, states of mind, and thought, in order to refine our responses.

Modern Mindfulness: a state of open, nonjudgmental acceptance usually associated with meditation.

• • •

Satipatthana Sutta: This is the original Buddhist text usually translated into English as *The Foundations of Mindfulness*.

the Sutta: a shorthand term for the *Satipatthana Sutta*.

sutta: an original sermon, talk, or discourse from the Buddha.

the Pali Canon: the huge collection of original *sutta* and monastic rules compiled in the Pali language about twenty-five-hundred years ago. The *Sutta* is the tenth in an important collection of 152 *sutta* called *The Middle-Length Discourses of the Buddha*.

satipatthana: the mind-training method taught in the *Satipatthana Sutta*.

the Theravada: the school of Buddhism found in Southeast Asia and Sri Lanka that is closest to the Pali Canon. The adjective is "Theravadin."

the Mahayana: the later schools of Buddhism found in Tibet, China, Vietnam, Korea, and Japan. These have their own scriptures independent of the Pali Canon. The Theravada and Mahayana are philosophically antagonistic to each other, like Catholic and Protestant, and are geographically isolated by the Himalayas.

vipassana: literally "insight" or "inquiry." This is a modern Burmese form of meditation based on the *Sutta*. It is the source of the popular ten-day Vipassana retreats now found throughout the world.

sampajjana: the accurate understanding of something. Evaluation and good judgment. An integral aspect of *sati* (mindfulness).

passaddhi: a state of body-mind stillness attained in meditation. Tranquility and the absence of anxiety or desire.

upekkha: a state of equanimity and philosophic detachment. The ultimate goal of most Buddhist practice.

zazen: the name for Zen sitting meditation.

shikantaza: the practice of "just sitting" (and "not thinking") that goes with the Soto Zen form of *zazen*. The Modern Mindfulness model derives more from *shikantaza* than from *satipatthana*.

emptiness: an alert, thought-free state of mind, most commonly attained in *zazen*. It is associated with stillness, passivity and a nonreactive openness to sensory experience.

Open Monitoring: the practice of monitoring the passing phenomena of the moment without focusing on anything in particular. A non-reactive, "just watching" state encouraged by Modern Mindfulness.

MBSR: mindfulness-based stress reduction. The eight-week training program in Modern Mindfulness that is the gold standard for research.

PART ONE

The First Foundation:
Mindfulness of the Body

1

The Standard
Meditation Practice

*How does a monk live contemplating the body? He
goes to the forest, to the foot of a tree, or to an empty
hut. He sits down cross-legged, holds his body erect,
and focuses on the breath in front of himself.*
—**Satipatthana Sutta**

The words "mindfulness" and "meditation" are often regarded as interchangeable, but can these activities occur separately? Can we meditate without being mindful, or be mindful without meditating? To help distinguish these two terms, I will start with an explanation of ordinary sitting meditation.

What people actually do when they meditate is very simple, and remarkably similar for nearly everyone. Meditating could be an innate biological function, like language or musical appreciation, that we are all capable of, given the right circumstances. The basic procedure, or the rootstock, is so uniform across cultures and eras that I call it "the Standard Meditation Practice."

This is how you do it (I'll now address you as a student): You sit in a chair—or on the floor, or you lie down—with your eyes closed for fifteen minutes or more. This is not sufficient in itself. You still need to "do" something with your mind. You now focus in a gentle but deliberate, exploratory fashion on your breath or on your body in some way. This is the mental function we call "selective, sustained attention." In Pali, this aspect of mindfulness is called *vitakka-vicara* (see chapter 14).

While focusing on your body, you are bound to notice unrelated thoughts periodically, but you try to engage with them as little as possible. You "notice" them but try not to "process" them. This trouble-shooting function is called "peripheral monitoring" or "distraction control," and it is a key attentional skill. It is just as important as sustaining focus on the body. No one can meditate well unless they also learn to manage peripheral thoughts economically.

Within ten minutes your body is bound to relax, even with intermittent focus. It will usually take an extra five minutes for your mind to settle. You are instinctively gravitating toward a place of inner balance. This is a homeostatic set point: the lowest degree of arousal and muscle tone possible without falling asleep. If you remain moderately alert and in control, as you should, your mind will also become much quieter than usual.

Occasionally you will go further than this. Your body will become extremely calm, and your mind will fall silent for shorter or longer periods. All anxiety and desire has vanished. When this occurs, we call it a state of "body-mind stillness." The Pali term for this is *passaddhi*, which is also translated as "tranquility."

This is the core of nearly all meditation practices: sitting still, eyes closed, focusing continuously on the body and monitoring peripheral thoughts for fifteen minutes or more. With practice you gradually improve your ability to remain focused and to weaken the process of active thought. These are the two essential skills in any meditation practice: sustained attention to the body and the control of thought.

These are like the skills necessary for driving a car. They are not complicated, but you can't approach body-mind stillness without them. They form the backbone for a huge range of practices. Yoga, Vipassana, Transcendental Meditation, mindfulness-based stress reduction, Tibetan, and Zen practices tick all of those boxes.

Of course meditation can be far more elaborate. It is easy to add mantra, visualization, special postures and rituals, or spiritual beliefs and aspirations to the Standard Meditation Practice. People do benefit from styles they find congenial. Likewise, many people find it useful to have at least one or two psychological props in place to meditate well: for instance a candle, a statue, incense, or a special cushion or piece of furniture.

I estimate that 90 percent of regular meditators do what is essentially a Standard Meditation Practice. Furthermore, 90 percent of the body-mind benefits of any meditation probably come from the Standard Meditation Practice component within it. The ideological packaging that makes up the extra 10 percent is far more prominent, but the Standard Meditation Practice is always the workhorse.

Whenever we think of meditation, something like the Standard Meditation Practice comes to mind, even for nonmeditators. Tai chi, yoga, prayer, positive thinking, chanting, and reflections on spiritual ideas can also be regarded as meditations, but we usually think of them under their own designations. I also train people to meditate with eyes open, in various activities, and for very short periods as described in my book *The 5-Minute Meditator*, but I know this is considered to be peculiar and "nonstandard." For most people, if you're not sitting down with closed eyes for several minutes you can't be meditating.

The Standard Meditation Practice is the universal paradigm. Stripped to its essence, "meditating" means "focusing continuously on the body." To do this means *not* pursuing your usual thoughts and *not* relating to the outer world. This primary emphasis on the body is reflected in the *Satipatthana Sutta*. Its large first section is called "Mindfulness of the Body," and it presents many different ways of focusing on the body.

TRANQUILITY AND MINDFULNESS

Let's now make a distinction. Buddhism talks about "tranquility" practices (Sanskrit: *samadhi*) and "mindfulness" practices (Pali: *sati*). The Standard Meditation Practice is a tranquility practice. Novice-level *samadhi* practice leads to a relaxed body with some degree of mental stillness and emotional calm. Expert-level *samadhi* practice leads to the four stages of absorption or trance called *jhana* in the Pali Canon (see chapter 18). "Mindfulness meditation" (*sati*) is not vastly different from tranquility meditation. It just adds a higher quality of observation to the meditation.

Mindfulness is metacognitive. This means that you don't just mechanically meditate and gradually feel better.

You also observe *how* you are meditating. This conscious perception of physical and mental phenomena leads to fine, intuitive adjustments that subtly accelerate the process. *Sati* also contributes to spin-off "insights" or bright ideas that are unlikely to occur in pure tranquility meditations.

To meditate on the breath is a Standard Meditation Practice (*samadhi*). However, we are also being mindful (*sati*) whenever we monitor what else is happening. When we check the quality of our focus, or resist distractions, or relax unnecessary tension, we are being mindful (*sati*) within a tranquility practice (*samadhi*). The Buddha said that to be mindful means that we know what is happening as it happens *and can describe it to ourselves* (see chapter 15).

Mindfulness, like any form of attention, has an important error-detection function. We notice the discrepancies and imbalances between where we actually are (slightly tense and worried, for example) and where we want to be. This recognition helps the body's homeostatic systems adjust toward the ideal. ("Loosen that shoulder. Soften the breath. Abandon that thought.") In other words, *sati* refines and accelerates the physiological movement toward stillness. If you just sit, and wait, and count the breaths with little reflection, your progress toward tranquility will be much slower and may not seem worth the amount of time involved.

We can make another distinction. Tranquility meditation is goal-directed. It aims for an ideal state of body-mind stillness—*passaddhi*, discussed in more detail shortly—that is usually dependent on long, seated meditation. When we are mindful, however, we notice what is happening *in the moment*, which is hardly ever that perfect or ideal. Mindfulness (*sati*) has a different orientation: to see and evaluate things accurately, while they are actually happening. And we can become mindful in an instant.

So can we be mindful without sitting down and meditating for several minutes? Of course we can. "To be mindful" in common usage—to pay attention to what we are doing—has no Standard Meditation Practice component at all. In mental health counselling, cognitive behavioral therapy develops a high degree of "mindfulness of thought" without a hint of meditation. Likewise, acceptance and commitment therapy recommends very short interventionist bursts of mindfulness as required. And, going back to the *Satipatthana Sutta*, the Buddha said that we should be able to evaluate and fine-tune our thoughts, emotions, and behavior at any time and in any activity. Even in Buddhism, mindfulness is not reliant on the practice of sitting down to meditate. So why do a formal meditation practice at all?

Although the principles are easy to understand, practice is essential for improvement. Attending seminars, or reading books on the subject, or even teaching it to clients, will increase our knowledge of mindfulness but not our ability to do it. The inertia of habit guarantees that we can't improve our level of skill in any domain without deliberate, self-monitoring practice over time. Learning to relax quickly and consciously is a physical skill. Learning to control attention and thought is a cognitive skill. Doing a formal sitting meditation is a good way to practice both at once.

BODY-MIND STILLNESS, OR *PASSADDHI*

A Standard Meditation Practice naturally gravitates toward a homeostatic ideal of inner stillness. This is a state in which the body is optimally relaxed: low muscle tone and low arousal. The body is no longer restless or primed for movement, and the mind is as calm and quiet as possible. The Buddha said that this inner stillness—*passaddhi*, in Pali—is the antidote to the mental hindrance that he called "agitation and worry." In other words, stillness dissolves anxiety.

This physical stillness matures into a mental silence. A well-directed, focused mind is not at the mercy of random thought, and the inner chatter really can stop for long periods. This mental control and inner stillness supports the delightful sense of space or freedom that meditators often report. A meditator may even say, "My mind was completely empty," but the reality is more nuanced.

The mind can feel very calm, but it is never empty or perfectly still. Our minds can no more stop completely than can our digestive or immune systems. The mind is obliged to continuously monitor sensory data and to process what has happened in the immediate past, even when we are asleep. In other words, thinking never stops. Physical stillness and inner silence is the state of optimal baseline cognitive functioning, but it is not complete vacancy.

Given these provisos, why is body-mind stillness (*passaddhi*) worth pursuing? Why is it so important to be able to sit down, do nothing, and be quiet? It is quite hard to do: Just ask any schoolchild. It is akin to boredom, and it doesn't seem very productive. It turns out that being calm, centered, and mentally controlled is foundational for many life skills.

Most of the psychological benefits of mindfulness start here. To sit still for long periods means learning to be "nonreactive." A meditator learns to stop the compulsive inclination toward thought or action. He can notice an emerging thought without elaborating on it. He can notice a physical impulse (for instance, toward food, drugs, or anger) and let it fade. He can notice pain or a bad mood dispassionately and accept its presence, rather than trying to fix it.

In meditation, this mental quality is often described as a "just watching" state, or as "nonjudgmental acceptance," or as the "observer mind." This leads to a sense of emotional detachment and objectivity toward what is happening. Psychologists regard this lowering of reactivity, and the retraining of it as a habit, as crucial for emotional health. And all these good results rely on the control of attention.

Body-mind stillness, emotional detachment, and the observer mind are values implicit in the Standard Meditation Practice, and they work synergistically. Stillness, as the lowering of arousal and muscle tone, is a *physical* skill. Detachment is an *emotional* skill. The observer mind is a *cognitive* skill. Being still and doing almost nothing may seem like a waste of time, but it has many spin-off benefits. When we finish our Standard Meditation Practice, we should be physically calm, mentally clear, somewhat refreshed, and above all, ready to reenter the world of action.

2

Anxiety and the Overactive Mind

How does a monk contemplate his states of mind?…
When his mind is caught in Desire, he knows: "This
is Desire." When his mind is free of Desire, he knows:
"This is the mind free of Desire." He carefully observes
how desire arises and passes away, and what causes
it to do so. He learns how to extinguish desire when
it arises, and how to prevent it arising in the future.
In the same manner, he examines the four other
Hindrances, namely Anger, Lethargy,
Anxiety, and Despair.
—SATIPATTHANA SUTTA

When I ask my students why they want to learn to meditate, one reason consistently comes out on top: They are too anxious. They have runaway minds and sleep poorly. They may also have chronic muscle tension, headaches, pain, and poor digestion. They feel off-color and irritable most of the time. Their mood is low. They feel mentally dull, unable to focus or to enjoy life. If they have tried sedatives or anti-depressants, those didn't seem to work.

This is the normal anxiety bundle. It involves the whole body and mind, not just mood. Psychologists try to improve mood but tend to neglect the body. Meditation takes the opposite approach. It tackles anxiety from the body up. It releases muscle tension, lowers agitation, and improves sleep as the crucial first steps.

Anxiety is a 24/7 state of chronic arousal and muscle tension. Anxious people remain tenser than they need to be, even while they're sleeping. Their cortisol levels remain elevated. They spend less time in deep sleep. They are likely to wake up frequently during the night, and they won't feel rested in the morning.

It can be surprisingly hard to recognize our own level of anxiety. It is easily masked by hyperactivity and a sense of excitement. When we're young, anxiety actually makes us more productive because of the effects of adrenaline and cortisol. Over time, however, anxiety can creep invisibly into our habits of thought and behavior in a way that becomes destructive. We can easily mistake it as a normal part of our character ("I was born anxious"). An anxious person never has anxiety-free periods. It is embedded in her body in the form of higher baseline levels of arousal and muscle tension.

When we finally recognize anxiety as a problem that could be solved, we've usually been anxious for years. We will still tend to underestimate or minimize its effects. Students who come to my classes often say, "I'm just feeling a bit anxious these days." Fortunately, their psychologist or doctor will often set them straight: "This is anxiety. It deserves to be taken seriously."

Pills and quick-fix palliative techniques are not much use against entrenched anxiety, but mindfulness is promising. If we build a habit of self-observation, we can gradually chip away at the problem. If we notice a clenched jaw or a runaway thought or an emotional overreaction, we can start to undermine it in that very moment.

This is the value of doing short, frequent "reset" meditations during the day. To release a tension "on the spot" is a small but very real improvement, and its effects are cumulative. It is much better to dissolve anxiety through hundreds of small adjustments rather than hoping that occasional long meditations will do it.

Anxiety naturally builds on itself. If we don't relax well, our baseline levels of arousal and muscle tension just keep increasing as the years go by. Trying to push on regardless can be an acceptable short-term solution, but it is dreadful in the long run. Trying to ignore the way we feel (that is, being unmindful) paradoxically increases tension, cortisol levels, and cognitive failings.

We can regard anxiety as maladaptive fear. Fear and worry in themselves can be helpful emotions. Fear enables us to respond rapidly to a threat. Worry helps us anticipate and prepare for future problems. Anxiety, however, is directed indiscriminately and ineffectually toward everything. We lose perspective, and even small problems can feel like crises.

Fear sharpens the mind and heightens our perceptions under threat, but anxiety just makes us agitated and confused. We feel bad and don't know what to do about it. Fear is short-lasting, and worry should come and go according to circumstances, but anxiety can set in for a lifetime. Because fear and worry are essential to our well-being, they tend to stay active in the brain and body long after they have ceased to be useful. We do relax a bit after a stressful email or the drive to work, but usually not much, and not very quickly. A new baseline will have been set.

After a high-energy event, we don't relax completely. We settle back into a state of mild overarousal that intuitively feels safe, given what has just happened. We remain partially fired up just in case another "predator" is lurking. This edgy, "looking around for danger" state makes it hard for us to focus adequately on what we are doing. If we are habitually more stirred up than we need to be for the task at hand, we can self-diagnose this as "anxiety" or "stress."

We are all descendants of African ancestors who responded quickly and without deliberation to potential threats either by fighting, fleeing, or freezing. This bias toward a knee-jerk response doesn't help when we have to make decisions more complex than "fight or flight." Anxiety makes us think too quickly to be productive. It is the *mental* equivalent of the fight-or-flight response.

Anxiety typically leads to an overactive, runaway, obsessive mind. Our thoughts take over. We can't stop them or direct them. We overreact to everything indiscriminately. Even when we are exhausted, the mind doesn't give up, and its incessant chatter can keep us awake at night.

Anxiety is like coffee. It increases arousal and energy consumption. It makes more energy available in the bloodstream, but we also burn through it more quickly. Coffee in the morning charges us up, but we can feel exhausted by midafternoon. Anxiety depletes us in the same way. This means that we can feel anxiety both as high-energy agitation and as low-energy dullness and muddle.

In the high-energy state, the mind is too fast. It jumps too rapidly from one thought to another on impulse, without reflection. It constantly scans the periphery for danger or advantage. It is easily distracted and can't concentrate. This rapid thought switching can give us the illusion of being busy and therefore productive.

Unfortunately, burning energy is not the same as doing things well. Shifting attention is always an expensive maneuver. We lose energy and a few seconds each time we shift focus and have to adjust our mental settings to another thought or action. If we do this several times a minute, we burn through our reserves very quickly. Multitasking is one of the most wasteful activities we can ever attempt to do.

If the mind is too speedy, it doesn't spend enough time with any one issue to process it adequately. We leave behind a trail of unfinished, ill-digested actions that we often have to return to and patch up afterward. For mental efficiency it is much better to slow down, pay attention, and keep the thought switching to a minimum. Just a few seconds more with any one issue would be a vast improvement.

Anxiety can also be a *low-energy* state. When our energy is depleted, the mind gets too tired to focus at all. It drifts uncontrollably from one thought to another at the mercy of any distraction, or it defaults to its habitual worries. It can't follow a train of thought productively and often just spaces out.

When we are tired and fretful, we can still function and apparently get through the day, but there is a price. We won't be mindful enough to adequately monitor what we are doing. We will probably be forgetful and neglect important details. Our mood will be poor, with little enjoyment or enthusiasm. We will also be worried that we are not functioning well, which is of course an accurate assessment.

This combination of low energy, dull attention, scrappy performance, poor recall, irritability, and foul mood can make us feel we are not coping well at all. In fact, this is a rule-of-thumb definition of stress. Whether the demands on you are heavy or light, you can say that you are "stressed" if you feel that you don't have the inner or outer resources to cope with them. One more email or harsh comment can make you snap.

An estimated 10 to 20 percent of the population of developed countries is likely to be suffering from anxiety at any one time, and it is a common component of other maladies. People with free-floating anxiety are often diagnosed as having a generalized anxiety disorder. About a quarter of such people will also face the horror of panic attacks. These sudden eruptions of paralytic fear can occur without any obvious trigger and are often mistaken for heart attacks.

Habitual anxiety, the high-energy state, often leads inexorably over the years into mild depression, the low-energy state. With no energy or enthusiasm, many people give in to a sense of futility. They get trapped in dull, obsessive, circular patterns of thought. They eat, drink, smoke, shop, watch TV, or sleep to excess, and with varying degrees of self-loathing.

Many fall into the roundabout of legal drugs (antidepressants and sedatives). For many people, these only seem to be helpful in the short term, and their benefits are by no means obvious. The legal drugs often have wide-ranging and unpredictable side effects over time. For many people, there is a significant risk that prolonged use is more likely to exacerbate their low mood rather than alleviate it.

All this anguish can start with feeling just a bit anxious. Since chronic anxiety naturally edges upward from existing levels of arousal, it is well worth trying to reverse it at an early stage. Fairly minor interventions are usually enough to maintain existing levels and prevent blowouts. With deliberate training, however, it is possible to reverse and virtually cure anxiety. It all starts with relaxing the body, and controlling attention and thought.

3

The Breath Meditation

Mindfully he breathes in and mindfully he breathes out. When inhaling a long breath, he thinks: "I am inhaling a long breath." When exhaling a long breath, he thinks: "I am exhaling a long breath." Likewise, he knows when he is breathing in or out a short breath. He is like a skilled turner who knows when he is making a long or short turn on the lathe.

—Satipatthana Sutta

We can define meditation very simply. It means to focus continuously on the breath or on the body in some way. This is a crude but remarkably adequate definition. There are dozens of possible ways of doing this, but they all have the same modus operandi.

Meditation trains us to feel our bodies more vividly from the inside. In particular we learn to read the real-time, ever-changing sensations coming from the musculature and the internal organs. This is how we become mindful of tension, arousal, energy levels, balance, pain, comfort, and the quality of our health at any moment. This cognitive process is called "interoception" (literally, "inner-perception"), and it makes our mental map of our bodies more accessible to consciousness.

The technical name for this mental map is the "body schema." Originally this term only applied to musculoskeletal information. I'm using it a broader whole-body sense, as many people now do. The body schema is in fact a composite image. Signals from the muscles are mapped in the somatosensory cortex of the brain. Signals from the internal organs—the viscera—are mapped in the insula. Other signals are mapped elsewhere in the brain. Nonetheless, we always sense the body schema as an integrated whole.

Over time a meditator cultivates a rich attunement to her body schema, almost without realizing it. Simply paying good attention to the body for long enough will eventually achieve this attunement. Many of the lasting benefits of meditation rely on this feeling of being "grounded" or "centered" or "embodied." This deeper, conscious familiarity with the body is another reason why it feels so good to meditate. Without this anchor, we can easily get caught in the world of perpetual thought.

Some people prefer to meditate on the breath. Others prefer to explore the body. This chapter will focus on breath meditations, and "body scan" meditations will be discussed in chapter 5. The distinction is somewhat arbitrary, since each implies the other. We couldn't focus on the breath without also being aware of the body, and vice versa. It is simply a question of which is consciously in the foreground and which is in the background. Focusing on either is guaranteed to strengthen our conscious perception of the body schema.

The breath meditation is easy to understand and do. Body scanning is more complex and detailed. In the *Sutta*, the Buddha starts with the breath meditation and develops it immediately into the body scan meditation. In two other important texts from the Pali Canon, *Mindfulness of the Breath* and *Mindfulness of the Body*, he treats them as entirely separate meditations. Each of these ancient practices has developed many variants, but the ten-day Vipassana retreats and the MBSR program that introduced mindfulness to psychology both derive from the original meditations as described in the *Sutta*.

Focusing on the breath is often presented as a complete description of meditation itself, but this is a mistake. Meditating is more about cultivating total body awareness and developing the cognitive skill of focusing itself. The breath is just one point of entry into the body schema. Nor does the breath meditation suit everyone. Many people actively dislike it and prefer scanning the body. Focusing on the breath makes some people more, not less, anxious, and many get caught up in the trap of trying to breathe "correctly."

We can make another distinction. The body scan is a superb way of releasing subtle *muscle tension*. It works directly on the musculoskeletal system. As soon as we notice unnecessary muscle tension, it is easy to start releasing much of it. To give the body more attention than usual, as we do when we meditate, accelerates the self-corrective feedback mechanisms, and this effect pervades the whole body (see chapter 5).

The breath meditation, by contrast, is more effective than the body scan at lowering *arousal*. It works through the visceral organs and the autonomic nervous system rather than through the musculature. Breathing is intimately connected to heart rate, blood pressure, and the secretions of adrenaline and cortisol. These are all governed by what is called the HPA axis (the hypothalamus, the pituitary gland, and the adrenal gland). High arousal increases glucose availability in the bloodstream and the rate at which we burn energy. We call this the "stress response" as opposed to the "relaxation response."

We can't control the stress response directly. We can't consciously lower blood pressure and heart rate, but we can do it through a proxy. If we consciously relax the breath, this will have an immediate ripple effect on the other components of the stress response as well. A sigh or yawn, for example, not only relaxes the breath. At exactly the same time, it slightly reduces blood pressure and heart rate. They are that closely connected. (We'll look more closely at the "miraculous sigh" in chapter 4.)

The breath meditation is traditionally regarded as a tranquility practice (*samadhi*). It tends to have a soothing, even sedating effect, and many people use it to fall asleep. The body scan, on the other hand, makes the mind slightly more alert and discriminating. You know where you're at, aches and pains and all, when you scan your body. It is more of a mindfulness practice (*sati*).

The breath meditation is popular for many reasons. The breath is comfortable and soothing to focus on. The gentle ebb and flow literally massages the internal organs. The breath gives us good immediate feedback on how wired up or relaxed we are. Tight grabby breaths indicate tension. Long, releasing breaths show we're relaxed. We also get our first conscious taste of physical stillness and mental silence in the gap between the out-breath and the in-breath.

The breath is a good anchor for other practices. It is transparent and accommodating. While focusing on the breath, we can easily scan the body or say a mantra or monitor thoughts or listen to sounds or do a visualization as well. Despite its apparent simplicity, the breath meditation is a practice that matures over the years and can last a lifetime. It is a straightforward entry point into the body schema. If you just did this one practice well and allowed it to evolve naturally, you wouldn't need anything else.

HOW TO DO THE BREATH MEDITATION

First, you choose your posture. Lying down or using a reclining chair is quite okay if you want to relax quickly and don't mind falling asleep. Sitting in a padded upright chair or on the floor will give you better focus and mental control. Start with two or three energetic sighs and a rapid scan of the body. It is remarkable how much tension you can shed almost immediately if you do this.

Now focus on the breath in a precise location in the body. Some people just "think" the breath, or ride up and down on it, but that approach is too vague. It is better to settle the mind down in one particular place so it doesn't drift. It doesn't matter where. It could be at the nostrils, the throat, the chest, the diaphragm, or belly. It is best to focus on the place where the breath is most vivid for you.

Good focus is not static. It involves a sense of gentle, moment-by-moment inquiry. This quality of quiet, steady investigation, called *dhamma-vicaya* in the *Sutta*, is integral to mindfulness. Your brain is intuitively seeking what feels most pleasant and satisfying. With a little practice, you will gradually notice the breath in much more detail than you normally would.

In the *Sutta*, the Buddha described the process this way: "When the monk is breathing in, he knows, 'I am breathing in.' When the monk is breathing out, he knows, 'I am breathing out.'" You should also be able to recognize when your breaths are short or long, smooth or irregular, comfortable or awkward. See if you can notice the split second when the breath seems to stop, and the split second it starts. These are indicators that you are really focused and are not getting distracted. Another sign of good focus is that time seems to slow down. You step out of twenty-first-century cybertime into the natural rhythms of body time, which hasn't changed in millennia.

Healthy breathing is naturally irregular and variable. The breath will intuitively find its own rhythm appropriate to circumstances and the person. For this reason, Buddhist practices usually don't try to control or shape the breath. This makes them quite different from many of the breathing exercises in yoga.

People commonly use mental props to stay on the track of the breath. These aren't essential, but they are excellent training wheels. You could try to silently count three or four breaths in a row, saying the count at the end of the out-breath.

If you still get distracted, you could double-count, saying the number on both the in-breath and the out-breath: in-breath, "one"; out-breath, "one"; in-breath, "two"; out-breath, "two"; and so on. If you don't like counting, you could just say "in . . . out" repeatedly as you breathe. These were the Buddha's instructions.

Alternatively, you could silently say an affirmation such as "let go" or "slow down" or "be still." You would say one word on the in-breath and one on the out-breath. If you used a single word, such as "relax," you would say it on the out-breath. Saying affirmations tends to have a more soothing effect than counting.

NAME THE DISTRACTION

Counting or saying affirmations may seem absurdly simple, but you shouldn't underestimate the power of your habitual thoughts to derail you. While focusing on the breath you still have to monitor the peripheral mental activity and respond to it as necessary. Most thoughts are light and trivial. They will just cruise by and disappear, and you get better at shrugging them off. Sometimes, however, you need a stronger strategy.

It goes like this. When you get distracted, don't get annoyed with yourself. It happens to everyone. I still get distracted after nearly half a century of meditation. Instead, stop and deliberately ask: "What is this?" "Naming the distraction" is like a micro-mindfulness technique inserted into your session.

You "hold the distraction in mind." You become "mindful" of that thought. You then name the content: "Food, TV, Josephine, sex, work," or whatever. To name a thought means you have to step outside the ongoing conversation and see it under its general category instead. To become fully conscious of the distraction in this way gives you more power over it.

To name or label something objectifies it somewhat and gives you the chance to evaluate it: Shall I stay with this thought or not? Most emerging thoughts can be abandoned on the spot once you are fully mindful of them. Others can be postponed or "shelved" or "boxed up" or put in the distance. (We'll talk more about this naming technique in chapter 6.)

No one can meditate well unless they have good, conscious strategies for managing distractions. Any distraction will always have more emotional charge and allure ("pay attention to me!") than focusing on the breath, which can seem quite pedestrian in comparison. Big distractions are most unlikely to fade away if you just try to ignore them.

BE MINDFUL OF THE RESULTS

While focusing on the breath, you should feel your body relaxing. This is one reason that you are meditating, after all. Your body may feel heavy or still or numb or even light. You may notice tingling or warmth or pulsing on the skin. You feel muscles continuing to relax. You may well feel your tiredness and aches and pains coming to the surface. Enjoy these sensations. They all confirm that you're on the right track.

Don't forget to monitor your mind and mood as well. The Buddha called this being mindful of your state of mind (see chapter 18). Are you focused, or is your mind drifting? Are you falling asleep and losing control, or are you fully tuned in to what is happening? Do you feel at home in your body and accepting of your mood, or are you unconsciously resisting it?

When you finish the breathing meditation, ask yourself: "Was that worth doing or not? Is my body relaxed? Is my mind calmer and more in control?" If you're not sure, or if the results were mediocre, or if the answer is "no," you probably won't have the motivation to continue. A meditation has to be sufficiently rewarding to justify the time you spend doing it.

FOR HOW LONG SHOULD I MEDITATE?

There is a good reason why a Standard Meditation Practice takes fifteen minutes or longer. It usually takes two to three minutes for you to break the habit of compulsive thought and actually start to feel the body schema. At some time within five to ten minutes, the body is likely to touch the point of sleep. You are definitely relaxing, and you know it!

However, the mind takes longer to truly settle. When the body relaxes, the mind typically gets sleepy. Every meditator knows the feeling of bobbing in and out of sleep. These few minutes of recovery sleepiness are often necessary, especially after a long day, but grogginess is hardly an ultimate goal.

Fairly soon a more satisfying state of mind should emerge. You feel alert, calm, and controlled. This tends to happen ten to fifteen minutes into a meditation. This is the ideal state: body relaxed, mind relatively calm and controlled. It still takes some effort to maintain, but it can be enormously rewarding. Once you've got it, how long should you continue? You will normally stop, as you should, when it intuitively feels right to do so, but it is good to have an approximate target.

I was trained to do meditations that were one hour, two hours, and sometimes three hours long. I now see that as having a monastic rationale: the longer you withdraw from the temptations of the world, the safer you are. My belief is that for most people the law of diminishing returns sets in after twenty or twenty-five minutes. A one-hour meditation is only slightly more profitable than a twenty-minute session. Long meditations can be truly beautiful, but they are also far more prone to sleepiness and mental wandering. People who only do long meditations may be unconsciously training themselves into states of relaxed fogginess rather than mental clarity. Long meditations may actually increase, rather than decrease, the time people spend in pointless, low-level rumination. If you have the time, short frequent sessions usually work better than single long ones.

4

The Miraculous Sigh

Meditation involves two skills. The first is physical: learning to relax rapidly. The second is cognitive: learning to pay attention. It does take a certain amount of time, about ten to twenty seconds, to significantly relax, but we can and do become mindful in an instant when we need to. This chapter will show you how to combine relaxation and attention into a powerful short exercise that you could easily do many times a day.

Some people think of relaxation as a state close to sleep. I'd like to propose a more sophisticated definition. We are "relaxed" when we have the optimal baseline levels of muscle tone, arousal, and attention for whatever we happen to be doing. Conversely, we are "tense," "anxious," or "stressed" when our muscle activity and arousal are higher than necessary.

The baseline changes continuously as we shift from one activity to another. Walking requires more lower-body tone and higher arousal than sitting. Talking requires more muscle tone in the face than being silent, but every activity will have an optimal baseline. When we're at the baseline, we feel relaxed, in control, well-paced, and mentally online.

If we check (and know what to look for), we will usually find we are a little, or a lot, more tense than we need to be for much of the day. To "relax," therefore, means dropping back to the optimal baseline for that activity. Once you know how, it rarely takes more than a minute to do this, but the benefits can be colossal. If we don't, we will mindlessly maintain those levels of excess tension and energy expenditure, and we usually crank them up further as the day goes by.

Relaxing quickly also has a huge cognitive payoff. If we're physically tense, our minds scatter and become too speedy to function well. If we're relaxed, however, we can give good, self-monitoring, economical attention to whatever we are doing. We will also be able to turn the quality of our attention up or down as required. We will know when to be extra sharp and focused and when we can safely cruise on "high-functioning automatic."

We really can become mindful in an instant, but sustained, good-quality attention depends on being close to the optimal baseline for much of the day. That's where we have to start. So how can we relax rapidly when we're habitually out of whack? We can use the breath to do it, as described in chapter 3, but here are some technical details to expand on that discussion.

Sympathetic arousal is a state of elevated blood pressure, heart rate, breathing rate, and secretions of adrenaline and cortisol. This arousal increases the rate at which we burn energy, and it makes us feel speedy. The only part of this autonomic nervous system network that we can control directly is the breath. Fortunately, if we consciously relax our breathing, that relaxation simultaneously slows down all the other aspects of arousal.

Here is a curious little fact: When we breathe in, our blood pressure and heart rate go up. When we breathe out, they go down. They go up and down over a single breath! This explains why, when we habitually hold the breath in (as we do when we're tense), arousal remains high. Conversely, when we let the breath go, as we do when we sigh or yawn, we relax.

The following are markers of *tense* breathing and high arousal: short, frequent breaths; longer in-breaths than out-breaths; breathing from the chest rather than lower down in the body; and holding on at the top of the in-breath. Conversely, the markers of *relaxed* breathing are these: longer, slower breaths; longer out-breaths than in-breaths; breathing from lower in the body; and usually (but not always) a space at the end of the out-breath. Once you can recognize these markers, it is easy to check. Just ask yourself at any time: "Do I seem to be holding on to the breath or letting it go?"

The fastest way to unlock your breathing is to sigh, but you need to do it well. So what makes a good sigh? We should think of a sigh as having three parts: in-breath, out-breath, and the pause at the end. If there's no pause, it's just a deep breath, not a sigh. Deep breaths are good, but sighs are so much more relaxing.

To get the hang of this, I suggest that you try doing an exercise I call "Three Sighs," and do it many times a day. Until you have more experience, one sigh usually isn't enough to break through the locked muscle tension and reset your level of arousal.

THREE SIGHS

The exercise goes like this. You sigh three times. The first big in-breath unlocks the tight chest. You then let the breath go without forcing it, and *wait* in the space at the end until you really need to breathe in again.

On the second sigh, it is good to have a fake yawn, and don't be surprised if this triggers a real one. A yawn slows down the breathing considerably by lengthening the out-breath. Don't forget to wait at the bottom of the out-breath for as long as is comfortable. This waiting really stretches the out-breath. On the third sigh, focus on releasing the breath completely and waiting at the end, until the next breath comes of its own accord. This whole process should take about thirty or forty seconds.

The meditation is now over. When you go back to natural, uncontrolled breathing you will find it has utterly changed. Your breathing will have shifted from tight, holding, chesty breathing, to looser, releasing, lower-body breathing. Your breaths will also be slower and longer, which is a clear marker of lower arousal, and your whole body will feel more relaxed.

It sounds easy, but without repetition and practice you won't get a great deal out of it. We don't break habitual levels of arousal that easily. They tend to rebound fairly quickly unless you repeatedly reset them. I suggest to my students that they try to do the "three sighs" at least ten times a day.

Here are some extra suggestions:

You can sigh reasonably well in polite company with your mouth closed if you linger at the end of the out-breath, thereby slowing your breathing down. However, if you have the chance, you will get far more mileage from sighing with your mouth open. This will unlock the jaw, resulting in a passive stretch of the lower face muscles and therefore accelerating the process.

You will get even more mileage if you yawn. You can think of a yawn as a turbo-charged sigh. A yawn will *actively* stretch all the face, neck, and throat muscles. Yawning will throw your shoulders back and open your throat to three times its usual capacity. The out-breath will drop so much deeper, and the space at the end will be that much longer.

A good yawn makes it quite impossible to maintain high levels of arousal and muscle tension. It *forces* you to relax. If you were a runner at the start of a race, fired up with isometric tension and ready to burst out of the blocks, but you then decided to have a big yawn, you would lose all your explosive edge. The gun would go off and you would come in last. No amount of willpower and determination can maintain muscle tension and arousal against a good yawn.

Try to do three sighs (openmouthed and with at least one yawn) whenever you start to walk somewhere. Choose somewhere you can do it nearly every time: when you get up from the computer, when you walk away from your car, when you walk out your door.

Don't forget to notice the mental benefit. After the three sighs, you may find that your mind is unexpectedly clear. Whatever you were thinking about before you started to sigh will have slipped off the mental stage. If we neglect a thought for ten to twenty seconds, it drops out of active mode into a resting state.

For this reason, giving full attention to three sighs is a marvelous way to detach yourself from a train of thought. It can be a punctuation mark in your day. You empty your head and prepare for the next activity. In neuroscience and sports psychology, this is called a "preparatory set." You see tennis players do it all the time when they prepare to serve. They sigh, bounce the ball a few times, and sigh again, in order to bring their arousal down to the level appropriate for serving. Only when they're ready do they serve.

You can easily do the same between one activity and another. A little exercise like this can bring you back into the present, reset the appropriate levels of muscle tone and arousal, and orient your mind to what is coming up. This is a great physical and mental outcome for a thirty-second meditation.

When you are experienced in doing three sighs, you will find that even a single sigh (ideally a yawn) can have a remarkable effect. You sigh, stop, reset your level of arousal, and get ready. A big conscious yawn will also drop you into a few seconds of physical stillness and mental silence at the very end of the out-breath. These moments of silence and embodiment can be pivot points in your day. They enable you to feel calm, focused, centered, and in control. When you move into action, you can do so when you're ready, in your own time.

5

The Body Scan

[The monk] trains himself thinking: "Conscious of the whole body, I breathe in. Conscious of the whole body, I breathe out. Calming the whole body, I breathe in. Calming the whole body, I breathe out."
—**SATIPATTHANA SUTTA**

Dozens of meditation practices are based on paying attention to the play of sensations within the body. Some call for systematically relaxing the muscles of the body from top to bottom. Some focus on subtle blocks and energy flows, as in yoga. In tai chi the focus is on moving the body in a fluid, harmonious way.

Despite their variety, these techniques all have a similar effect: they strengthen and harmonize the mental map of the body (the body schema, discussed in chapter 3). "Scanning" the body slowly—that is, undertaking a careful mental exploration of the sensations present in the body—brings mindfulness of hidden tensions, and this alleviates many of them within seconds. It is like gently combing the knots out of a tangle of long hair—and discovering with amazement how many knots there actually are.

A good way to structure a body scan meditation session is to scan slowly and systematically, three or four breaths in each place. For example, you could spend four breaths while mentally exploring the sensations in each of the following places: scalp and forehead; face; neck, throat, and shoulders; arms and hands; chest; diaphragm; belly; hips; legs and feet. That would keep you occupied for several minutes, and you could easily vary this format at will.

After a slow scan, you can scan more rapidly up and down to more generally integrate the body schema. Let your mind explore tensions, blocks, imbalances, and discomforts whenever it seems useful to do so. Conversely, you can amplify pleasant sensations by focusing on them. This can be very enjoyable and rewarding work with remarkable psychological and physical benefits. Although this may be hard for a novice to understand, some people spend hundreds of hours doing this.

Scanning in detail can so alter our perception that some people will feel that they are sensing their bodies "as they actually are" for the first time. They sense not just their usual body, more clearly, but a kind of body that is qualitatively different. They feel an "energy body" of fluid sensations rather than the usual lumpish flesh and bones. The state of mind that induces this effect is often called "just watching" or "bare attention," but this is only half the truth.

Being mindful always improves some aspect of what we are focusing on. This is the biological purpose of attention, even if we don't consciously target that outcome. Just to notice a subtle tension or a disturbing mood or a repetitive thought invariably leads to a reappraisal and adjustment, whether we intend it or not. The act of sensing the body leads to highlighting what is "bad" and orienting us to what is "good." Attention to the body helps us notice subtle deviations from the homeostatic optimums and instinctively reorient toward balance. This means that exploring the body in detail will integrate and balance it in ways that we can't even imagine until we become proficient. This effect is continuous and subliminal throughout any good meditation practice, and the results are cumulative over time.

When being mindful of something induces a positive change, psychologists refer to this as being an automatic or "implicit" reappraisal rather than a conscious or "cognitive" one. Because the transformation is not a deliberate act, it may seem as if we've done nothing at all—as if we really were just noticing something in a state of nonjudgmental acceptance.

In fact we did do something: We chose to become mindful of that sensation in the first place. We focused on it for long enough for an implicit reappraisal and an adaptive response to occur. We probably wouldn't continue with the "just watching" mode if that positive change didn't occur. We always need a subtle sense of reward to continue with anything we do, even if we don't consciously register it.

After ten to fifteen minutes a good meditator will usually feel that he or she has arrived at some degree of body-mind stillness (what the *Sutta* calls *passaddhi*). At this point the formal instructions can and usually do take second place to a deeper kind of guidance from within. Beginners are often apprehensive about getting the instructions right. They are afraid that if they tweak anything, the promised magic will fail. What will happen if they breathe through their mouth instead of their nose? Or if they accidentally touch their thumbs to the second fingers rather than the first? Thousands stop meditating altogether because they can't afford the prescribed time span of twenty minutes or forty minutes or an hour, depending on where they got their first instructions.

The body schema is a fully integrated, real-time map of the state of the body. It is highly dynamic and rich with feedback mechanisms. That is to say: Relaxing the scalp will help relax the feet. Unlocking the jaw will reduce cortisol output. Noticing sadness will soften the face. Breathing out will lower blood pressure, and so on.

The body will naturally gravitate toward homeostatic set points if we let it. It never forgets what perfect health and well-being feel like. Buried in the depths it holds a detailed template of that goal. It compares where we are at in any moment against those foundational templates. The body knows where it needs to go. It continuously makes judgment calls: This feels bad. This feels good. If I do this, it feels better. We accelerate this process by being well focused and mindful of the sensations within us.

"Homeostasis" means having optimal tone in every muscle group, optimal functioning in every organ, optimal balance, and arousal, and so on. The process toward homeostasis is subtle but very dynamic, and it never stops. We can dimly sense this inner intelligence at work, even though most of it occurs out of sight.

The mind also has homeostatic ideals and will gravitate toward them when we let it. This process is mostly preconscious, but most people do have at least an instinct for what a healthy, balanced, well-functioning mind feels like. It is a memory, if nothing else. When we meditate, we can intuitively direct our attention in ways that feel compatible with these inner guidelines. If we are mindful of what we are doing, we will also be able to evaluate whether this inner play is truly useful or just another distraction or escape.

BODY SCAN VARIATIONS

People often achieve a good degree of body-mind stillness and wonder "Is this it? Is this all there is?" This is the time to let go of whatever we were led to expect, and follow our imagination instead.

The possibilities are limitless. We may feel an inclination to go deeply into one place; or to notice an arising emotion or memory trace; or to integrate an emerging image or color into the scanning; or to notice weird little bad sensations or peculiar new good ones; or to catch a visceral insight; or to realign ourselves in imaginal space; or to examine a mood; or to shift from one body-based practice to another; or to examine a problem through nonverbal feeling; or to just have fun with what we find. To playfully enjoy what feels worth doing, whether in meditation or not, has a very strong antidepressant effect. It may be the best antidepressant of all. Here is a list of body scan variations.

Scanning Down or Up

Scanning down from head to feet is a relaxing approach to the body scan. It works with the releasing effect of the out-breath, but it can make you sleepy. Scanning up, starting distantly with the feet and untangling sensations on up through the core of the body and into the head, is more energizing. It is more likely to keep you awake.

Scanning in Stages
It is useful to deliberately scan through the same stages repeatedly. This will train you to accurately target your attention. How you divide the body from top to bottom is up to you. You are likely to have more divisions if you scan slowly, and less if you scan quickly. You can also scan by visualizing what you understand of your anatomy.

Slow Scanning
To scan slowly, taking fifteen minutes or more from top to bottom, is good for beginners. We shouldn't underestimate how long it takes to actually "see" what is happening deep in the body. It may take weeks before you can sense each place in any detail.

Rapid Sweeping
After a slow scan it is good to sweep in rapid and somewhat random fashion up and down the body. This leads to subtle changes that improve balance, open the body, and integrate the body schema. Fast scans are economical in terms of time invested, and you're likely to do more of them once you get the knack. I do dozens of quick scans each day. Most of them are less than a minute long, and some consist of just a single sigh.

Scanning Only the Upper Body
The face, shoulders, and chest are psychosomatic areas. They

tense up easily but also relax fairly quickly. Scanning just the upper body can be more satisfying than going all the way down to the feet. You get strong positive feedback from the upper body that what you are doing is working, and this encourages you to continue. This isn't the case lower in the body. The buttocks and thighs, for example, will automatically relax if the upper body does, but the feedback signs are much less obvious. They therefore have a weaker confirmatory effect.

Counting and Affirmations

Props are often essential to keep yourself on track. You can always count three or four breaths silently to each stage, or repeat an affirmation while you breathe, as I described in chapter 3.

Visualization

Focusing on the body is like illuminating it from within. It's just a small step further to imagine gradually filling the body with light or a color or nectar or spiritual energy. The Japanese Zen master Hakuin (1686–1769) suggested imagining a ball of aromatic butter on your head gradually melting throughout your body. (Hakuin is also famous for the saying "Meditation in the midst of activity is a thousand times superior to meditation in stillness.")

The Central Axis

When you become very still and calm (*passaddhi*), your mind may want to go deeper inside. When scanning it will tend to move up and down the "central axis" of the body. We usually feel this as being slightly in front of the spine. The central axis is not a genuine anatomical structure; it is a mental concept. It is how we imagine ourselves as being straight and balanced.

Chakras

Along the central axis you will find places where your mind naturally wants to rest: the point behind the eyes; the center of the chest; the center of the hips, for example. Let your mind go to these places. In yoga these are called "chakras." These are not anatomically real locations, but the feeling of being centered is very real. Don't worry if your apparent chakras don't exactly match the five or seven chakra models of the various yogic or Tibetan systems. The fact that these are not compatible with each other makes it obvious that they are not an absolute spiritual anatomy. They are just frameworks to hang your experience off. You don't need to force your actual experience to conform to either of these.

Deep Point Focus

If your mind wants to go to any particular place, let it do so. It will be attracted in particular to the "negatives"—to whatever is painful, awkward, or out of balance. Focusing on those areas helps to correct them.

Searching for Pain

Home in on what feels bad and let the sensations there come to the surface. Mindfulness typically acts as a troubleshooter. Error detection is one of its major functions. We often have to become fully conscious of unnecessary tension or a runaway thought or a disturbing mood, and let it emerge fully in consciousness, in order to relax at all.

Breath Body

Use your breath as a probe for scanning your body—you can imagine "breathing through the body" or "breathing into" areas of pain or tension. This will help you create a sense of space and openness throughout the body, thereby inducing the so-called "breath body" experience.

Attention to the Positives

Because the lovely states of mind are more subtle than the negatives, they can easily be missed. When they do occur, make sure you notice them: deep stillness, inner silence, bliss, vision, sensory delight, mental clarity, and control. Don't forget why you're meditating: You do want to feel better. Keep the goal in mind and enjoy any unexpected rewards that come along.

ACCEPTING THE BODY

Body scanning can be profoundly enjoyable. It still surprises me that physical bliss can coexist with the inevitable discomforts of having a human body. Some of my students even say that severe pain and illness are no obstacle and can even help. Because scanning is so therapeutic, however, people often try to force the process. This can lead to frustration: "I couldn't make my shoulders relax no matter how hard I tried!"

The most helpful attitude is a loving and tolerant curiosity toward the body just as it is—that is, "nonjudgmental acceptance" (a term we'll return to often throughout this book). Nonjudgmental acceptance is an excellent response toward things that we can't immediately change. All we can do is pay attention to the body and gently explore. We usually can't force it to feel exactly the way we would like. If we can feel comfortably at home in our less-than-perfect bodies, we stop fighting ourselves and automatically relax.

There can be hundreds of things that we don't like about ourselves—sensations, thoughts, moods, and habits. In meditation, we meet them one by one as the minutes go by. Each one gives us a chance to let go a little more of our habitual negativities, to become more tolerant of negative affect. The minor physical discomforts are a good place to start. Learning to do this enhances our capacity for what psychologists call "distress tolerance" or "pain tolerance."

The results can be truly amazing. Although body scanning illuminates our discomforts, it is also the royal road to bliss. We can feel every part of the body, and all the systems within it, orienting toward a state of health and balance. Beneath the discomforts, the body can feel tranquil, radiant, and alive.

IS IT WORKING?

Some psychologists say that we should practice meditation without aiming for any particular outcome. "Just accept whatever happens, good or bad." Such universal acceptance is a goal in itself, but I'm not sure that it's a good one. This approach certainly wouldn't make us any better at golf or mathematics. Learning any skill is rewarding, but it does take effort. We will only stick with it if it seems to be worthwhile. We know that most students of any subject need frequent positive feedback on their progress or they're likely to get discouraged. This is exactly what happens to most people who attempt meditation. They fail to look for the benefits.

Meditation is about learning to relax rapidly, to focus better, and to manage thoughts and emotions more intelligently.

These are skills that we can readily improve if we know how to assess our progress. Let's look at just the first of these: relaxing consciously. Beginners often doubt that focusing on their bodies will relax them. We usually get sleepy and less conscious as we relax, so we are rarely alert enough to notice how pleasant it feels. So how can we tell if we are succeeding or not?

The shift from the stress response to the relaxation response, from sympathetic arousal to parasympathetic recover, creates dramatic effects throughout the body. Several signs will indicate that this process is at work:

Muscle tension releases. We can easily feel the little muscles around the eyes, lips, and jaw soften. The shoulders drop. The loss of tone throughout the large muscles of the body induces a feeling of heaviness. As tension fades, the body loses its jumpy, ready-to-move quality. It starts to feel genuinely still.

Tingling, warmth, and pulsing arises. The relaxation response diverts the blood flow from the large fight-or-flight muscles to the skin and the digestive system. The skin often feels tingly and warm, and the pulse may become more prominent. Stress shuts down the digestive system, but relaxation wakes it up, sometimes with gurgling and mild nausea.

Physical discomforts emerge. Stress and cortisol mask our aches, pains, and fatigue. Relaxation brings them to the surface. Their presence can be regarded as good signs of progress. Focusing on the body naturally amplifies sensations, and the brain will always give priority to unpleasant signals over pleasant ones.

Arousal drops. We sense this most clearly in our breathing. We shift from tense, holding, rapid, upper-body breathing to soft, releasing, slower, lower-body breathing. When this happens we know that heart rate and blood pressure will also be returning to balance. We also get our first taste of stillness and silence in the gap between out-breath and in-breath.

You know you're on the right track during any meditation if you feel heavy or light, soft, tingling, warm, tired, sore, still, or any combination of these sensations. In being "mindful of the body," you may also feel your breathing soften, notice more saliva in your mouth, watering in the eyes, a gurgling stomach, a sense of inner space or flow.

Mentally you may still be a bit distracted or sleepy, or you may feel fully calm and controlled. Your bad mood may have utterly changed, or it may just have weakened. You are likely to feel more grounded and in tune with your emotional state. Ideally you feel a stronger sense of agency after a meditation. You are more able to choose where to direct your attention rather than being at the mercy of whatever arises.

When we meditate, our quality of focus naturally fluctuates according to inner and outer forces that we usually can't see or control (biology, weather, stress, fatigue, cognitive overload, sickness, emotional cross-contamination, and so on). But still, we're not helpless.

None of us can focus perfectly for long, but we can certainly get better with practice. It is simply a matter of being "mindful of your state of mind" and repeatedly checking. It starts with a simple question: "Am I focused or not? Am I paying attention to the body as I intended to do, or am I distracted by some thought?" If we become mindful that we're not focused, it is easy to correct it. If we don't recognize it, we're as lost as a tennis player who endlessly repeats an error.

If we notice when our attention is good, we can amplify it. Just to recognize that "this is good focus" and to embed that feeling in memory is sufficient. It lays down a positive template for the future. As the Buddha said in the *Sutta*, "Recognize when a good state of mind is present and learn how to amplify it."

Even acknowledging that your mind is hopelessly scattered is better than not recognizing it at all. To notice that something is wrong is the essential first step toward improvement, even if nothing happens immediately. The Buddha said that if you repeatedly recognize bad states of mind and store them in memory, you will eventually come to see what triggers them and what helps them fade.

6

Controlling Thought

It is easy to relax the *body*. It takes no great skill or effort. We only have to sit or lie down and close our eyes for long enough. This sends a potent message to the body that we have disengaged from the world. Our muscles no longer need to be primed for action. Just closing our eyes gives the muscles permission to relax, and they do. Everyone lowers their muscle tension and arousal to some degree when they meditate, even the most unskilled practitioner.

Unfortunately, our minds don't relax so easily. We don't stop thinking just because our bodies have stopped moving. The freed-up mental capacity gets redirected into the "virtual action" of thought. Whenever we have nothing to do, we don't switch off the mind and rest. Our default behavior is to think over what we've just done and to plan for future actions. While this is an essential mental activity, we frequently overdo it to our detriment. Sitting down and closing our eyes certainly doesn't switch off that default habit. The brain is hardwired to revert to thought in the absence of immediate action.

AUTOMATIC THINKING

Cognitive psychologists have various names for this perpetual mental activity. They call it the "automatic processing system" or the "default network" or the "narrative network" or the "interior dialogue" or the "stream of consciousness." We can regard this mental activity as the stream of *automatic* cognition that underpins our *conscious* thought. Whether we are aware of it or not, automatic thinking never stops, not even when we periodically shift into conscious, goal-directed thinking. We can think both automatically and consciously at the same time. (Cognitive psychologists explain this according to what is called the "dual process theory.")

Automatic thinking is complex and powerful. It processes many issues simultaneously, operating on parallel tracks continuously day and night. It is the mental equivalent of the digestive system. It thinks over, digests, sifts through, files away, and organizes all the information we take in each day. It discards the junk, clears the decks, and primes us for coming activities.

This is the huge substrata of automatic and unconscious cognition that keeps our lives on track. We would be in a lunatic asylum or dead without it. While conscious, directed thought does certain things much better than automatic thought, it is just the luxury top end of the vast factory of cognition. Thinking is thus a continuous, automatic, and mostly beneficial process. Nor do we have to decide to think. It happens by itself just like breathing does. It would be futile to try to shut it down, or switch it off, or blank it out as many people would like to do. By meditating, we just learn to inter-act with the process of thinking more effectively.

We control automatic thought in several ways when we meditate. As we *calm* our bodies down, the mental noise and busyness diminish. As we *slow* our minds down, we become more able to choose which thoughts to follow. By getting *sleepy* we dull our thoughts out—not a ideal strategy. By becoming *mindful*—by seeing what actually happens in the mind—we understand how it all works.

Meditating calms automatic thought through the way we direct our attention. In particular, we focus *toward* the body and *away* from our habitual thoughts. We give *more* atten-tion than usual to the flux of bodily sensations and *less* atten-tion to our thoughts. We feed X by starving Y. This results in our automatic thoughts becoming weaker, less emotionally charged, and easier to ignore or tolerate.

Where attention goes, energy follows. Because energy is a limited resource, giving more to our mental representations of the body (the body schema) means less is available for runaway thought. When starved of oxygen and glucose, our background thoughts, and the neural networks that support them, become weaker. Their emotional charge declines, and the chains of thought break apart more quickly.

FOCUSING AND MONITORING

Focusing on the body disarms most intrusive thoughts, but they never completely disappear. Nor would that be a useful goal. We don't want to go mentally blank. It is much better to lightly monitor that peripheral stream of cognition and data. It could contain something we need to respond to (for instance, the house is burning down).

This means that "paying attention" is not as single-minded as it might seem. It consists of two mutually supporting skills. We can call them "focusing" and "monitoring." We *focus* on the body while *monitoring* the peripheral activity. Nor do we have to toggle between them. We both focus and monitor simultaneously. As the instructions say: focus on the body while noticing thoughts with detachment. We *consciously* focus on the body, while monitoring the *automatic* thinking in the background.

Paying attention to something always divides the world into two: what we focus on and everything else. The body and the thoughts. Foreground and background. The center and the periphery. Figure and field. The path and the scenery. What we regard as most important in the moment, and what we see as potential distractions to that.

Attention highlights one thing alone. This is critical whenever we try to do something physical. Action is always unitary. Our thoughts can scatter and fragment, but we can't walk in five different directions at once. We have to make continuous this-and-not-that choices to do even the simplest action.

Even when we meditate and apparently do nothing, we still split our attentional resources. One part of our attention looks inward. We use conscious, top-down, controlled "selective attention" to focus on the body. The other part looks outward. We use automatic, bottom-up, reactive "monitoring attention" for the peripheral thoughts that push their way onto the mental stage.

"Selective attention" involves making a conscious choice to focus for longer and more deeply than usual on the sensations of the body. Although this calms us down, it is also surprisingly dynamic and enjoyable in a quiet way. It is "approach" behavior guided by the reward circuitry of the brain.

"Monitoring attention," on the other hand, is vigilant and dismissive. It is "withdrawal" behavior. Monitoring involves noticing, evaluating, and mostly discarding the peripheral thoughts, sounds, and emotions as rapidly as possible.

Monitoring attention is economical and aims to conserve resources. It "notices" but doesn't "process" or "elaborate" on the peripheral data any more than necessary. It is a space-maker. It aims to keep the mental stage uncluttered for the chosen task of focusing on the body. Most of the peripheral input can be dismissed instantly, but some will be important enough to be briefly processed ("Don't forget to make that phone call!").

Ideally we give whatever arises just the right amount of attention it needs: no more but also no less. If we give it too little attention or try to ignore it, it may continue to niggle at us from the sidelines. If we give it too much attention, we will lose focus on the body. The few seconds or milliseconds it takes to process a peripheral stimulus is not enough to break the body-focused flow of a meditation. In fact, by processing potential distractions rapidly, it keeps the meditation running smoothly.

This focusing-monitoring duality is reflected in most meditation instructions. For example: Focus on the body and let everything else go. Focus on the body while noticing thoughts with detachment. Focus on the breath while noticing everything else with nonjudgmental acceptance.

There are many rule-of-thumb instructions relating to the monitoring of peripheral data: Just watch. Be an observer. Let it all pass by like leaves in a stream or clouds in the sky. Notice thoughts without reacting to them (or without processing them, or without elaborating on them). Accept whatever happens with an open, curious mind.

The mindfulness-based stress reduction approach, derived from Zen, is slightly different. It cultivates an "open" or "empty," unfocused state of mind. Although thoughts invariably arise, they are to be seen as the unimportant epiphenomena that go with being alive. An instructor will tell you that there is no need to either attach to or resist these thoughts. You are encouraged to let them simply pass through the mental space.

Often, however, these gentle and encouraging instructions are not enough. Trying to lightly brush aside unwanted thoughts, or contain them through acceptance, or let them pass through, is a strategy that can only go so far. Some of our thoughts and our patterns around them are so obsessive that they won't readily submit to such mild treatment. Just ask any anxious person if they find it easy to "let thoughts gently float away."

My students often complain that they're not thinking well (too scattered, can't focus, can't remember, can't stop). Although we all would like a quick fix, the first step toward controlling thoughts is to remind ourselves that we can't just switch the mind off. (Thinking is a continuous automatic process.) Nor can we focus better by trying harder (too stressful and tiring). We can't argue ourselves out of runaway thought or force ourselves to go to sleep. (The brain usually ignores top-down commands.) Nor can we pretend that all thoughts are unimportant (some of them obviously are important). Nonetheless we can still learn to control our thoughts much better than we normally do.

WHAT HAPPENS WHEN YOU MEDITATE?

When you start to meditate, you will find that it takes at least half a minute to mentally settle into your body. You have to shift attention from outer to inner, from thought and action to internal body sensations. That's a big shift. It takes time to activate the mental map of your body, so don't expect it to happen instantly.

Eventually, you connect well with the breath. You feel it rise. You feel it fall. You feel the beginning and end of each breath. This is mindfulness as "selective, sustained attention." You gently explore the moment-to-moment sensations of the breath. This is good-quality attention, and it feels satisfying to do.

Sooner or later, however, you're likely to get sidetracked. You may revert to a previous thought, or to something that seems much more important than the breath. It could be last night's TV program, or lunch, or the mortgage. When you realize you've been distracted, you've got a choice. You could continue thinking about that subject for as long as you normally would. Or you could say, "Not now. I need to relax." So you tick that thought off and refocus on the breath.

It might take only a second to do this, but a lot will have happened. You were mindful of the thought and you stopped the conversation with it. You evaluated it as useless. And you deliberately abandoned it. This is good economical "monitoring attention" at work: perception + evaluation + response. It didn't take long enough to seriously distract you from your primary focus on the breath. You were tempted but you didn't succumb. Only when you stay with a thought for more than ten seconds does it start to become a serious distraction.

So you recommit to the breath. You feel it rise. You feel it fall. You feel the breath starting to loosen up. Your whole body starts to feel good, but before you know it, another thought captures you. When you are mindful of this new distraction, you go through the same procedure. You stop that thought, evaluate it, tick it off, and return to the breath. This is the natural rhythm of any meditation. You focus, get distracted, dismiss the distraction, refocus, and so on.

Fairly soon you realize that it is quite pleasant to return to the breath. It is a much quieter place than chasing your thoughts. The pleasure principle now kicks in. At a gut level you start to understand the value of focusing, and the sense of mental control is quite lovely. You feel the mind settling and the body relaxing, and the positive sensory feedback makes it so much easier to stay on track. Peripheral thoughts will still tempt you, but they won't be such a problem. They will have lost their "stickiness," their usual emotional charge. This is the ideal place in any meditation. You are actively focused on the breath while "noticing" but not "processing" your thoughts.

Sometimes, however, a thought truly becomes a capital-D Distraction, and you need a better strategy than noticing it and letting go. Unless you also learn to manage strong, intrusive, and often important thoughts, your meditation will always be liable to disintegrate.

NAME THE THOUGHT

Good thought control starts with learning to manage an *individual* thought that has grown into a "distraction." To do so, we have to bring that thought out of automatic runaway mode into full consciousness. The best way to do this is to become mindful of it–to "hold it in mind"–and verbally identify it. As the Buddha said, you are mindful if you know what is in your mind, *and you can describe it to yourself.* In the *Sutta* he gives precise examples of how to do this, as you will see later in this book.

I briefly introduced this technique in chapter 3. The strategy is simple but immensely powerful. We just ask: "What is this? What am I thinking about?" and we come up with an appropriate word to describe it: "work" or "money" or "Daniel." This is called "naming" or "categorizing" or "labeling" or "noting." To do this, we have to stop the momentum of the thought and hold it in the mind for long enough to classify it.

This has the effect of objectifying the thought. Naming a thought puts it "outside" the body (which remains the main focus of attention) and gives us a choice about how to respond. Shall I give it more energy or less energy? Shall I feed it or starve it? Shall I process it further or refocus on the body? To name a thought is not to suppress it. Nor is it a way of consciously reappraising it, as we would, for instance, with cognitive behavioral therapy. It means that we recognize its presence while nonetheless suspending our tendency to engage further with it.

This is what psychologists call "nonjudgmental acceptance"—a kind of cunning, strategic, let-it-be laziness. If we stop processing a thought for more than a few seconds, it starts to fade. Even if it remains in consciousness, the neural networks that represent it decline from the active processing state to a passive, waiting state. The thought drifts from center stage to the wings. If we don't feed the stray cat, eventually it wanders off.

Naming works so well because it inhibits the emotional charge that powers the thought. To use language engages the brain's left-hemispheric prefrontal cortex. This region is essential for rational, verbal thought. When activated, it has an inhibitory effect on the limbic system deep in the brain where emotions are generated. This means that the act of naming saps the emotional energy from the thought. (The chapter "Painful Emotion" looks into this mechanism in more detail; see page 193.)

I confess that it took me years, aided by my studies in cognitive psychology, to realize how potent this technique is. I find that my students generally fail to take it seriously, as well. It might seem relatively simple, but "naming a thought" is a skill that benefits from being done with precision. When I ask my students how they named a troublesome thought, they usually don't give me a name. They give me instead a description, which is often quite lengthy, of what they were thinking about!

This tells me that they were still elaborating on it. I often have to prompt them by saying, "The name for this thought is 'work' or 'shopping.'" To name is to give a single word label to something. It is the kind of word you would put on a filing cabinet file. It is not about resolving the issue or understanding it more deeply.

To be mindful of something also means holding it *still*. If you don't actively feed it, it will naturally shrink in importance. To categorize a thought, and to see it outside of yourself, is quite enough to weaken the vast majority of your thoughts. Students gradually learn to notice the difference between elaborating on a thought and "just seeing" it.

When all else fails, however, the Buddha said that holding a thought in mind also means "holding it *down*," in the way that "a strong man forces down and subdues a weaker one." This use of willpower, however, is only a last resort after the gentler strategies have failed. Willpower is never as potent as we would like it to be, and it is always a limited resource.

Many people find it a revelation to understand that they don't have to respond to every one of their thoughts. If they are fully mindful, they can make an executive choice about whether to follow a thought or not. This is a crucial life skill, since giving energy to any one thought necessarily excludes others which may be more valuable.

For some people, using imagery can work just as well at this task as language. "Naming" a thought "captures" it in a word and "boxes" it up. It is very natural and intuitive to use imagery to enhance this process. As human beings, we "think" with pictures just as much as with words. If our thought is about Daniel, we could see also "see" him as an image (like a computer icon).

Once we have converted a thought into a word or a picture we can manipulate it. We can put it "outside" of ourselves or in the distance. We can put it on a shelf or a mental list or in a rubbish bin or in a filing cabinet. We can schedule it for a time in the future. We can place a thought in the geographical space around us, left or right, up or down, near or far. We can bury a thought, or put it into a thought-bubble, or throw it off a cliff, or grind it under our feet or throw it back into the stream of consciousness. You can be confident that any image that spontaneously occurs to you about how to manage a thought is likely to be useful.

Another strategy to escape a thought is to switch obsessions. We can disengage from a thought by actively thinking about something else that is strong enough to hold our attention. This is not a last-resort strategy. It is a way of practicing the vital cognitive skill of attention switching. The Dutch Renaissance thinker Erasmus called this "using a nail to extract a nail."

An even more drastic approach is to continuously stonewall thought or to "play a dead bat" or to basically say "no" to everything indiscriminately. Meditation as a monastic tradition places high value on inactivity and emotional withdrawal: "Be firm and unmoving like a mountain." This sweeping indifference to all worldly vanities may lead to a dull mind, but that could be better than mental chaos. Experienced meditators occasionally take this too far. They cultivate an automatic "do nothing" response to everything.

Some thoughts are so important (sick child, big decision, recent catastrophe) that they do need to remain somewhere in consciousness. Naming allows you to quarantine an important thought off to the side. It will still draw some energy, but you don't need to get entangled in it. While still aware of it, you can continue with your main work of focusing on the body. This is an important Stoic skill: You plod on philosophically amid the natural turmoil of life.

If all else fails, however, it is best to stop meditating altogether. There is no point in struggling with the inner tar baby. It is better to get out of your head and distract yourself with some fully engaging activity. Exercise or a conversation or some physical activity can be excellent diversionary options.

Most of these strategies still rely on having a primary focus on the body. We can only escape a thought by having somewhere else for our attention to go to. Focusing on the body is the ultimate escape from thought, and naming the distractions is basically a way of patrolling the borders.

You might realize that most of the strategies in this chapter have little in common with nonjudgmental acceptance as it is recommended by many psychologists. These strategies all correctly imply that getting tangled up in thought is not a good thing at all. Runaway thought can make us very miserable indeed—it is a core ingredient of anxiety—and some people have their lives destroyed by it.

The language of traditional Buddhism describes thoughts and behaviors as being either right or wrong, healthy or unhealthy, "skillful" or "unskillful." *Sati*, which I translate throughout this book as "the conscious perception and evaluation of something," is what makes those discriminations. The purpose of mindfulness is to make us better at deciding what is good or bad in any situation and to steer us toward advantage and away from danger. The quality of our lives depends on it. As the Buddha said, our actions follow our thoughts "as the cart follows the ox."

In the long run you may still have to tackle the problem of destructive thought closer to its source. If your quality of mind is persistently bad, then tackling individual thoughts is not going to fix that. If you are drifting into depression and your life is starting to suffer, you might need to also work on the preceding causes. In the *Sutta* the Buddha said, "Be mindful of what causes good and bad states of mind to arise." Here are some good long-term solutions to consider:

Let the brain rest. Fatigue is a guaranteed cause of poor thought, so try to get more sleep or downtime. An extra hour in bed each night, even if you're still half-awake in that time, will vastly improve your ability to think the next day.

Don't tax your brain unnecessarily. Cut down the information overload and be ruthless about it. How much media junk and gossip do you really need? The brain has to waste energy processing it all no matter how trashy it is.

Spend more time alone, even if you're not actually meditating. It may be a little boring and antisocial, but that's when your brain has a chance to tidy the mental desk and put out the rubbish.

Avoid conflict whenever possible, even when you are right. It often triggers a hurricane of thoughts. It's sometimes better to be a relaxed loser than a stressed-out winner.

Finally, learn organizational skills to make your life more orderly and less cluttered. If necessary, dump activities and people from your life. You can't expect meditation alone to give you a calm, well-functioning mind.

7

Why Focus on the Body?

If one thing, O monks, is developed and cultivated,
the body is calmed, the mind is calmed, discursive
thoughts are quieted, and all wholesome states
that partake of supreme knowledge reach fullness
of development. What is that one thing? It is
mindfulness directed to the body.
—**Mindfulness of the Body Sutta**[1]

Meditation is based on paying sustained attention to the breath or to the body. Ten-day retreats, yoga, the MBSR program used by psychologists, and most traditional practices ask us to devote a huge percentage of practice time to observing the body. So why is the body so important?

The answer is not at all obvious. There is little consensus in either the spiritual or the scientific literature. A common argument is that the body is a refuge from thoughts. "If you get distracted by a thought, let it go and place your attention gently back on the breath." This suggests that any other object would serve just as well, which is obviously not the case. There are in fact dozens of other meditation objects in the literature, but most are relics or curiosities or add-ons. The body trumps them all.

We can only focus well on something if it seems to be worth the effort. People often struggle to focus on the breath because it seems so pointless. In fact, the more frequently they get distracted the harder it becomes to refocus. Researchers call this reluctance the "inhibition of return" and can even measure it. We can't keep refocusing on something that seems of little value, and why on earth would we? We actually focus on the body for reasons that are far more convincing than the "breath as anchor" argument, but these are quite hard to explain in words. They often seem trivial until they are well grounded through practice.

Focusing on the body can produce some very satisfying results. In particular, it can induce fine pervasive pleasure throughout the body, even in the presence of residual pain. Body scanning disarms the habitual tension and overarousal that make many of us unconsciously miserable all day long. It can make us feel good and often very good indeed. This alone is sufficient to explain why meditation is such a good antidote to anxiety. The Buddha was adamant that deep physical pleasure is almost essential for progress. It is the reward for good work, the proof of success, and the motivation for further effort. Pleasure induces the body itself to make a judgment: "Meditating is good! Keep doing it!"

VIPASSANA RETREATS

If you focus more deliberately than usual on the body, what do you find? On the ten-day retreats I did between 1975 and 1992, we spent as many as ten hours a day sitting still and focusing on the body. The retreats mostly followed the same formula, which originated from two or three Vipassana teachers in Burma and Thailand.

For the first three days we were typically asked to focus in microscopic detail on the changing sensations of the breath at the nostrils: pulsing, tingling, itching, aching, warmth, coolness, and so on. In other words, we were learning the skill of selective, sustained attention (Pali: *vitakka-vicara*) directed at the breath. This strong focus simultaneously weakened our natural mental inclination toward action or random thought.

From the fourth day onward we would repeatedly scan the whole body with the same fine quality of attention we gave to the breath. An hour to scan down. An hour to scan up. Two hours to scan down. Two hours to scan up. We would notice pleasure, pain, warmth, pulsing, flow, knots, dullness, expansion, tightness and softness, darkness and light.

I always found it easy to stay focused. The work was fascinating and rewarding. A general rule in meditation suggests that "focus improves function." If you pay good attention to what you are doing, whether that is meditating or something else, the activity invariably becomes more efficient and satisfying. This principle certainly operates when you focus your attention on the body.

By repeatedly scanning, I could feel my body softening, rebalancing, opening up, letting go of chronic tensions, and discovering new sensory pleasures. I also noticed the subtle emotional resonances, the verbal scripts, the imagery and memories embedded within those physical sensations. By observing my *body* carefully I could see in much finer detail what was happening in my *mind*.

In other words, focusing on the body was not confined to the purely physical. Detailed body awareness jumps that body-mind divide. The Buddha said that profound training in mindfulness of the body inevitably flows through into mindfulness of emotions, of states of mind, and of thought itself. When we could feel each part of our bodies with a high degree of sensitivity, we were then told to sweep up and down more rapidly, to integrate our mental maps of our bodies. Focusing on the body still took effort, but it certainly wasn't boring.

At this point in the Vipassana format, we were usually encouraged to contemplate the Buddhist theory of suffering and its causes. I don't know how many of us actually did that. The arguments the teachers presented struck me as childish and unconvincing. They were also quite incidental to the remarkable and unexpected benefits I got from meditating.

GAINING EXPERTISE IN BODY AWARENESS

We know that the acquisition of any skill correlates closely to hours of intelligent (that is, not mindless) practice. Most people can't afford to take ten-day retreats, but practicing steadily over a year can clock up just as much time. So what distinguishes an experienced meditator from a novice? What is the result of the hundred hours of practice you get from a retreat?

Meditation profoundly enhances the way we feel our body from the inside. This data is integrated into a detailed map, or series of maps, of the body held in the brain. This is the mental map we have talked about as the "body schema" in earlier chapters, and it is extremely fluid. It constantly adjusts to new information via feedback mechanisms. When we reach out or smile or burp or get angry, the body schema instantly mirrors those events.

One part of the body schema is "proprioceptive." That is to say, it reads the signals from our muscles, tendons, joints, and cartilage to give us an inner picture of where our body is in space. Proprioception tells us which part of the body is doing what, how tense or relaxed we are, and how easy or hard, how effective or faulty, any movement is. It also connects with our sense of balance.

Because proprioception comes from the musculoskeletal system, we can control much of it with considerable precision. Meditators often make countless subtle adjustments while they sit that would be invisible to any outside observer. More commonly, however, they simply notice external or musculo-skeletal sensations, and this awareness alone induces fine changes. Every one of those tiny shifts is likely to improve the sense of comfort and ease in the body, and the effect is cumulative over time.

The other big part of the body schema is "visceral." This emanates from our cardiovascular and respiratory systems and from our digestive tract. This information tells us, in particular, about our levels of arousal (that is, blood pressure and heart rate), which are the key indicators of stress.

The viscera also convey many of our emotions and moods to the brain. They are the biological sources for our intuitive sense of good and bad, right and wrong, about anything at all (see chapter 19 for a fuller discussion about optimizing emotions). These "gut feelings" explain why being more grounded in the body helps us to make better judgments. Detailed body scanning puts us in touch with the substrata of sensations and emotions that support and inform our conscious mental activity.

Unlike the visible body, the body schema will change enormously during the day. Your body as you walk into a restaurant looks much the same as the one that walks out. But if you ate or drank too much, your body schema would be utterly different. Similarly, a relaxed body feels different from an anxious one. A joyful body is different from a depressed one, and these different states can be worlds apart.

Because body awareness is nonverbal, it is mostly outside of consciousness. We all have a functioning body schema or we couldn't negotiate our way through a room, but our ability to tap into this mental map varies enormously. A child can move with ease, agility, and precision because of her good sense of body and the surrounding space. An old, sick person is likely to grope and fumble at least partly because of his impaired body schema. He doesn't "see" or "feel" himself as clearly as he once did.

Some people have good body awareness but most don't. Some people barely feel their bodies except when in they're in pain. Other people live totally in their heads or in their actions, and some deliberately split off from their bodies. People who rarely notice their bodies will have rudimentary, underdeveloped body schemas. They won't be able to detect signals of stress, pain, fatigue, hunger, or even their emotions, until these become extreme. They may realize they have a problem only when they start having panic attacks.

On the other hand, athletes, musicians, performers, tradesmen, people who work with their bodies, and those who exercise consciously are bound to have more detailed and functional body schemas. They are more "embodied," at least in the domain of their particular abilities. Having a good body schema also makes it more likely that a person will be happier, more emotionally aware, and able to make better decisions.

THE REWARDS OF BLISS (*PITI*)
AND CONTENTMENT (*SUKHA*)

Regular meditators inevitably develop their body schemas over time, even if they think they are doing something altogether different. Since our attention naturally orients itself to what is problematic, when we focus on the body we first notice the "negatives"—the stress, pain, fatigue, and imbalances. Over time these negatives diminish, the body schema becomes balanced, and the "positives" become more prominent.

The positives that we feel in meditation can be quite splendid. The Buddha said that mindfulness of the body is the source of the most profound bliss (*piti*) and contentment (*sukha*) possible in this unsatisfactory world. Personally, I believe that there are superior pleasures, but a good meditation is right up there near the top.

The historical Buddha is correctly seen as a somber, world-renouncing ascetic, but that's not the full story. Two of his key texts, *The Foundations of Mindfulness* and its companion work, *Mindfulness of the Body*,[2] were designed to induce profoundly positive states of body and mind. These are called the absorption states (*jhana*), and they can help answer the question "Why do we focus so much on the body?"

Both of these key texts start with the same 1-2-3-4 stages: Focus on the breath. Calm the breath. Focus on the body.

Calm the body. The relief that comes from reducing arousal and muscle tension to its minimum is followed by the subtle pleasure of body-mind stillness (*passaddhi*). The Buddha said that this sense of tranquil embodiment was the indispensable foundation for what follows.

At this point, the *Satipatthana Sutta* branches out to explore emotions, states of mind, and thoughts (the other three foundations of mindfulness), while *Mindfulness of the Body* goes more deeply into the absorption states, or *jhana*. Let's follow this latter route.

The instructions go like this. First establish sustained point focus on the breath (as in the first three days of a ten-day retreat). Then become absorbed in the body schema by scanning in minute detail (as in the last seven days of a retreat). Sooner or later a sense of subtle bliss (*piti*) will start to occur.

The term *piti* covers a vast range of dynamic body sensations ranging from mild pleasure to ecstasy, not all of which are pleasant. *Piti* typically has a radiant, bubbling, alive quality within the body. Its emotional quality is described in terms such as delight, joy, exhilaration, rapture. The word "bliss," which implies both its physical and emotional qualities, is probably the best one-word definition of *piti*, but the range of *piti* is so wide that we need to hold its definitions lightly. We can, however, say three things about it.

First, it is a very positive state that arises from transformations within a tranquil body. *Piti* can be thought of as the very best of the sensations that accompany relaxation. Second, it is hard to continue meditating or see any point in doing so without experiencing at least some degree of *piti*. Why would you meditate if it didn't feel good to do so? Third, *piti* can be so subtle that we may not even notice it when it is present. Many people get dull and sleepy when they meditate, so they can miss it. *Piti* can be life changing, but it is usually profound and pervasive, rather than flashy or exciting.

When people feel that meditation can heal the body, this fine internal effervescence is the source of their intuition. The term *piti* roughly corresponds to the yogic term *prana*, and the Chinese *ch'i*, and the Greek *psyche*. These all refer to a sort of "life force" that manifests as a real-time, ever-changing play of sensations rather than a concept.

Over time an even richer state than *piti* will emerge. This is *sukha*, which translates from the Pali most inadequately as "contentment" or "happiness." *Sukha* involves an uncritical acceptance of the moment: "Whatever happens is okay." *Sukha* implies a complete absence of mental disturbance or conflict, even in the most extreme situations. It roughly correlates to the sense of mystic union with the world found in other traditions.

Mindfulness of the Body presents a string of vivid metaphors that describe what good body scanning feels like. For instance, it says, the monk "makes the rapture (*piti*) and pleasure (*sukha*) born of seclusion drench, steep, fill and pervade his body so that there is no part of his whole body"[3] that is unpervaded by it. Body scanning intuitively aims for this kind of total body harmony.

Here is another metaphor from the text above. The monk's body is said to become like a lake with no inflow. The waters well up from an internal spring so that every part of the lake is pervaded with cool water. In the Pali Canon, coolness symbolizes freedom from the passions, which presumably are "hot." And here is another metaphor: The monk's body is said to be like a lotus that grows entirely beneath the surface of the lake, so that cool water will "drench, steep, fill and pervade" the whole lotus from tip to roots.

Among serious meditators, this sense of upwelling or enveloping bliss is quite common. It typically occurs, as the text says, "in seclusion," with "no inflow" from the outer world. This explains why doing retreats and being cut off from the world for a time is so valuable. It has the paradoxical effect of being both dynamic (*piti*) and deeply soothing (*sukha*). (Many other practices, from Kundalini yoga to the elaborate visualizations of Tibetan Buddhism, try to evoke the same thing.)

Although *piti* ("the pleasure born of seclusion") is most likely to become obvious on a retreat, the first signs of bliss are very ordinary. They occur whenever we relax. We shift from the tight, holding on, blocked, slightly painful, awkward sensations of tension toward a softer, flowing, gentler way of being in our bodies. When people say that they meditate to "relieve stress," they are intuitively seeking this shift toward pleasure and ease. This shift is why we unaccountably feel so much better when we meditate.

In the *Sutta* the Buddha asks us to notice not only the presence of positive states such as *piti* and *sukha*, but also what precedes them and what causes them to arise. The most primary and necessary cause of *piti* is enhanced body awareness. Absorption states rarely last very long, but even regular ordinary meditations will cultivate a rich and detailed mental map of the body over time.

THE MENTAL BENEFITS OF BODY MINDFULNESS

I've described the physical reward of good embodiment, but there are powerful cognitive benefits as well. The Buddha describes mindfulness of the body as being like a fortress against the world. If your mind completely pervades your body, it is like a door made of heartwood. It repels temptations as if they were balls of string thrown at it. This suggests that a good meditator can escape the tyranny of thought by retreating to the sanctuary of his body. Nor does he require constant interaction with the outer world to feel good. He really can sit quietly in his room and be blissful.

The Buddha then described good embodiment as the basis for directed attention. He said that the mind grounded in the body is like oil within a jar. When you tip the jar, the oil will flow out smoothly in that one direction only. This means that good embodiment allows you to focus effortlessly on whatever you choose without your attention splattering.

In a similar metaphor, he says that mindfulness of the body is like having a team of thoroughbred horses harnessed to a chariot at the crossroads, ready to go anywhere. A man with a well-trained mind can go out on any road as far as he wishes and return at will. In other words, a mindful person can investigate any thought safely because he remains grounded in his body. He is too strong to be ambushed or tempted by mental detours. He can also disengage from any train of thought and return to body-mind stillness (the crossroads) whenever he wants.

The Buddha also said that mindfulness of the body is the essential base for all intuitive knowledge. Because the body mirrors the mind, good body awareness is thus the foundation for understanding our emotions, our states of mind, and thoughts. (He then goes on to list another twenty metaphors and benefits that come from enhanced embodiment, many of them magical!)

We can now understand why the "breath as anchor" argument is so inadequate. If our attention sits too lightly on the breath it will soon flit off to something more interesting. The breath is almost too simple to focus on. The body as a whole is more engaging. Trying to focus on the breath to avoid thought can be far too cerebral and unrewarding a reason to stay there.

For many meditators, the breath is most valuable as a proxy entrance into the body schema. A good breath meditator will simultaneously feel his whole body and the state of the life force within it. This positive somatic feedback will strengthen focus, and the benefits just mentioned can start to appear.

Whether we focus on the breath or scan the body, the primal underlying object of meditation is always the body schema: our unified, real-time, proprioceptive-visceral mental map of the body. Research using brain scans tells us that regular practice strengthens this mental map and bulks up its neural correlates in the brain. That part of a violinist's brain that maps his fingers becomes larger and more richly connected over time. Similarly, a good meditator will develop a strong, integrated image of his entire body.

Over the years this familiarity with the body schema builds into a disposition in which we maintain body awareness whether we happen to be meditating or not. This explains how sitting down and apparently doing nothing can be so valuable. It ultimately gives us a rich, flexible, and enhanced mental map of who we are in the moment. It makes us "present."

We now have many good reasons for focusing so much on the body: Rapid relaxation. Dissolving stress and anxiety. Body-mind stillness (*passaddhi*). Physical bliss (*piti*). Deep contentment (*sukha*). Immunity from temptation and distraction. Strong sustained focus (*samadhi*). A sense of embodiment (*kayagatasati*). The capacity to follow any thought or action as far as we want and then return to baseline. Emotional awareness and the ability to make good judgments. I could go on, but I think that's enough.

Don't be surprised if all of this seems unfamiliar to you. It is hardly ever mentioned in the modern literature. Psychologists and popular writers invariably privilege mind over body. They tend to present mindfulness as being purely cognitive: an ideal state of nonjudgmental acceptance or "the observer mind." This parallels the way that Tibetan Buddhism and Zen tend to seek out an underlying or transcendental purity of mind while devaluing its contents.

Many of the early writers on psychological mindfulness were even hostile to the idea that physical effects such as relaxation could be at all beneficial. They saw relaxation as an epiphenomenal side effect of little importance. This is presumably because, as specialists in the field of mental disorders, they preferred to emphasize the mind as the causative agent in therapeutic change. You'd be hard-pressed, however, to find an experienced meditator who would subscribe to the claim that all satisfaction happens in the mind.

Good meditators tend to be equally critical of the trivializing, quick-fix, "change your mind and be happy" approach of the self-help literature. A novice really can meditate from scratch and get good results within minutes, but cultivating strong body awareness is analogous to sports training: It takes months of steady, self-monitoring practice. We don't become more embodied by flicking a mental switch or by thinking to ourselves "just be present."

8

To Sit or Not to Sit

*Furthermore, when walking, a monk thinks:
"I am walking." When standing, he thinks: "I am
standing." Likewise he knows when he is sitting
or lying down. He calms his breathing and his
body in each of these postures.*

*He is equally mindful when coming and going;
when looking forward or around him; when bending
and stretching; when wearing his robes and carrying
his bowl; when eating, drinking, chewing, and
tasting; when defecating and urinating; when
walking, standing, sitting, and lying down;
when falling asleep and waking up; when
talking and remaining silent.*
—**Satipatthana Sutta**

For most popular writers, psychologists, and meditators, "mindfulness" describes a formal meditation practice and nothing else. The sit-down, eyes-closed Standard Meditation Practice described in chapter 1 is assumed to have trickle-down effects in ordinary life, but these spin-offs are rarely regarded as part of the mindfulness practice itself. Most people assume that meditation *always* involves sitting down. It *always* involves having the eyes closed. This is not what the Buddha taught, but it seems to have become the universal paradigm in the West.

Likewise, the psychological definition of mindfulness as "a state of nonjudgmental acceptance" relies on sitting still. We couldn't maintain this passive, nonreactive, "open" state once we start to move. Even the most routine action requires a stream of subtle judgments and decisions. We couldn't cross the road safely or even do the dishes adequately in a state of nonjudgmental acceptance. So what are we to make of the Buddha's instructions in the *Sutta*? They seem completely counterintuitive.

The Buddha regarded "the systematic four-stage training of attention" as a continuous practice, independent of any formal posture. Learning to maintain good body awareness throughout the day is just the first of the four foundations of mindfulness. Mindfulness of the body is the essential support what follows: the real-time perception and evaluation of emotions, states of mind, and thoughts as they come and go in all circumstances. In other words, *satipatthana*—the art of continual self-observation—is purposeful. The *Sutta* addresses monks who were striving for enlightenment. We strive in some way for a more satisfying life. We can only achieve this through the skillful, discriminatory use of our attention.

The Buddha insisted that the monk should train himself to meditate equally well in *four* formal postures: sitting, walking, standing, and lying down. Likewise, a modern meditator is perfectly capable of attaining body-mind stillness (*passad-dhi*), bliss (*piti*), and deep contentment (*sukha*) while walking or standing. Feeling inwardly still while physically moving is not an oxymoron. Athletes call this "dynamic balance," and it is a defining characteristic of flow states.

Once the monk had perfected body-mind stillness in each of those four standard postures, he was then instructed to expand that quality into *every* activity. The Buddha gave a few examples: getting dressed, eating, bathing, urinating, and defecating. We don't usually think of urinating as an activity suitable for meditation, but the Buddha really did mean it. The development of inner balance, bodily comfort, mental stillness, and self-observation should not be confined to the ghetto of a formal exercise.

A monk of the Buddha's time may well have trained himself to do formal walking meditations, as people often do nowadays on ten-day retreats. However, the fourth-century commentator Buddhaghosa correctly spelled out the Buddha's intentions. He said that formal practice was good and usually necessary at first, but *informal* practice was superior.

A monk might practice formally by walking twenty paces back and forth in front of his hut, as they still occasionally do nowadays. A skilled monk, however, could maintain his detachment and cultivate his purity of mind while "walking across a plowed field" or through a busy town. This would mean the monk who "graduated" from novice to expert was no longer reliant on any posture or situation. His practice could in fact be invisible to others. People wouldn't know whether he was meditating or not. He could be mindful anywhere and at any time. Sitting meditators, on the other hand, remain stuck at the first stage. Their meditation is separate from the rest of their life.

We can guess from the *Sutta* how the systematic development of the postures would have happened. The monk would first meditate *sitting* with eyes closed under a tree; then doing the same with eyes open; then *walking* to and fro in front of his tree; then *walking* to the local village to beg some food. He would then meditate while *standing* outside a rich man's home until lunchtime, when a servant would notice him and bring him food. He would then *walk* mindfully back to his tree; eat mindfully; *lie down* and rest.

These are the four formal postures: sitting, walking, standing, and lying down. These are acknowledged if not practiced by nearly all Buddhist schools. The monk would surely have done each of them with erratic and unreliable self-awareness at first. Like all skills, they would need to be separately and repeatedly practiced. Being an accomplished *sitting* meditator doesn't automatically spill over into being a good *walking* or *standing* meditator. All skills are far more context-dependent than we usually assume.

Unfortunately, learning to walk mindfully doesn't seem worthwhile to modern meditators. Many aspiring models, not to mention yoga practitioners, gym junkies, politicians, and celebrities, are more conscious of how they walk and stand than are meditators. How many experienced meditators exhibit a sense of ease, balance, and flow when they walk? The Buddha described this as a noble accomplishment. According to legend, the emperor Asoka was inspired to make Buddhism the state religion by seeing a monk walking serenely through the gory aftermath of a mighty battle.

The Buddha's instructions have been extremely important for me personally. After discovering them in 1975, I developed the forty-two exercises in my 2005 book, *The 5-Minute Meditator*. Twelve of these are walking meditations that can be practiced invisibly on any street. These exercises, and many I've developed since, are the broad-based foundation of my own discipline. I still enjoy sitting. I discovered recently that I can still sit cross-legged for seven hours a day with no discomfort. Nonetheless I am not fixated on this one posture. I meditate in all the four formal postures nearly every day.

JUST SITTING, NOT THINKING

Almost no one nowadays knows about the instructions from the *Sutta*, or takes them seriously if they do. The standard sitting meditation described in chapter 1 is the universal paradigm, and to be honest, there are some good reasons for this. For the rest of this chapter, I'll be the devil's advocate and argue the opposite point of view to the Buddha.

Long sitting meditation under good circumstances can lead to exceptionally beautiful states of body and mind. These are called the four *jhana* (absorption or trance states). The *jhana* states are characterized by an extreme stillness of body and mind (*passaddhi*), physical bliss (*piti*), deep contentment (*sukha*), and a profound sense of philosophic and emotional detachment from the world (*upekkha*, or equanimity).

The Buddha regarded the state of absorption, or trance, as the finest pleasure available in this uncertain world. Although he may have viewed *jhana* as an essential springboard for ultimate attainment, he repeatedly warned against mistaking it for enlightenment itself. The "tranquility practice" of *jhana* was a common attainment of the many non-Buddhist schools of his time. The Buddha distinguished his teaching from these by his emphasis on mindfulness (*sati*) and insight (*vipassana*). Nonetheless, there remains a long tradition within Buddhism of infatuation with *jhana* as the ultimate attainment. This inevitably leads to a heavy emphasis on sitting meditation.

The thirteenth-century Zen philosopher Dogen is the most articulate exponent of this approach. Dogen founded the Japanese school of Soto Zen, which is solidly anchored on sitting meditation (*zazen*). He invented the practice called *shikantaza*, which literally translates as "just sitting." The Japanese word is actually more emphatic. A better translation would be "absolutely nothing but sitting" or "just sitting very firmly."

In a rich and compact early text called "Fukanzazengi" (which translates as "universal recommendations for *zazen*"), Dogen explained how to do *shikantaza*: "Sit firmly. Think of not thinking. How do you think of not thinking? By not thinking! This is the very essence of *zazen*."[1] Dogen gave demanding prescriptions on how to sit properly: straight, alert, and only cross-legged on the proper Zen cushions, in full-lotus or half-lotus posture. No other posture was acceptable in the pursuit of enlightenment. A hair's breadth of deviation from this ideal, and the Way is as distant as heaven from earth.

For serious meditators, this emphasis on the sitting posture can verge on the fanatical. Many of us in the 1970s and 1980s were encouraged to strive for the ideal and to sit through the pain. It was regarded as a great virtue to sit for hours with screaming knees and backs. (The insightful Zen writer Susan Moon recently commented that there seemed to be a disproportionate number of dedicated meditators requiring knee operations in later life.)

When criticized by monks of rival schools for ignoring the other three classic postures of Buddhism (walking, standing, and lying down), and for sidelining *all* Buddhist philosophy and tradition, Dogen argued that *zazen* was the most direct route to enlightenment: "The character of this school is simply devotion to sitting, total engagement in immobile sitting. Although there are as many minds as there are men, still they [all] negotiate the Way solely in *zazen*. Why leave behind the seat that exists in your home and go aimlessly off to the dusty realms of other lands?"[2]

Dogen even described sitting meditation as the *entire* practice of Buddhism. The scriptures were irrelevant. The practice alone was the attainment. Just to do *zazen* was to be enlightened in that very moment. Dogen said, "*Zazen* is the ultimate practice. This is indeed the True Self. The Buddha-dharma is not to be sought outside of this."[3]

Dogen goes on: "Cast aside all involvements and cease all affairs. Do not think good or bad. Do not administer pros and cons. Cease all the movements of the conscious mind, gauging of all thoughts and views. Cease from practice based on intellectual understanding, pursuing words and following after speech, and learn the backward step that turns your light inward."[4] Dogen repeats this point about abandoning all judgment and discrimination hundreds of times in his voluminous writings. Kabat-Zinn's definition of mindfulness as "a state of nonjudgmental acceptance" almost certainly derives, directly or indirectly, from Dogen. That is, Modern

Mindfulness reflects the approach of *shikantaza*, not the instructions of the Buddha from the Pali Canon.

Shikantaza is similar to *jhana* but a little different as well. *Jhana* in the Indian tradition typically turns inward, and disconnects from the outer world. *Shikantaza* is more open to ordinary present-moment experience. The Chan Buddhist Master Sheng Yen (1930–2009) says, "Be clear about everything going on in your mind, but never abandon the awareness of your whole body sitting. Whatever enters the door of your senses becomes one totality, extending from your body to the whole environment."[5]

In the practice of *shikantaza*, you try to become "empty." You allow thoughts and sensations to pass through your mental space. You aim for a passive, nonstriving state of mind: no active thought, no judgment, no likes or dislikes, no attachment or avoidance—just an unfocused openness to experience. Eventually, "body and mind drop away" and the sense of separation between self and the world vanishes.

The Mahayana tradition calls this state *sunyata* (emptiness) or *bodhicitta* (buddhamind) or *anatta* (no-self) or "nonduality." Literally thousands of pages in praise of it fill the Mahayana scriptures of Tibet, China, and Japan. Kabat-Zinn echoes this tradition when he says that that meditation is "the direct realization and embodiment in this very moment of who you already are, outside of time and space and any concept of any kind, a resting in the very nature of your being, in what is sometimes called the natural state, original mind, pure awareness, no mind, or simply emptiness."[6]

Kabat-Zinn trained extensively in Zen before developing MBSR. *Shikantaza*, the practice of "just sitting, not thinking" is identical to MBSR in many respects: the emphasis on still-ness and nonreactivity; long sitting meditations; the deval-uing of thought and the abandonment of judgment; and the idealizing of an "open," uncritical acceptance of present-moment experience.

The Zen conception of meditation has largely super-seded the more substantial Theravadin tradition, at least in the West. Our popular conception of Buddhist meditation comes almost entirely from Soto Zen and Vipassana. Both disciplines emphasize long and repeated sessions of seated meditation. Both emphasize the superiority of direct experi-ence over tradition and learning. The mind of a Zen master is assumed to be identical to the mind of the Buddha, so this makes the scriptures irrelevant. They might as well be used as firewood (as at least one Zen master did to shock his stu-dents). This authority from intuition has also enabled Zen to abandon large swathes of traditional Buddhism while still claiming to manifest its essence.

Dogen's Zen is a halfway house between the asceticism of the Buddha and the more accommodating, secular med-itation practices of today. As a late reform movement in Buddhism, it downplays ideas that many Westerners find dis-tasteful. Karma and reincarnation are reduced to metaphors. Emptiness (*sunyata*) has replaced suffering as the big idea. Sense-restraint, moral training, and monastic values become optional. Stillness and "being present" replace the earnest drive for enlightenment. And the four classical postures of early Buddhism are reduced to just one.

Modern Mindfulness is often criticized as being a form of "Buddhism lite," but Dogen's Zen had already established the new ground rules. Modern Mindfulness really can claim some Buddhist descent, but it derives from a stripped-down, "be here now" form of Buddhism that is more acceptable to Westerners than the ascetic original.

9

Mindful Action

This chapter is not about meditation. It is about our common English-language use of the word "mindful." The word "mindful" goes back to the fourteenth century. Most of us will use it occasionally, and we certainly understand what it means. As native English speakers, we "own" this word as part of our lexical heritage. We shouldn't let psychologists and popular writers obscure its original meaning with their new interpretations.

In the English vernacular, "to be mindful" means "to pay attention." The phrase is particularly targeted at one's *actions*. It usually means: to focus on what you are doing to avoid mistakes or improve performance. As an adjective, "mindful" means "alert" or "attentive." It works just as well as an imperative: "Be mindful!" means "Be careful! Don't make mistakes!" Acting mindfully is the opposite of being thoughtless or clumsy or mindless or inadvertently offending others. It suggests a fully conscious, discriminating quality of mind.

We are always mindful for a purpose. Anything we consciously notice has already been preselected by the brain as potentially important, so we only give high-quality attention to things that could be significant for our well-being. We focus on something in order to better evaluate and respond to it. When we do so, we usually shift our attitude or behavior toward it in some way, however slight. We refine our judgment. Paying attention would be a waste of mental energy otherwise.

We have to be sufficiently mindful to accomplish any kind of task: getting dressed, eating, driving, having a conversation, working, managing children, answering emails, shopping, doing exercise, seeking entertainment, or doing whatever other details of daily life need to be attended to. All of these actions will suffer if done thoughtlessly, and each one requires a certain level of self-monitoring attention to be accomplished at all. If we're too careless or distracted, we can't even reliably pick up a spoon. We're just as likely to knock it off the table instead.

Some activities are so routine and automatic that we can virtually do them in our sleep. Others demand more focus. Situations of novelty, danger, temptation, or inner conflict will all prompt us to become more mindful. We also sharpen up in situations that could go wrong, in those with high potential for reward, and in those where clear thought or finesse are essential for success.

We become mindful spontaneously when we need to. Mindfulness is commonly a "stop and look before you act" mechanism. This slows us down, if only for a nanosecond, so that we can reflect on what we are doing. To be mindful means that we notice when we have eaten enough, so we stop. We notice when an unintended tone of sarcasm enters our voice. While in the supermarket, we recognize the conflict between our desires for pleasure and good health.

To be mindful also means noticing and (ideally) resisting impulses that it is best not to act upon: the tendency to grab that food, to shop recreationally, to space out, to quit, to stare, to get self-righteous, to give in, to complain. Mindfulness is a huge part of what we think of as self-control.

Mindfulness helps us to make thousands of small yes-or-no judgments each day to keep us out of trouble. It can be thought of as the habit of self-observation or self-reflection or self-monitoring. Without it, if we were mindless, we would be at the mercy of every temptation and impulse, and we wouldn't even know why things were going so badly wrong. This wouldn't stop us from finding plausible reasons: bad luck, upbringing, karma, discrimination, genes, conspiracy, God's plan.

Because mindfulness of action is built on learned routines, it can work quite smoothly for hours at a time. We monitor and self-evaluate our behavior almost without realizing it. However, when it comes under pressure this routine, low-level mindfulness becomes fragile and prone to collapse. The Buddha encouraged us to monitor our states of mind (the third "foundation" of mindfulness, discussed more in chapter 18) to preempt this danger.

Our capacity to pay sufficient attention suffers under suboptimal states of mind. These occur when we are tired, sick, hungry, emotionally aroused, overloaded with information, obsessing about something, worrying about a chronic problem, or when we have just made too many demanding decisions in the preceding hours (decision fatigue). All of these will weaken self-control and make us more likely to act thoughtlessly.

At certain times we simply don't have the cognitive capacity to think straight, any more than we can drive safely when we're drunk. We can try hard to perform well, but no amount of effort or worry or need or coffee will bring us up to scratch. When we become mindful that we are a liability to ourselves, we need to restrict our activity to tasks that are simple and routine, or just go to bed. This retreat from activity would not be a failure of will—it would be a decision to act wisely instead of foolishly.

MINDFULNESS HAS MULTIPLE PURPOSES

Mindfulness is not a free-floating state of mind, a pure awareness, or mirrorlike consciousness. "To pay attention" is a transitive verb: it always has an object and it interacts with it. We have to focus our attention on *something*, and the consequent interaction is for a *purpose*. The flavors of mindfulness differ immensely according to what we focus on and what our purpose is. Let's now look at how different objects and purposes shape our understanding of mindfulness.

The "Man in the Street"

To an ordinary person in everyday life, being mindful means paying attention to what one is doing. The *object* is invariably an action and the *purpose* is to avoid mistakes and improve performance. It is also mindfulness directed *outwardly* rather than inwardly.

The Monk

The Buddha said that we should pay attention to the body, emotions, states of mind, and thoughts, but he omits action from this list except when it is unavoidable. A monk is trying to bring all thought and action to a halt, not improve them. This is mindfulness directed *inwardly* for the *purpose* of physical stillness and emotional detachment.

The Professional Athlete

In the West, attentional training has been most fully developed in sports, the performing arts, and the military. A soccer player, for example, has to focus both *inwardly*, monitoring arousal, muscle tone, and energy, and focus *outwardly* as well. He learns to flexibly switch attention from inner to outer, and from single-point focus to wide-angle focus as the moment requires. This is high-quality, high-energy attention for the purpose of winning. A person can make a lot of money out of well-trained mindfulness.

The Mother

Any good mother learns to focus well on her child's physical and emotional behavior, and on her own response to that. She's not interested in serene detachment (like the monk) or in winning (like the football player). Her goal is closer to that of the ordinary man in the street: good daily functioning.

The Soldier

Learning to self-monitor and pay attention has been integral to military training for centuries. In the Far East we see it in the close links between the samurai and Zen. A sniper needs very low arousal and muscle activation while also remaining vigilant. His goal is to kill without getting killed. Conversely a soldier in the field needs the ability to pace himself under pressure. Soldiers can pay the supreme price if they are distracted when it matters. Being mindful is not just a baby-boomer indulgence.

The High-Stakes Specialist

Many people such as doctors, pilots, or operators of machinery have to develop sustained, self-monitoring attention as part of their professions, or catastrophes can occur in an instant. This is another high-stakes form of mindfulness.

The Psychologist

A psychologist will see mindfulness primarily as a therapeutic tool. Her goal will usually be to help another person lower arousal, enhance self-control, and better manage thoughts and moods.

The Student

Long before the psychological bandwagon took off, mindfulness was promoted as an essential metacognitive skill for students. Attention is critical for any kind of learning, from babyhood onward. We have to be able to "hold something in mind" for long enough to store it in memory.

The Connoisseur

People who deeply enjoy music, art, movies, travel, nature, or other pleasures will have given a lot of high-quality attention to them over the years. The object of their mindfulness is beauty. Their purpose is delight.

The Contented Person

Sustained, uninterrupted attention is essential for states of deep pleasure and "flow." Social scientists now speculate that frequent flow states in one's life are good indicators of subjective well-being, while the absence of flow correlates with depression. Conversely, it is almost impossible to feel good if one's mind is constantly scattered, distracted, restless, or confused.

MINDFULNESS IS DOMAIN-SPECIFIC

These kinds of mindfulness all involve attention, but this is not readily transferable from one activity to another. You don't want your surgeon to be in a state of serene monastic detachment. Empathy and affection are ideal for a mother, but not for a soldier. The intense point focus of a sniper will not necessarily help you raise a toddler. Nor can a mindful mother instantly switch to being a mindful soldier or a mindful nun.

Skills are invariably domain specific. Each skill comes embedded with different physiological markers, emotional tones, learned behaviors, and values. A surgeon needs strong sustained point focus. A mother needs wide-angle trouble-shooting attention. A meditator wants a low-arousal, low-muscle-tone state with minimal awareness of the environment. An athlete needs high arousal, constantly modulated muscle tone, and strong environmental awareness.

Learning any skill is time-consuming, so we naturally select what seems most profitable to us personally. A mindful person such as a meditator is likely to have specialized in focusing on one kind of object (the body) for one kind of purpose (mental calm). She may not even be aware of other possibilities. Even after reading this book, I am sure that many readers will continue to think of mindfulness as referring to meditation alone. So which of these is "real" mindfulness? I hope this survey shows you that the uses of mindfulness can be much more diverse than you may have expected. The concept of mindful action doesn't have to be squeezed all into one box.

MINDFULNESS FOR ENHANCED PERFORMANCE

Mindfulness keeps us out of trouble, but it is also essential if we want to *improve* what we do. Mindfulness is often incorporated into sports and military training. Top athletes consciously develop a wide range of attentional skills. A team player needs to be able to switch from a tunnel-visioned, spotlight focus (for instance, when making a shot) to a wide-angle fluid attention (when sensing what is happening on the whole field). We also have to switch our attention from narrow to wide when we leave the computer or a book, and attend to our children or our friends.

An athlete needs to be able to mobilize what is called "preparatory attention." This is when he stops, clears his mental space, and imagines a few seconds ahead to a desired outcome. Likewise, in everyday life we need to learn how to put aside a previous task and psychologically prepare for a new one.

A good athlete is able to turn his level of arousal up or down as required. He can recognize when he needs maximum arousal and when he can mentally cruise (if the ball is far away). High arousal sustained for too long will make him brittle and jumpy. This is when athletes choke. Low arousal, on the other hand, leads to boredom and distraction. Similarly, we need to recognize the signs of mind-numbing anxiety (high arousal) or a severe lack of interest in what we are doing (low arousal).

All of these attentional skills are essential for the conservation of physical energy. With poor self-monitoring, an athlete will run out of juice before the end of the game, and so will parents and office workers. Athletes are frequently taught attentional skills to help them avoid this. Nonspecialists like the rest of us tend to haphazardly learn them as required over a much greater range of activities, but the process is similar.

Sati, the Buddhist word for "mindfulness," literally means "memory." If we do something on automatic pilot we forget it immediately. If, however, we pay good attention to a task for just a few seconds, it gets a foothold in what is called "working memory." If we do that task particularly well or badly it then gets stored for future reference.

The next time that we do that task, a faint functional trace of that memory returns. It reminds us how to do the task better or how to avoid the same mistake again. This is how the sportsman gradually improves a maneuver and how we improve our performance in a vast range of social and practical skills. We learn to do things well by recognizing, acknowledging, and remembering our *mistakes*. Educators call this "error-based learning." Mindfulness as a kind of self-monitoring, or metacognition—that is, thinking about thinking—enhances these positive outcomes.

Because meditation emphasizes stillness, "just watching," and nonreactivity, we can easily forget that it is a skill like any other. It is training in not reacting. We have said before that the four foundations of mindfulness are more accurately translated as "training disciplines." The *Sutta* itself contains thirteen exercises, each of which is designed to be practiced individually until they are all well consolidated in memory. Learning any skill requires intelligent self-criticism, but we tend to assume this doesn't apply to meditation. A meditation model of passivity and nonjudgmental acceptance, an attitude of "just being, not doing" and "nothing to achieve," is now far more dominant in meditation than it was in the Buddha's time.

HOW TO BE MINDFUL IN ACTION

To be mindful of something means to consciously perceive and evaluate it. We can train ourselves to be mindful of our actions by asking two simple questions: "What am I doing?" and "How well am I doing it?" These few seconds of perception and evaluation have the potential to improve an action or ameliorate any bad outcomes on the spot.

It is good to check what we are doing as we do it—psychologists call this "supervisory attention." It is even better if we look back over what we've just done—called "retrospective attention." For example, we can ask: "What did I just do? How well did I answer that question or drive through that intersection or process the emails? Was it adequate?" This metacognitive monitoring helps to remember good and bad performances for future reference.

To reliably improve our performance, we need to make these assessments consciously and repeatedly. Top athletes in training can commonly describe what they have just done with great accuracy and in the appropriate technical language. As the Buddha said, you are mindful if you know what you are doing *and can describe it to yourself.*

Let's now be more systematic. If we want to, we can become mindful in a flash. We simply have to ask, "What I am I doing?" and "name" that action. The next question is "Is this worth doing? Yes or no?" When we consider the matter, it is usually perfectly obvious either way. This evaluation leads to the response. If the answer is "no," we stop doing it. If the answer is "yes," a new question arises, namely, "Can I do this more efficiently?" Let's now streamline all the above into the following mindfulness exercises.

NAME THE ACTION

One way to improve your actions at any moment is to just ask yourself: "What am I doing?" Then "name" it: it could be driving, shopping, reading a magazine, eating breakfast, surfing the web, or whatever.

Then ask: "Is this worth doing at all?"

If it isn't, you drop it. If you judge it to be worthwhile, you ask: "How well am I doing this? Could I do it better?"

Let's now go a step further. It is useful to regard thinking as a kind of virtual, miniaturized action, a mental playacting that falls just short of observable behavior. Fundamentally, there is little difference between the questions "What am I doing?" and "What am I thinking about?" except that the latter is more subtle. This leads into the next exercise.

NAME THE THOUGHT

This time the sequence goes as follows. When you realize you are mentally confused, just ask: "What am I *thinking* about?"

Then "name" it: work, money, getting fat, Angelina Jolie, the tennis tournament, what the president just said.

Next ask: "Is this worth thinking about at all?"

If it is, you ask: "Could I think about this more productively?"

If it isn't, you drop it and ask: "What shall I switch my attention to now?"

Mindfulness of action typically happens on the run. We crank up our mindfulness levels as required while doing something. These quick exercises in making conscious choices about our actions and thoughts take next to no time at all. I do dozens of these self-monitoring exercises each day.

Of course this doesn't look anything like a Standard Meditation Practice. I'm not sitting down for twenty minutes focusing on my breath. I'm not even particularly calm or relaxed. I'm just more focused and present than usual. So does this mean that mindfulness of action is not "real" mindfulness? Do you still feel that you have to do formal meditations to "really" get into the perfect mindful state that psychologists and popular writers talk about?

10

A Journey into
Open Monitoring

In 1984 I did a seven-month retreat in a tiny hut high on a mountainside in the Southern Alps of New Zealand. My hut was fifteen minutes' walk above a small retreat center, which was itself fifteen minutes above a dead-end valley road about twelve miles from the nearest village. Each Wednesday afternoon I hauled my week's supplies up from the road, and I usually spent that evening with my girlfriend in her hut nearby. Otherwise I enjoyed six days of total isolation each week—just me, the possums, and the wild pigs. The panoramic views extended eighty miles to the east, and I never saw or heard any other human activity.

So what did I do each day? Seven or eight hours of sitting practice, some yoga, housework, and long walks. I got up about 2 or 3 AM and sat until the first spark of sunlight cut the eastern horizon. I usually had a late-morning sleep and a midafternoon sleep, and went to bed about 10 or 11 PM.

For the first month or two, I did various Tibetan practices, including the first half of the so-called foundation work, also known as "training in the preliminaries." This involved doing 108,000 full-length prostrations complete with mantra, visualization, and philosophical speculations. However, *satipatthana*–the Buddha's training in continuous, targeted self-observation–was always my primary practice. The conditions were perfect. I'd never enjoyed such an undisturbed, open-ended opportunity until then, and never have since. I investigated my body sensations, thoughts, emotions, moods, dreams, and biological rhythms for weeks at a time. I did this while sitting, walking, standing, and lying down, and during all the activities in between.

Through weeks of body scanning I gradually became transparent to myself. I illuminated every part of my body from the inside. I "saw" and felt everything about the muscles, bones, organs, and other physiology that it was humanly possible for me to feel. I directed that same sharp quality of vision toward my mental activity, as the Buddha recommends in the *Sutta*. I certainly didn't need any external stimulus to stay interested. Silence, stillness, and time were quite enough. The inner movies never stopped. The drama was all there within my skin, and the surprises kept coming.

Seven months of (essentially) looking in the mirror was not boring for a moment. I was delighted, irritated, astonished, and disgusted, but never bored. At that time (and *never* since), my mind had a powerful instinct to go further and further back into the past. I recovered an immense store of memories that I thought I had lost forever. I'm sure some of them were fictions, but since I was also exploring my mind's imaginative capacities, this hardly mattered. The many sublime and ecstatic states that occurred over those months were superior to anything I'd known from my younger ventures in taking LSD, which is saying a great deal. The insights into myself and the world came in the hundreds.

I believe the retreat cured forever any tendency I might have had toward depression, which is always a risk for a loner and an introvert. I also had minutes and hours, but never more than a day, of what seemed to be absolute insanity, except that I always recovered more cheerful than before. I felt confident with the process. I developed something akin to religious faith in the self-preserving intelligence of the mind. I felt as if I was in good hands, even if I didn't know whose hands they were.

Over the seven months, I got to see my mind's vast library, repertoire of stories, and bags of tricks in unimaginable detail. The luxury of this retreat was that I had ample time to see and appraise literally everything that made up "me," down to the most fleeting emotions and assumptions. I came to know who I was and what I felt, at least in that moment. I discovered which ideas and emotions were natural to me and which were cultural viruses. This gave me the grounding to deal intelligently with my biggest issue, which was: "What am I going to do with my life?"

I remained throughout a keen follower of the Buddha's method in the *Satipatthana Sutta*. There is a beautiful phrase in the literature: *ehipassiko*, which means "Come and try it out for yourself"–with the implication "and you will see that this teaching is true." That is, if you do the practice and develop a strong, calm, insightful mind, you will see the world just as the Buddha did.

I did what the Buddha recommended by following his instructions in the *Sutta*. I developed that trustworthy state of mind, but when I looked at the world, I found that the Buddha had got it wrong. He said his truth was universal, but in fact it turned out to be only *his* truth. It certainly wasn't mine. He saw life as nothing but suffering, misery, and ugliness. I couldn't for the life of me understand what he was complaining about. Meditating just made the world more beautiful and fascinating for me. I knew that was never going to change, and it never has.

I ended the retreat only because the snow arrived. My hut was not insulated and had no source of heat. After several freezing days wearing all the clothing I owned, including my sleeping bag, I realized that I had no choice but to leave. I felt somewhat half-cooked, and I promised myself another seven months sometime, but it hasn't happened yet.

That retreat was the turning point in my life. Prior to that, I had spent three years in Asia. I had also spent eight years living a back-to-the-land lifestyle, complete with gardens, orchards, beehives, and a hand-built house, in a place with like-minded neighbors. After the retreat, the limitations of that rustic idyll were nakedly obvious. Nor was I ever going to take the logical next step and become a monk. Isolation from society, playing Thoreau, and navel-gazing could take me only so far, and I knew I'd gone far enough. Freud said, "Love and work are the cornerstones of our humanity," and I knew I was lacking in both. So I came to Australia and opened up the Perth Meditation Centre. I've been teaching meditation and writing books ever since.

I was apprehensive when I left the retreat. My state of mind felt superb, but could it only exist within the nursery of a retreat? Was it like a plant reliant on a precise biological niche? Would it survive the plunge back into the barbaric world of money, work, sexual relationships, information overload, and the seas of faceless humanity?

My fears were justified. I was not surprised to find that the reentry was even tougher than I could have imagined. My life had been peaceful but intellectually poor for many years. I could see that a rich quality of life comes with a price. If I couldn't usefully meditate after an argument with a girlfriend or during another financial emergency, there wasn't much point in it. I didn't want meditation to become just a hobby, an escape, a way to relax, or a nostalgic memory of earlier, carefree times.

OPEN MONITORING

Fortunately, my main practice was *satipatthana*. On retreat, I trained myself to become mindful of–to "hold in mind" and evaluate–every thought, sensation, emotion, mood, quality of mind, memory, dream image, and intuition as they occurred. This is the full development of the *satipatthana* method, and it doesn't require isolation or long sitting meditations. *Satipatthana* could adjust to post-retreat life in a way that the Tibetan practices couldn't.

A meditation similar to *satipatthana*, and easier to understand, is what psychologists call "Open Monitoring" (OM). Done systematically, Open Monitoring is still based on a normal breath or body scan practice. It is essentially just a shift in emphasis from a "closed" focus on the body toward an "open" monitoring of peripheral thoughts, sensations, and moods. When doing OM, we still focus on the body but we give ourselves more license to notice what else is in consciousness at the same time. We don't need to actively search for anything. We just wait for the next thing to arise, for the next item to float along the stream of consciousness. Many writers regard OM as the best way of describing Modern Mindfulness as a meditation practice.

There are a variety of Open Monitoring techniques in the literature. For instance, the Indian anti-guru Krishnamurti (1895–1986) promoted the concept of "choiceless awareness," which he described as an ego-free, nondiscriminating, effortless, "observing without an observer" state of mind. On my seven-month retreat, I also did the advanced Tibetan practice called Dzogchen (Sanskrit: *Mahamudra*). The approach of Dzogchen involves a fifty-fifty split between the focusing and monitoring functions, and I suspect that this is ideal.

Modern Mindfulness is sympathetic to both Dzogchen and choiceless awareness and uses their terminology. All three approaches are simpler than the Buddha's approach in the *Sutta*, but the family resemblance is obvious. They all have the same open-ended, all-inclusive quality. A defining characteristic of Open Monitoring is that you don't preselect what you will pay attention to. While remaining consciously grounded in the body, you give your remaining attention to whatever else arises in the moment. The quieter your body and mind become, the more attention is available for this activity.

Zen and Tibetan Buddhism commonly assume a fundamental duality of body and mind. They have a theory that "mind" is intrinsically pure, luminous, and empty, and that thoughts and perceptions defile this purity. This pure "buddhamind," also called *sunyata* or emptiness, is assumed to be eternal and transcendental, as opposed to everything else, which is subject to decay and death.

A meditator tries to approach this absolute state by cultivating a pure, disengaged "observer" mind. The technique implies a belief that there can be an observer consciousness that is separate from what it sees—that mind can be separated from the contents of the mind. Modern Mindfulness tends to idealize this nonreactive, "just watching," "empty" state of mind. Unlike *satipatthana*, Modern Mindfulness also minimizes the value of deliberate attention. Once you feel settled, you are encouraged to let go into a free-floating, "open" state of choiceless awareness. Many writers now seem to regard this passive, nonjudgmental acceptance of present-moment experience as what mindfulness "really" is.

But is it actually possible to attain a dispassionate, "just watching" state of mind? That was certainly not my experience on retreat, and I doubt if any meditator attains anything that resembles it for long. In science, the idea of unbiased observation is regarded as a cognitive fallacy. Scientists, with the help of elaborate protocols, work extremely hard to minimize this effect, but they never expect to eradicate it completely. This subtle, continuous interaction of subject and object is also going on when we meditate.

An observer always interacts in profound and mysterious ways with what he observes. He has his goals, hopes, expectations, and prior knowledge. These invariably shape what he sees, as indeed they should. We also now know that the brain splits every incoming perception into thousands of subcomponents. These are then reconstructed along with all relevant past- and future-oriented data before being presented half a second later to consciousness. Even the simplest perception is inextricably coded with an immense body of memory-based understanding. There is no possible way of reversing all this to return to a state of "bare attention." All we can attain is a state where we don't elaborate on it further.

Even at the level of consciousness, and if we are honest with ourselves, we will have to admit that when doing Open Monitoring, the "watching mind" doesn't "just watch." It is subtly selective and discriminating. It is not pure and impersonal like a mirror (which is a common metaphor) reflecting things "just as they are." It always gravitates toward what is most interesting or salient, as it should. It is not passive or disengaged (like a mountain). We can't dismiss or "just watch" everything indiscriminately (like objects floating downstream). Life is too important to let it all drift past unexamined. Nor can we revert to seeing things innocently the way a child is assumed to do (in Zen this is called "beginner's mind"). We know too much. We can see things *differently*, and in more detail, but we can't go back to scratch.

The "watching mind" is not a kind of "bare attention" or primordial consciousness cut free from cognition, memory, and emotion. No matter how refined and detailed our perception of something is, it will always have associations and filters unique to us. We are also likely to have well-embedded ideological filters and preferences. Modern Mindfulness and Zen, for example, automatically give high value to arising sensations and discriminate against arising thought. They also regard the ideal state of mind as more important than the phenomena passing through it.

So why try to do Open Monitoring at all? It turns out that what does happen is very useful indeed. Even when we apparently "just watch," we invariably reappraise and reorient ourselves toward each object. We engage and "process" each thing we notice, if only to a tiny degree, through lightning-fast feedback systems. ("Is this really what it seems to be? How important is it really?") Even if we abandon it in a milli-second, which is the fate of most stimuli, we still evaluate it first. This evaluation is mostly automatic and effortless, but it can't be avoided. If we are alert, we are likely to be aware of it happening dozens of times each minute.

Open Monitoring makes this natural process more con-scious and therefore more accurate. It slows down the video to catch the detail. OM means holding and reappraising any interesting stimulus for a few seconds longer than usual. A well-controlled mind can easily do this without losing its pri-mary focus on the body. This enables us to grasp that arising object and "know" it more precisely than before.

Nor does monitoring involve only thoughts. We "reframe" many other kinds of stimuli to put them in their broader per-spective. We recognize a subtle overreaction or bad mood, and it starts to dissolve. We notice an ancient memory and see it from a different angle. We realize that we are holding on to a grudge, or are worrying about something unnecessar-ily, and the problem starts to shift. Open Monitoring scales whatever we notice up or down in value, and doing this more consciously can vastly improve the outcomes.

Most of these fine reappraisals are done within a few sec-onds or less. This isn't long enough to lead us into open-ended "elaborative" thought. If we are well-grounded in the body, a brief examination of something else is not long enough to break that anchor. These reappraisals are likely to be small, but there may be hundreds of them. OM brings those homeostatic adjustments closer to the surface. This is one reason why we mysteriously feel so much better as we meditate.

Meditation almost always involves both *focusing* (on the body, for example) and *monitoring* (the periphery, the "not-body"), but we can choose how we distribute our metabolic resources between these two functions. New meditators have to give most emphasis to the focusing function, and at first they may not even have a clue about monitoring. Open Monitoring is usually regarded in the traditional literature as an advanced practice to be done only after good body-mind stillness is established.

Good *focusing* alone brings enormous benefits. These include relaxation (optimal muscle tone and arousal), balance, comfort, pleasure, and mental control. Once a meditator has attained good body-mind stillness (*passaddhi*), he can maintain this with a more routine level of focus. This gives him more freedom to deliberately *monitor* what else is happening in his mind without getting lost in thought.

Open Monitoring is a tolerant and welcoming practice. In theory, nothing is excluded. In theory at least, nothing is a distraction if it can be appropriately held in mind. Without good grounding in the body, however, an OM meditation can easily degenerate into little more than randomly thinking about whatever comes to mind. If the body is not genuinely still, the mind can easily wander everywhere. Trying to "watch the stream of consciousness" without mental calm can actually *increase* the amount of time that meditators spend thinking about themselves each day. It can *amplify* rather than reduce their tendency to ruminate.

TO FOCUS AND EVALUATE

Satipatthana can be regarded as an Open Monitoring practice, but one that is more sharp edged. *Sati*, the word we translate as "mindfulness," literally means "to focus on and evaluate" something. Whenever we pay attention to anything at all, we do so for extra clarity of vision and a clearer understanding. We want to know more about it to inform our response. This dynamic of perception + evaluation + response applies equally to the hundreds of stimuli that we notice coming and going in an OM meditation.

To be mindful means: to hold a thought or idea in mind; to hold it still, without elaboration; and to hold it as a "clear and distinct image" (or "mental representation"). This feeling of holding something in the spotlight, and holding it separate from everything else, is quite unmistakable once you get it. It's a feeling that something has "clicked" into place. You feel face-to-face with the object. This feeling is often accompanied by a remarkable sense of stillness, lightness, and space in the body.

Here are other ways of describing this experience. The body is calm and still; the mind feels like a clear, open space in front of you; and the object being held in mind hangs in the center of that space. (Alternatively, your body itself can seem like that open space.) This state of mind is often called "emptiness," and it certainly feels empty. Emptiness is a good metaphor, but in the Mahayana it is reified into a spiritual absolute. I think it is best to regard emptiness as simply a figure of speech that helps describe a particular uncluttered quality of mind.

Compared to Open Monitoring, the full practice of *satipatthana* means being able to see *all* the contents of consciousness with this kind of clarity. In the *Satipatthana Sutta*, the Buddha suggested we approach this task systematically. Once body-mind stillness has been established, he said we should train ourselves to notice individual thoughts; states of mind; valences (the positive or negative affective charges of stimuli); emotions; and the continuous flux of body sensations.

On my long retreat, I started by investigating the infinity of inner and outer sensations. I then naturally moved on to explore finer and finer gradations of feeling and mood—the background weather of the body-mind. Some of these were anchored to memories or images, while others arrived for no apparent reason at all. I also spent hours exploring the hypnagogic dream world between waking and sleep. Time became elastic, both contracting and expanding. Most of this inner drama was quiet, delicate, and miniaturized. It was in water colors not oils. It was like Beethoven played on a clavichord rather than a concert grand.

Although I often lost the plot, fell asleep, and fell down rabbit holes of thought, the feeling of being truly mindful—fully focused and aware of something—was quite unmistakable. No matter how peculiar, subtle, gross, fleeting, massive, or minute a particular mental object might be, the feeling of clear perception was always much the same. It seemed to be grounded in a particularly stable physiological state. This sense of lucid perception, of having a mind-state as clear and accurate as possible, was perhaps the most valuable discovery I made on that retreat.

But where do you stop? I could easily have accumulated terabytes of information about my inner world, but to what purpose? The amassing of information is endless. A scientist can easily spend a lifetime investigating aquatic snails or arctic lichen. Charles Darwin spent eight years studying barnacles, but like any scientist he did so in a highly discriminating fashion.

We have been saying that to be mindful means to consciously perceive and *evaluate* something. When we are mindful, we are able to see and evaluate the true worth of anything in relation to our larger goals. We always have to make judgments, and we do this so automatically that we rarely notice it happening. Attention is the currency, the hard cash of the brain. When we become mindful of something, we automatically evaluate it: How much longer shall I stay with this? How much attention does this deserve? This attribution of value is even quantifiable and fungible. You may give one object five seconds and another ten seconds. This means that you intuitively see one object as being twice as important as the other.

In an Open Monitoring meditation, we notice one stimulus after another, and we have to decide how long to stay with each one. If we are mentally dull, we will just drift. We get bored with one thing and somehow drift toward something else. This is our normal state of automatic, low-quality, impulse-led judgment: not this, not that, maybe this, try out that—until it is time to finish. This incoherent drifting is always a danger with Open Monitoring.

The *satipatthana* method calls for a brighter and more purposeful mental quality. When something arises, we orient toward it until it clicks into place (*sati*). We see it in more detail, with clarity and understanding (*sampajjana*). At this point the judgment is usually clear: let it go (low value) or give it a few more seconds (higher value). Even if we abandon it in an instant, it has still been slightly "processed," as cognitive psychologists would say. We have understood it a little more clearly, and it goes back into the cerebral database more differentiated than before.

This is how I understood the process on my long retreat. I had reduced the stimuli from the outer world to an absolute minimum for those seven months. This enabled my inner activity to emerge in all its ragged glory. My brain slowed down so much that I could stop, hold, and come to know tens of thousands of individual stimuli, one by one. It was like an exceptionally detailed spring cleaning, room by room, shelf by shelf, corner by corner, of a mansion the size of Gormenghast.

Learning how to usefully direct my attention at the microscopic level was very valuable, but it wasn't quite enough in itself. I still had to make the macroscopic decisions: How would I make a living? Should I become a monk? Was I going to stay with my girlfriend or not? These higher-order deliberations are also part of the *satipatthana* method, but they go beyond Open Monitoring. I'll explain how that kind of advanced thought works in chapter 20, "Embodied Thought."

PART TWO

The *Satipatthana Sutta*

11

An Overview of the *Satipatthana Sutta*

I t is now time to become more familiar with the *Satipatthana Sutta* itself. In the Pali Canon, we have more than three thousand of the Buddha's sermons, ranging in size from brief poems to multipage narratives. We probably have more words directly attributed to the Buddha himself than are found in the entire Judeo-Christian Bible. Most of these sermons are exhortations to abandon sensual pleasures and worldly pursuits and to lead a pure, ascetic life. Other sermons are philosophic, argumentative, or autobiographical. Only a handful of the *sutta* in the Pali Canon give particular prominence to meditation, and the *Satipatthana Sutta—The Foundations of Mindfulness—*is the most important of these. It presents the first, and still the most inclusive, description of mindfulness as a practice.

The *Satipatthana Sutta* has four sections, addressing (1) mindfulness of the body, (2) mindfulness of emotion, (3) mindfulness of states of mind, and (4) mindfulness of thought. These are the four "foundations of mindfulness"—or "training disciplines" or "contemplations" or "applications" or *satipatthanas*—that make up the *Sutta*.

The first of these, mindfulness of the body, is essentially what we think of as "meditation"—covered extensively in the first ten chapters of this book. Being able to meditate well is so valuable that many people may not want or need to go beyond this substantial first stage.

My explanation of meditation in those first ten chapters, and the way I teach it in class, differs hardly at all from the way the Buddha described it twenty-five hundred years ago. Meditation is clearly an organic, transcultural practice, almost as natural as breathing, which explains why so many people (including me) have managed to teach themselves to meditate with virtually no instruction at all.

Mindfulness, however, is more than just meditation. The three other foundations of the *Sutta* make it a truly comprehensive mind-training discipline. These are the graduate levels. In the next chapter I will present my translation of the *Sutta*. It is not difficult to understand, but to help with this first reading, I will give you a rough outline of its historical setting and its argument. Some aspects are bound to remain mystifying, but I will unravel them in coming chapters.

THE ARGUMENT OF THE *SUTTA*

The *Sutta* opens with a bold statement: "The systematic four-stage training of attention is the *only* way to enlightenment." The Buddha addressed this sermon to a group of "wanderers" or "homeless ones." They weren't really what we think of as monks. They were itinerant and usually solitary holy men.

There may have been no established monasteries at this time. Nonetheless these men had already renounced what they saw as the evils of sensuality and worldly life, and they were committed to the complete extinction of suffering in this and future lives.

The first foundation, mindfulness of the body, starts with seated meditation, but it doesn't stay there. Its purpose is to help the monk develop a continuous, refined, detailed attunement to his body throughout the entire day. This ever-present body awareness would keep the monk stable and calm and give him the platform for what follows. Included in this section are three "memento mori" contemplations to help the monk overcome his attachment to his body and the world. They are hardly ever practiced by Western meditators today.

What we would call "emotion" is examined in both the second and third sections of the *Sutta*. The actual mindfulness of emotion section confines itself to one small but pervasive aspect of emotion: the "valence"–the emotional charge or feeling tone–that accompanies every perception. To be mindful of valence means being able to verbally identify the "pleasant" or "unpleasant" tone, however subtle, of any sensation, thought, emotion, or action.

Other aspects of emotion are found in the third section: mindfulness of states of mind. This section presents the "five hindrances"–the Buddha's short list of "bad" emotions: desire, anger, lethargy, anxiety, and despair. He gives instructions on how to hold, identify, and eventually extinguish these emotions, in the present and in the future.

Once the negative states of mind are tranquilized, the monk can freely develop the positive states of mind, called "the seven factors of enlightenment." These seven factors shouldn't be confused with good emotions or moral virtues. They have a more specific focus. They are the ideal meditative qualities of mind necessary for the breakthrough to enlightenment. These are most easily cultivated in deep meditative states (*jhana*) and in the seated posture.

These seven ideal qualities of mind all need to be present for the purpose of attaining enlightenment, but they can also be regarded as a sequence culminating in the last. We have already discussed most of them, but here is a quick runthrough: The first is *sati*, or mindfulness itself. The second is *dhamma-vicaya*—the quality of active, sustained investigation (such as occurs in a body scan meditation). The third is *viriya*: energy and will (which we'll talk about in later chapters). The fourth is *piti*, the bliss described in chapter 7. The fifth is *passaddhi* (body-mind stillness). The sixth is *samadhi* (uninterrupted, blissful concentration).

The final culminating quality of mind is *upekkha*, which is usually translated as equanimity. It implies a state of extreme philosophic detachment and the extinguishing of all emotional responses to the world. The monk first achieves this in deep meditation, but he eventually consolidates it as an enduring state of mind that never leaves him. Equanimity is frequently regarded as the ultimate achievement, the final escape from suffering.

For the Buddha, however, equanimity was only the penultimate state. The purpose of all the training presented in the *Satipatthana Sutta* becomes obvious in the fourth section, which discusses mindfulness of thought. The monk now has the mental stability to engage in profound, intuitive, directed, penetrating thought (*vipassana*) into the nature of life—or into any question that he sets himself.

The fourth section includes three contemplations. The first presents the Buddha's "bundle theory" of the self as being composed of transient, unstable elements. This underpins his key idea of *anatta*, or "no-soul." The second maps out his idea that all suffering starts with attachment to sensory things. The third is the famous Eightfold Path. This is the full package of Buddhist philosophy, morality, and practice.

In the West, "the Enlightenment" is a term applied to an era when scientists and scholars were determined to think and figure out the truth about the physical world and human existence for themselves, based on hard evidence, without reliance on political or religious authorities. The *Sutta* is a comprehensive mind-training discipline that aims at just this kind of self-reliance and mental vigor, and we can easily target it toward our own personal goals.

The Buddha, however, had a narrower purpose. In climbing his own Mount Olympus he leaves nearly all of us behind. He said that the only subject worth thinking about was his own doctrine about the nature of existence. The monk finally awakens only through profound insight into the Buddha's teaching.

12

The Foundations of Mindfulness
(the Satipatthana Sutta)

When the Buddha was in the land of the Kurus, he told the monks: The systematic four-stage training of attention is the only way to overcome suffering, to purify the mind, to enter the true path and attain Enlightenment. What are these four?

The monk lives intently contemplating his body, clearly understanding and mindful of it, having abandoned all desire and aversion toward the world. Likewise he lives examining his emotions, his states of mind, and his thought. He lives alone, reliant on no one, attached to nothing in the world.

MINDFULNESS OF THE BODY (*KAYA*)

How does a monk live contemplating the body? He goes to the forest, to the foot of a tree, or to an empty hut. He sits down cross-legged, holds his body erect, and focuses on the breath in front of himself.

Mindfully he breathes in and mindfully he breathes out. When inhaling a long breath, he thinks: "I am inhaling a long breath." When exhaling a long breath, he thinks: "I am exhaling a long breath." Likewise, he knows when he is breathing in or out a short breath. He is like a skilled turner who knows when he is making a long or short turn on the lathe.

He trains himself thinking: "Conscious of the whole body, I breathe in. Conscious of the whole body, I breathe out. Calming the whole body, I breathe in. Calming the whole body I breathe out."

He carefully observes his own body and the bodies of others. He observes how bodily sensations arise and pass away, and what causes them to do so. He focuses on his body solely for the purpose of understanding its true nature. And he lives alone, reliant on no one, attached to nothing in this world.

Furthermore, when walking, a monk thinks: "I am walking." When standing, he thinks: "I am standing." Likewise he knows when he is sitting or lying down. He calms his breathing and his body in each of these postures.

He is equally mindful when coming and going; when looking forward or around him; when bending and stretching; when wearing his robes and carrying his bowl; when eating, drinking, chewing, and tasting; when defecating and urinating; when walking, standing, sitting, and lying down; when falling asleep and waking up; when talking and remaining silent.

He surveys his body upward from the soles of his feet, or downward from the hairs of his head. He examines the thirty-two constituent parts of the body and sees them all as repulsive. He analyzes the body in terms of the four elements.

If possible, he will examine a corpse throughout the nine stages of decay, thinking: "My body is just like that one and cannot escape its fate." In these ways a monk contemplates the nature of the body.

MINDFULNESS OF EMOTION (*VEDANA*)

How does a monk observe the valences of phenomena? When he experiences a pleasant feeling, he knows: "This is pleasant." When he experiences an unpleasant feeling, he knows: "This is unpleasant." He also recognizes those valences that are neither pleasant nor unpleasant. Likewise, he is aware of the positive, negative, and neutral valences that accompany thoughts.

He carefully observes how valences arise and how they pass away, and what causes them to do so. He observes this both in himself and in others. He pays attention to valences solely for the purpose of understanding their true nature. And he lives alone, reliant on no one, attached to nothing in this world.

MINDFULNESS OF STATES OF MIND (*CITTA*)

How does a monk contemplate his states of mind? He recognizes the mind that is caught in desire and the mind free of desire. He recognizes the mind that is caught in anger and the mind free of anger. He recognizes the mind that is caught in delusion and the mind free of delusion. He recognizes the shrunken mind and the distracted mind; the undeveloped mind and the supreme mind; the restless mind and the settled mind; the mind that is not free and the liberated mind.

He carefully observes how these states of mind arise and pass away, and what causes them to do so. He observes this both in himself and in others. And he lives alone, reliant on no one, attached to nothing in this world.

He lives observing *The Five Hindrances*. When his mind is caught in Desire, he knows: "This is Desire." When his mind is free of Desire, he knows: "This is the mind free of Desire." He carefully observes how desire arises and passes away, and what causes it to do so. He learns how to extinguish desire when it arises, and how to prevent it arising in the future.

In the same manner, he examines the four other Hindrances, namely, Anger, Lethargy, Anxiety, and Despair. He sees how they arise and pass away, and what causes them to do so. He learns how to extinguish them when they arise, and how to prevent them arising in the future.

He lives observing *The Seven Factors of Enlightenment*. When he is Mindful, he knows it. When he is not Mindful, he knows it. He carefully observes how mindfulness comes and goes, and what causes it to do so. He learns how to strengthen mindfulness when it is present, and how to bring it forth when it is not present.

Likewise, he contemplates the other *Factors of Enlightenment*. He carefully observes how Investigation, Energy, Bliss, Stillness, Absorption, and Equanimity arise and pass away, and what causes them to do so. He learns how to strengthen each one of these qualities when it is present, and how to bring it forth when it is not present.

He carefully observes how *The Seven Factors of Enlightenment* arise and pass away, and what causes them to do so. He observes this both in himself and in others. And he lives alone, reliant on no one, attached to nothing in this world.

MINDFULNESS OF THOUGHT (*DHAMMA*)

How does a monk live fully conscious and in control of his thoughts? He contemplates the five aggregate parts that make up his sense of self. He understands how the body, perceptions, feelings, action tendencies, and consciousness arise and pass away. He investigates how attachment occurs through the contact of sense organs and sense objects, and understands how to break free from that attachment.

The monk reflects on *The Four Noble Truths* that lead to Nirvana. He understands by direct experience that: Life is suffering. The cause of suffering is desire. Desire can be extinguished. The Eightfold Path of training extinguishes desire and leads to the end of suffering.

Anyone who practices these four Foundations of Mindfulness for seven years or seven months or even seven days may expect one of two outcomes: complete enlightenment in this life or, if some trace of clinging to the world still remains, no rebirth after death.

The systematic four-stage training of attention is the only way to overcome suffering, to purify the mind, to enter the true path, and attain Enlightenment.

13

The History of Translation

With a little effort the *Satipatthana Sutta* is not difficult to understand, yet in the twenty-first century it is almost completely neglected. It is rarely mentioned in the psychological or popular literature except as the iconic primal source. Even people with a serious interest in mindfulness seem reluctant to examine it, and if you tried to read it yourself, you would soon find out why.

The standard translation, originating in the Victorian era, has a semi-biblical, true-believer tone that is quite discouraging. It uses phrases like "sorrow and lamentation," "sloth and torpor," and "the purification of all beings." It comes from a bygone age. It probably doesn't help that nearly all available commentaries on the *Sutta* in book form are written by Western and Asian monks who are not native speakers of English.

The first and by far the most important translator of the *Sutta* was T. W. Rhys Davids (1843–1922), a British administrator in Ceylon (now Sri Lanka) in the late nineteenth century. Davids established the Pali Text Society (PTS) in 1881 to make the massive quantity of original texts available in English. It took Davids and his scholars over forty years to translate the whole Pali Canon, but the PTS is still going strong today.

The next translators emerged from a tiny group of Westerners who became monks in Ceylon before World War II. The first of these was the monk Soma Thera (1898–1960), who was born in Ceylon to Latin parents and who became a major proselytizer of the *Sutta* after his conversion to Buddhism. Soma Thera's 1949 translation and commentary, *The Way of Mindfulness*, was the first such exploration of the *Sutta* to appear in book form. Unfortunately, Soma Thera adopts the exhortatory manner of an Old Testament prophet, which would nowadays deter all but the hardiest reader.

Soma Thera was assisted with his book by Nyanaponika Thera (1901–1994), a senior monk of German birth. Later, Nyanaponika produced his own translation of, and commentary on, the *Sutta*, titled *The Heart of Buddhist Meditation: Satipatthana*, published in London in 1962. Nyanaponika's intelligent, thoughtful book is a little awkward to read, but is still perfectly serviceable. It has been the foundational commentary for most Vipassana students since the 1960s.

And the lineage continues. Nyanaponika's younger associate, the American monk Bhikkhu Bodhi (born in 1944), became and still is the most respected current editor/translator of the Pali Canon. He edited the latest PTS version of the *Sutta* in 1995 as part of the collection *The Middle Length Discourses of the Buddha*. Bodhi's student, a German monk named Analayo, produced his own superb commentary in 2004 titled *Satipatthana: The Direct Path to Realization*. This book is technically superior to the works of Soma Thera and

Nyanaponika, but it still exhibits all the caution and conservatism of a young scholar monk.

Monasticism is dying out in the West, and Western Buddhist monks are an infinitesimally tiny population. Nirvana as the Buddha described it now seems to be a dead goal even for Asians (although it would be impossible to tell for sure). However, the translators of the *Sutta* just outlined did or do take nirvana very seriously. They were or are monks translating what another monk, the Buddha, said to his own monks about the only way to enlightenment. Their deep conviction and allegiance to the monastic life comes through in their commentaries.

As translators, however, they are all limited by their excessive respect for the style and authority of Rhys Davids. We don't get five different translations from these five men. We just get a succession of minor tinkering with Rhys Davids' original. We can think of it as the Standard Pali Text Society translation. There has been no substantial change to it since it first appeared.

Rhys Davids was a late Victorian who understandably wrote like one. He liked archaisms such as "lamentation" and "abide" and preferred language with a spiritual or biblical flavor (for example, "mindfulness" instead of "attention"). Half a century later, in 1941, Soma Thera didn't translate the *Sutta* from the original Pali as he could have done. (He was always compulsively busy.) With the help of the German monk Nyanaponika, he simply cleaned up Rhys Davids' rather prolix original translation.

Nyanaponika in his 1962 book used the same translation he had worked on with Soma Thera two decades earlier.

Likewise, Bhikkhu Bodhi in 1995 presents the same translation with minor variants, as does his student Analayo in the 2004 book. Even Thanissaro Bhikkhu, an American monk in a Thai rather than Sri Lankan lineage, leaves the standard PTS text largely untouched.

It is easy to understand why these translators relied so unashamedly on Rhys Davids' fine pioneering work. This was partly out of respect, but they would also have faced huge difficulties doing their own translations had they attempted to do so. The original texts are written in Pali, which was a local vernacular cousin of Sanskrit. Pali was an oral language with no written form until three centuries after the Buddha died. The texts of the Pali Canon were memorized before that time. Pali now survives only as the language of the Buddhist texts.

Pali scholars have three ways of interpreting the meaning of any word: from its context, from the huge commentarial literature, and from its equivalent meaning in Sanskrit. In practice, this means that only simple Pali words have straightforward definitions. Important words are more likely to be "defined" by a sprawling body of often contradictory meanings, references, and associations. Pali and Sanskrit also use a common rhetorical device of using a string of similes to express an idea. This makes the precise meaning of any word even more difficult to nail down.

Pali scholarship is an impenetrably dense thicket of competing interpretations about minutiae, which I personally find very discouraging. For example, early Buddhist psychology (in a series of texts called the *Abhidhamma*) is capable of analyzing a single moment of perception into thirty-seven constituent parts. Reverential nit-picking analysis has been the style of Buddhist scholarship from the very beginning. It is particularly obsessed with lists and the cross-referencing of lists. This approach brings to mind Ajaan Chah's criticism of certain meditators: He said they were like people in a chicken shed who mistakenly collect the droppings rather than the eggs.

Another reason that Westerners are discouraged by the *Sutta* is that its Buddhism is not at all what they are used to. It is "hard" uncompromising Buddhism, fleshed out on a skeleton of core beliefs. It never mentions compassion. It is not the "soft" sentimental Buddhism of popular media and books, with the bar set so low that anyone can stumble in ("just be kind"). The *Sutta* is what the Buddha actually said. It is serious stuff.

We encounter this original Buddhism in the first words of the *Sutta*, asserting the Buddha's aversion to the world, and I'm sure many people are repelled by it. The *Sutta* is logical, well-argued, and psychologically astute. It is also self-oriented, pessimistic, and world denying. I argue that it is quite easy to extract the superb mind-training techniques from the Buddha's personal values and beliefs, but I'm not surprised that few people ever persist long enough with the *Sutta* to do that.

A NEW TRANSLATION AT LAST

Here are a few comments on my translation. Pali itself seems to have been a homely language of the people. It definitely wasn't like its cousin: highborn, literary, philosophic Sanskrit. The *Sutta* reads as a self-development manual: How to attain nirvana in thirteen stages.

The Buddha seems to have called a spade a spade whenever he could. He was talking to a preliterate people in a language that had no written form. I've tried to restore that directness in my own translation. To translate the *Sutta* using archaisms, spiritual words, and neologisms obscures its eminently practical character and gives undue authority to its monastic interpreters.

I regard it as a failure on the part of a translator if he or she uses terms that appear mystifying or esoteric to a reader. I know this is occasionally unavoidable, but jargon words are certainly not necessary in the case of the *Sutta*. I was determined to offer a translation of the *Sutta* in vernacular English that could be at least roughly understood on a first reading without the use of a glossary or a commentary.

I first encountered Soma Thera's *The Way of Mindfulness* in 1975. I had a degree in English literature, so I was used to interpreting strange old texts in ways that made sense. I was so impressed with the underlying value of the *Sutta* that I converted Soma Thera's translation into modern English and memorized it. Over the years, I continued to refine my own working version of the *Sutta*, and now, more than forty years on, it has emerged in this book. I think this is also the first English translation and commentary on the *Sutta* in book form that is not written by a monk. I am sure this will help to make it more useful and readable.

Perhaps the most striking difference is that my translation is very short. It is less than one-fourth as long as Bhikkhu Bodhi's authoritative 1995 version. People who have compared the two have asked me, "Have you left something out?" and I have. The original contains thirteen liturgical refrains of about one hundred words each. Bodhi omits or abbreviates a few of these. I omit nearly all of them, and I omit many other numerous but shorter repetitions as well.

Likewise, Bhikkhu Bodhi gives nearly eight hundred words to three practices that I cover in eighty words. I think that meditating on corpses and the repulsiveness of the body have only antiquarian interest nowadays. Rather than provide the full details of these practices for the sake of completeness, I chose to bring out the clean functional lines of the training itself, which can easily get lost in the detail. For those who are keen to know more about meditating on corpses, Bodhi's translation is readily available.

The *Sutta* consists of an introduction and four training disciplines, or "foundations." Years ago, to help myself understand the text, I made an internal change to this structure. Despite its immense authority, the *Sutta* looks like it was shaped into its present, final form by a committee, which it probably was. All the Pali texts were originally held only in the memory of monks. The *Sutta* was only put into written form about three hundred years after the Buddha composed it. The individual components and subsections of the *Sutta* are almost certainly accurate representations of the Buddha's words. We find them repeatedly elsewhere in the Pali Canon. However, the organization of the *Sutta* itself seems awkward. Its last two categories are confused and illogical. I don't know for sure, but my guess is that this confusion is probably due to an error of judgment in the final editing.

For example, two subsections called "the five hindrances" (gross emotions) and "the seven factors of enlightenment" (refined states of mind) are usually found in the fourth section, on "thought." Because we more naturally think of these as "states of mind," I have transposed them down to that third section where they seem to belong. In fact, the five hindrances are very similar to many of the states of mind already described in that section. It is obvious that the third section is the natural home for the hindrances.

Since the *Sutta* is modular in structure, nothing is lost by relocating those two subsections. I've just made the categories more logical. This shift also makes what remains in the fourth section much more coherent, and it makes the word "thought" a more exact title for it. This section now contains the Buddha's "five aggregates" theory of identity, his theory of perception, and the Four Noble Truths. These are all concepts that the monk is being asked to think about in a rational fashion.

I've also re-labeled the usual translations of the four foundations of mindfulness. The objects of these four are usually translated in the following ways: *kaya* as "body"; *vedana* as "feeling" or "sensation"; *citta* as "mind"; and *dhamma* as "mind-objects." I've tried to make sense of these category names for years, but I've finally given up. The science and philosophy I've been reading in recent years has made me even more intolerant of semantic obscurity. I now regard the last three of these four category names as wrong, vague, and meaningless respectively.

Vedana does not mean "feeling" or "sensation." It means "valence" or "emotional charge," which is something quite different. Likewise, "mind" is far too vague and protean a term for *citta*. Even Nyanaponika (and other commentators) realized that the term "states of mind" is more appropriate.

He changed other terms in the standard translation created by Rhys Davids, but he was too respectful to change this one.

Dhamma has multiple meanings in Pali, and previous translators and commentators have understandably failed to find any one English equivalent: For the most part, they simply leave it untranslated and unexplained. Nonetheless, it seems fairly obvious that whatever *dhamma* means elsewhere in the Pali texts, in the *Sutta* it refers to conscious, goal-directed thought. The Buddha is asking the monk to inquire deeply into both his own teaching (called *Buddhadhamma*) and into the nature of life itself. This is why I translate it as "thought."

As far as I know, my interpretation of *dhamma* as "thought" is unique to me, and I doubt if it will be favorably regarded by monks and scholars. Similarly, my transposition of the two subsections from the fourth foundation to the third will be regarded as sacrilegious by many. The Buddhist texts including the *Sutta* are almost exclusively used in the East as magical and ceremonial chants. Many people would regard my change to the structure as tantamount to rewriting a spell.

Despite these changes, I have not tried to rewrite the *Sutta* from scratch. Rhys Davids did a good original job on it, and I have retained those elements of style, voice, and structure that still work perfectly well in the twenty-first century. I'm not a Pali scholar, so my translation, like all the others just mentioned, is still a grateful descendent of Rhys Davids' original.

My slim and economical version of the *Sutta* is intended to make it comprehensible to a nonspecialist. Very few people, apart from Buddhists and devotees, are able to use the

PTS text in any practical way. The PTS translation remains stranded on the shoals of its late-Victorian, semi-biblical idiom and its monastic orientation. It hasn't quite made it over into serviceable English. The PTS text doesn't serve the Buddha well in the twenty-first century. It doesn't allow his voice to be heard by the ordinary Westerner. It is a magnificent and indispensible resource for scholarship, but it is too unwieldy to be used as the practical manual that it is.

My translation of the *Sutta* is not orthodox, but I believe it is readable, accurate, and structurally clear. It can also be used immediately as a manual, both within and outside its Buddhist context. I also hope that this translation can be of practical use to meditators, particularly those who do Vipassana retreats that claim to be based on the *Sutta*, and for psychologists and popular writers who would like to understand more about the long-neglected sources of mindfulness.

14

Sati: The Analysis of a Word

For a text that is twenty-five hundred years old, the *Sutta* is remarkably easy to understand, so why is it so neglected? Part of the reason is the mistranslation and consequent misuse of its key term. In this chapter, I'll try to answer just one question: What did the Buddha actually mean by *sati*, the word we now translate as "mindfulness"? As a result, this chapter is full of technical details and quotes from the traditional authorities. If you are new to the field, you don't need to totally understand this pedantic analysis. It is quite sufficient to get the general drift. In particular, you will find that the original meaning of *sati* differs remarkably from the way modern writers describe mindfulness.

My principal sources for this analysis are Buddhaghosa's monumental fourth-century Theravadin commentary on the *Sutta*, translated by Bhikkhu Nanamoli as *The Path of Purification* (1991); Soma Thera's 1949 book, *The Way of Mindfulness*; Nyanaponika Thera's 1962 book, *The Heart of Buddhist Meditation*; Analayo's 2004 book, *Satipatthana:*

The Direct Path to Realization; Thanissaro Bhikkhu's 2008 article, "Mindfulness Defined," from the Buddhist website Access to Insight; and a 1992 guide to Vipassana meditation, *In This Very Life*, by Sayadaw U Pandita, the successor to the great Burmese Vipassana theorist Mahasi Sayadaw.

It is obvious that the word *sati* is used in the *Sutta* in a way that corresponds very well to the English word "attention." *Sati* is also intimately linked to words that mean evaluation (*sampajjana*), goal-directed effort (*atapi*), and memory. These words are all found in the same sentence of the *Sutta* and are traditionally analyzed together. This cluster of functions matches what we understand from the field of cognitive psychology. Attention never occurs as an autonomous function. Attention, judgment, memory, and purpose all work together as the key executive skills of any rational adult.

Although *sati* clearly means "attention" in the *Sutta*, T. W. Rhys Davids thought he could improve upon it. Rhys Davids was by far the most important translator of early Buddhist texts. In 1881 he decided to translate *sati* not as "attention" but as "mindfulness." As an adjective, "mindful" has been in the English language since the fourteenth century, but Rhys Davids chose to revise the archaic noun form "mindfulness" as a translation for *sati*. It could even be argued that Rhys Davids is the inadvertent inventor of the modern word "mindfulness."

Choosing "mindfulness" as the translation has had the unfortunate effect of changing the way we think about *sati*. It shifts it from a cognitive *function* (that is, something we do) into a *thing* (that is, a state of mind, or a meditation practice, or a philosophy). The ambiguities around the modern conception of "mindfulness" start right there.

The choice of the word "mindfulness" was a poor decision, but we are now stuck with it. It is a workable term but awkward in so many ways. Bhikkhu Bodhi is the most authoritative modern translator, and he has no fondness for "mindfulness." He was the editor of the Pali Text Society for many years, and was therefore the custodian of Rhys Davids' legacy. Despite his undoubted loyalty, he still describes mindfulness as "a makeshift term."

The Western monk Thanissaro Bhikkhu also dislikes the word "mindfulness." In his essay "Mindfulness Defined," he speculates that Rhys Davids chose the term because "being mindful" would have associations with Anglican prayer for his late Victorian audience. As a Buddhist proselytizer, Rhys Davids tailored his language to that audience.

As a result of Rhys Davids' efforts, "mindfulness" gradually came to mean not "attention" but a narrower subset. He presented mindfulness as being good in a moral sense—as referring to "*right* attention" (*samma-sati*) rather than just "attention" (*sati*). Rhys Davids saw mindfulness only as the kind of attention that is directed to a moral or spiritual goal. A sniper, in other words, would be seen as exercising "wrong attention" (*miccha-sati*).

Likewise, modern writers and psychologists invariably talk about mindfulness as a "special kind of attention," or as "paying attention in a particular way," and they frequently qualify it with adjectives. Buddhist writers also like to retain the Buddhist moral associations of "mindfulness" rather than let it revert to its true meaning,

I think this is a mistake that confuses and cripples the concept. It tangles up the universal cognitive function of attention with particular Buddhist or psychological goals. Let me emphasize this point: *Sati* just means "attention," and, as the Buddha's original terminology recognizes (*samma-sati* versus *miccha-sati*), attention can be used for good or bad purposes.

SUSTAINED ATTENTION

The German monk Nyanaponika was also uncomfortable with Rhys Davids' term "mindfulness." He affirmed the primary meaning of *sati* as "attention" in his influential 1962 book, *The Heart of Buddhist Meditation*: "Mindfulness is not a mystical state. It is on the contrary something quite simple and common, and very familiar to all of us. Under the term 'attention' it is one of the cardinal functions of consciousness without which there cannot be perception of any object at all."[1]

Since *sati* suggests a cognitive function, not a state of being, it more accurately means "to pay attention to" or "to focus on" something. For example, *sati* is used in the title of another meditation text called the *Anapanasati Sutta*. This title translates in an uncomplicated fashion as "paying attention (*sati*) to the breath (*anapana*)." In other words, "to be mindful" is "to hold something in mind" or "to focus on something."

The traditional commentators usually describe *sati* as what we would call *sustained* attention. For example, the Standard Meditation Practice as described in chapter 1 involves paying sustained attention to the body. In "Mindfulness Defined," Thanissaro Bhikkhu says, "Continuous attention is what mindfulness is for. It keeps the object of your attention and the purpose of your attention in mind."[2] In his

1992 guide to Vipassana, the Burmese monk U Pandita said, "The function of mindfulness is to keep the object always in view, neither forgetting it nor allowing it to disappear."[3]

Soma Thera articulated the same concept in his book *The Way of Mindfulness*: "When one is strongly mindful of an object, one plants one's consciousness deep into it, like a post sunk into the ground, and withstands the tempestuous clamour of the extraneous by a 'sublime ignoring of non-essentials.' Mindfulness sticks to the business at hand."[4]

Reaching back further in time, Buddhaghosa describes *sati* as having the characteristic of "non-distraction," of "not floating" or "not wobbling"[5] (that is, not drifting or spacing out or fantasizing). To be mindful is to focus on an object and stay with it against all the temptations to wander.

Buddhaghosa, and many teachers since, describe training the mind as like tying a wild elephant (or an ox or a calf or a puppy!) to a stake in order to tame it. At first the elephant will try to break free and return to the forest. Eventually it will lie down by the stake and become a docile and obedient servant. In a similar metaphor, Buddhaghosa says, "When a monk wants to tame his own mind which has long been spoilt by being reared on visible data," he should "tie it up . . . to the post of in-breaths and out-breaths with the rope of mindfulness."[6]

Buddhaghosa also describes mindfulness as "seeing the object face to face." U Pandita glosses this as "walking straight towards someone who is walking towards you."[7] The Buddha uses a similar full-frontal metaphor in the *Sutta*: The monk focuses on the breath in front of himself. In our Western tradition, the French philosopher René Descartes (1596–1650) likewise described meditation as holding a "clear and distinct idea" on what he thought of as "the stage of the mind." Because this mental space is invariably imagined as being *in front of* the body, it implies a sense of objectivity and clarity of vision.

The Pali texts contain many other metaphors, all of which imply judgment and discrimination. *Sati* is the mental quality of a shepherd watching over his flock. It is like a soldier on a watchtower, "looking for the glint of armour." It is the guard at the city gate who decides who can enter and who can't, and who directs the right visitor to the king. It is the skillful charioteer who can steer attention and control the passions. It is even compared to "a waggoner who ties the oxen to the waggon's yoke, greases the axle, and drives the waggon, making the oxen go gently."[8] These examples show that *sati* is always mindful for a purpose. It is certainly not a disengaged, mirrorlike state of nonjudgmental acceptance.

Despite the mental effort involved, we can still distinguish *sati* from the one-pointed concentration called *samadhi*. With *sati* we typically retain a sense of the body and self, and a subject-object relationship. We still see and evaluate the object within the larger context of our long-term goals. *Sati* is characterized by discrimination, evaluation, and self-monitoring. *Samadhi*, on the other hand, is a more extreme quality of focus. It results in total absorption and a tunnel vision that loses sight of everything else. This trancelike state is a valuable experience, but it is different from *sati*.

To summarize, to be mindful is to pay attention to something, to hold it in mind, to hold it "in front of you," and even "to hold it down." The Pali texts use words like "grasp," "apprehend," "lock on to," and "penetrate into." This is *sati* as selective, sustained attention.

EVALUATION AND JUDGMENT

In the Pali Canon, the word *sati* is frequently combined with the term *sampajjana* into the phrase *sati-sampajjana*. The word *sampajjana* literally means "accurate understanding." In practice it means "evaluation" or "good judgment," since this is its purpose. I've translated *sati-sampajjana* in the *Sutta* as "clearly understanding and mindful of." It is more usually translated as "clearly comprehending and mindful of." This phrase is so important that it occurs as a refrain throughout the *Sutta*.

Buddhaghosa said that well-established mindfulness is as immovable as "the king of mountains." This metaphor refers to the importance of body-mind stillness (*passaddhi*) for good attentional control. "Whatever subject the monk adverts to, consciously reacts to, gives attention to or reviews, he will be able to enter deeply into it and understand its essence."[9] This deep understanding (of a thought, emotion, state of mind, or behavior) is *sampajjana*. But why would a monk want to achieve this?

Attention is never pure or disinterested. Whenever we pay attention to anything (*sati*), we do so in order to consciously or implicitly evaluate it prior to a response. This evaluation is *sampajjana*. At an absolute minimum we have to decide "Is this useful or useless? Is this worth giving more attention to or not?" We have to make these judgment calls hundreds of times a day. Everything that grabs our attention demands a yes-or-no response.

Where our attention goes, our actions follow. As the bestselling author Joseph Goldstein puts it, "With clear comprehension [*sampajjana*], we know the purpose and appropriateness of what we're doing; we understand the motivations behind our actions."[10] If we don't make *conscious* decisions at critical points, our *automatic* impulses will decide for us.

The Pali word *pajjana* means "to know something." The prefix *sam-* acts as a reinforcer. *Sampajjana* therefore means the right or true or accurate knowledge of something. For the monk, *sampajjana* meant recognizing what was good and bad, useful or useless, in even the smallest matters, so he could control his behavior and achieve his goals.

Sampajjana is also used in the sense of "seeing in depth" or "seeing the essence" of something. It has connotations of brightness and alertness (that is, full consciousness). It implies accuracy in judgment. *Sampajjana* fully developed is thus the capacity for the discriminating thought that is the precondition for enlightenment. Analayo points out that *sampajjana* "can range from basic forms of knowing to deep discriminative understanding."[11]

Ultimately, *sampajjana* is associated with the important Sanskrit word *prajna*, which means "wisdom" or "direct knowing" or even "enlightenment" itself. In particular, *sampajjana* means seeing things "as they really are." A monk would see everything as suffering, impermanent, and devoid of self. This important insight is said to result in profound disgust and a resolution to abandon the world.

In *The Way of Mindfulness*, Soma Thera says *sati* acts like "the Chief Adviser of a King, who is instrumental in distinguishing the good from the bad, the worthy from the unworthy."[12] The word *sati* implies this aspect of discriminating judgment even more strongly than does our English word "attention." This is why I usually translate *sati* as "the conscious perception *and evaluation* of something." The English word "attention" on its own is not strong enough to carry the sense of discrimination and purpose inherent in *sati*.

Even when *sati* appears alone in the texts, *sampajjana* is always implied. Recalling a discussion he had in the 1990s with the elderly Nyanaponika, Bhikkhu Bodhi said they were in full agreement that *sati* and *sampajjana* are both necessary for "right mindfulness" (*samma-sati*).[13] The functional unity of *sati* and *sampajjana* is always taken for granted by commentators. *Sati-sampajjana* thus means "to hold an object in mind in order to accurately evaluate it prior to a response." This is what is implied by the frequently repeated phrase in the *Sutta*: "clearly understanding and mindful of it."

In Nyanaponika's seminal book from 1962, he describes *sati* as the "stop, look and see clearly" function that preceded intelligent action. *Sati* allows the shift from the *automatic* judgment that accompanies any perception to a more conscious and accurate judgment. Nyanaponika says, "By pausing before action . . . one will be able to seize that decisive but brief moment when mind has not yet settled upon a definite course of action, but is still open to receive skilful directions."

Nyanaponika goes on to say, "Mind has to choose, to decide and to judge. It is Clear Comprehension (*sampajjana*) . . . which is concerned with that greater part of our life, the active one. It is one of the aims of the practice of Satipatthana that Clear Comprehension should gradually become the regulative force of all our activities, bodily, verbal and mental."[14]

Soma Thera likewise described *sati-sampajjana* as "the analysis, reflection, vision, sagacity, the discernment that leads to right, penetrative insight and clear comprehension."[15] He adds, "Mindfulness . . . produces lucidity of thought, sound judgment and definiteness of outlook." Notice that the word "mindfulness" (*sati*) in the sentence above *includes* the meaning of "sound judgment" (*sampajjana*). Soma Thera doesn't try to make any distinction between *sati* and *sampajjana* and doesn't need to. They are traditionally seen as a functional unity.

PUTTING IT ALL TOGETHER

Let's summarize where we are up to. *Sati* means sustained attention. *Sampajjana* means evaluation or judgment. *Sati-sampajjana* means attention combined with evaluation, or "to focus on and evaluate" something. The word *sati*, just like the English word "attention," always implies an evaluative purpose, but *sati-sampajjana* spells it out unequivocally.

We can apply *sati-sampajjana* to anything. We could focus on a body sensation such as fatigue or pain or pleasure, a behavior such as eating or watching TV, a decision to stop or start some activity, a sense perception such as seeing a beautiful woman or feeling a gust of wind, an emotional impulse, a mood such as sadness or frustration or elation. It could even be a thought or problem or a philosophic concept that deserves deeper analysis.

The Buddha suggested that we systematically contemplate our body sensations, emotions, states of mind, and thoughts until we can do those contemplations consciously and under all conditions. These four contemplations are goal-directed training disciplines, the four so-called *satipatthanas*. This is a huge task, and no one would undertake it out of disinterested curiosity. We become mindful because it is useful to do so.

Few of us are now trying to extinguish all our passions and attain nirvana, but *sati* has many other more tangible benefits. For example, focusing on the body helps us to relax at will (as discussed in chapters 1–8). Focusing on our actions will improve the outcomes (see chapter 9). Focusing on emotions helps us modulate them up or down, and understand our deepest values (see chapters 16, 17, and 19). Focusing on states of mind helps us boost the good states and dissolve the bad ones (see chapter 18). Focusing on thought and reflecting on how we think leads to the goal-directed, insightful thought that the Buddha valued so highly (see chapters 20–22).

MEMORY

It is obvious from its use in the *Sutta* that *sati* correlates almost perfectly to our English word "attention." Nonetheless, its etymological root is actually "memory." Not surprisingly, this has confused many modern writers. The way we currently use the word "memory" in English is apparently quite different from its use in the Buddha's time. Nonetheless, I'll try to unravel this. We can say that *sati* relates to memory in four ways.

First, *sati* refers to the cluster of associations that unconsciously supports every one of our perceptions. Without this, we wouldn't be able to identify what a thing was or what it meant to us.

Second, *sati* refers to what cognitive psychologists call "working memory." We noted earlier that to be mindful means "to hold something in mind" (working memory) in order to evaluate it. If we hold it there long enough, it will get a foothold in short-term memory, and we will be able to recall it later. If we do this repeatedly, it will eventually move from short-term memory (in the hippocampus) into long-term memory (in the cerebral cortex). *Sati* is the goal-directed, discriminating attention—"don't forget this!"—that is essential for all learning, and the *Sutta* is nothing if not a mind-training manual.

Third, *sati* means remembering our good and bad experiences in order to learn from them. *Sati* was regarded as essential for moral training and sense restraint. It was described as being the monk's gatekeeper, or like a sentinel on a watchtower. *Sati*'s role was to guard the monk's five sense-doors—as Buddhaghosa says, "so that states of desire do not invade, pursue and threaten his virtue."[16]

The monk is expected to be mindful of his bad states of mind when they occur, but he should also notice and *remember* what leads up to them. He eventually controls his lust or anger not through heroic acts of will but by *remembering* their antecedent causes. ("There are too many pretty girls down that street. Remember what happened last time!")

Finally, *sati* means memory in the sense of "keeping in mind" one's goals and intentions in the face of contrary temptations. This is a very ordinary cognitive skill. It involves remembering what you are doing so that you don't get sidetracked en route. It suggests staying focused and completing whatever you plan to do. For a monk, this meant remembering his goal of enlightenment. For modern-day meditators, it means remembering what we are trying to achieve in both the short term and the long term.

Sati as a memory function was far more crucial in the Buddha's time. The first monks didn't have books or monastic routines to remind them what to do. They had to literally memorize the teaching to carry it with them as they roamed. Even the most junior monks would be able to recite certain texts such as the *Sutta*, while some monks were famous for developing phenomenal mental libraries. In the commentaries, this was regarded as an integral aspect of *sati*.

To summarize, *sati* implies memory in several ways. It means holding something in working memory or focusing on it; it means remembering what is important so we can learn from our experience; and it means remembering our values and goals to guide our actions. These uses of *sati* are all spelled out in other texts and in the extensive commentarial literature. They are all the natural consequences of deliberate attention.

PURPOSEFUL EFFORT

Sati has another dimension that is definitely missing from the modern understanding of mindfulness. It has a driving, purposeful energy to it. A monk is mindful because he is aspiring to nothing less than total awakening. This means that *sati* is frequently linked with words that mean "intense, vigilant, ardent." The word *atapi*, meaning a strong intention, or a goal-directed effort, relates to *tapas*, the sacrificial fire of Vedic rituals. Metaphorically it refers to the inner heat, energy, and ecstasy that the dedicated yogi generates to burn out his spiritual impurities. The persistent effort of *atapi* also leads to the blissful sensations (*piti*) that can occur in longer meditations.

The Burmese monk U Pandita (1921–2016) was perhaps the most important modern authority on Vipassana. In his

1992 meditation guide, he says, "'Mindfulness' has come to be the accepted translation of *sati* into English. However, this word has a kind of passive connotation that can be misleading. 'Mindfulness' must be dynamic and confrontative. . . . I teach that mindfulness should leap forward onto the object, covering it completely, penetrating into it, not missing any part of it. To convey this active sense, I often prefer to use the words 'observing power' to translate *sati*, rather than 'mindfulness.'"[17]

This approach may seem extreme, but you can see his point. *Atapi* is the capacity for sustained mental effort in pursuit of a goal. In the example from U Pandita, the goal is direct knowledge or insight into an object. With *atapi*, a goal is always implied, or its energy would be destructive. *Atapi* also implies that discrimination (*sampajjana*) and ultimate purpose are integral parts of *sati*.

Finally, there are four other Pali terms that reflect different aspects of *sati*. *Vitakka-vicara* is a form of *sati* that literally means "selective, sustained attention." *Vitakka* means the circling around, or the orienting of the mind, toward the object. (Cognitive psychology tells us that this is the first stage of focusing on anything at all.) *Vicara* adds the meaning of sustaining the attention, or locking on the object and staying with it uninterruptedly. *Vitakka-vicara* leads to the undistracted streaming of attention in one direction, and it is regarded as the entry into the first of the *jhanas*, or trance states.

The concept of *dhamma-vicaya* (the second of the seven factors of enlightenment) explains why you would do this. *Vicaya* means looking deeply into the mental phenomena that arise (*dhamma*) in meditation. For a monk, *dhamma-vicaya* is the understanding that every single perception is impermanent (*anicca*), a potential source of suffering (*dukkha*), and devoid of any lasting identity (*anatta*), and should therefore be abandoned. We are not monks, so when we examine any sensation, thought, impulse, or emotion, we are likely to have different interpretations, but the same principle applies. When we look into something (*dhamma-vicaya*) for long enough, be it a few seconds or a few minutes, we will accurately know its true value for good or ill in our lives.

When we put all these different aspects of attention together as a mind-training program, we have *vipassana*, a term that literally means "repeated deep seeing." *Vipassana* is sometimes translated as "penetrating insight," suggesting the kind of purposeful drive that is reflected in U Pandita's comments.

MINDFUL VERSUS MINDLESS

The Buddha understood *sati* as discriminating self-observation for the purpose of awakening. The *Sutta* says, "The monk lives intently (*atapi*) contemplating his body, clearly understanding (*sampajjana*), and mindful (*sati*) of it." *Sati* is "attention." *Sampajjana* is "evaluation." *Sati-sampajjana* is "the conscious perception and evaluation of something." The primary role of *sati* is to make good decisions in all matters, big or small. Above all, the *satipatthana* method trains the executive functions of a mature adult: attention, judgment, memory, willpower, and goal-directed effort.

So how did mindfulness come to be viewed as "a state of nonjudgmental acceptance"? Today's writers are often likely to describe it as savoring the present, tasting the raisin, firmly resisting the lure of thought and action. As Jon Kabat-Zinn puts it, "You are already everything you may hope to attain, so no effort of the will is necessary. . . . You are already it."[18]

Although this is nothing like *satipatthana*, we do find it throughout Buddhism, almost from the beginning. Its most obvious sources nowadays are Burmese Vipassana, Tibetan Dzogchen, and Chinese Chan and Japanese Zen. These are the so-called "tranquility" or "no-thought" practices based almost entirely on sitting. These practices typically emphasize stillness and passivity; an abandonment of thought, analysis, discrimination, or learning; and an uncritical acceptance of the flow of the moment.

These practices usually aspire to a so-called nondual, mirrorlike state of pure consciousness. Buddhism has literally dozens of technical terms and metaphors for this ideal state: buddhamind (*bodhicitta*), luminosity, bare attention, emptiness (*sunyata*). Despite their intellectual poverty, tranquility meditations are often regarded by their practitioners as being the very quintessence of the Buddha's teaching. As Dogen put it, "*Zazen* is the ultimate practice. This is indeed the True Self. The Buddhadharma is not to be sought outside of this."[19]

In contrast, many scholars, monks, and the Buddha himself have criticized these practices as being more mindless than mindful. They are narcotic and potentially addictive. A no-thought meditator is seen as doing "dead stump" or "bronze buddha" practice. He has "fallen into emptiness" or is suffering a "Zen sickness." Buddhaghosa would probably regard this kind of complacent tranquility as "the near enemy" lurking within *any* meditation practice. According to the Buddhist scholar Robert Sharf, the eighth-century Indian teacher

Kamalashila said there is a special hell for yogis who believe that the goal of meditation is no-thought: they will face five hundred eons in the zombie realm of beings without minds.[20]

Tranquility meditations, as an escape from the world and its rational reference points, can easily reinforce a kind of narcissistic self-absorption. As Sharf puts it, the practitioner "can lose touch with the socially, culturally and historically construed world in which he or she lives."[21] The "nonjudging" aspect can also suggest he has abandoned his moral compass and sense of common humanity. A modern meditator can easily lapse into a kind of mystical, "be here now" ideology. This quietistic abnegation of thought and action can be found in many religions, including Christianity. It is related to virtues such as faith and surrender, but it is a very long way from the *Satipatthana Sutta*.

Tranquility meditations are satisfying, healthy, and restful, and their simplicity makes them easy to market. They are a good and probably essential first step for any meditator, but they are also a honey trap for tired and lazy minds. Above all, they can blind us to the full dynamic potential of mindfulness.

15

How the *Sutta* Works

In the last chapter I described *sati* as sustained, purposeful attention. I will now explain how this concept is applied throughout the *Sutta*. Before I do so, I have to address an uncomfortable issue. The Buddha's techniques are exquisitely practical, but his values are not ours. Above all, he was a monk with little sympathy for the "householder" life. If you read the Pali Canon texts, it is obvious that seeking nirvana entails physical seclusion, emotional detachment, a horror of sensuality, and an indifference toward the world.

Hardly anyone swallows this original Buddhist formula whole nowadays. It is far too cold and bitter, and the benefits don't seem to justify the enormous sacrifices involved. This is partly why the *Sutta* and the original texts are so neglected. Every writer on Buddhism draws lines between what they accept from the tradition and what they don't, even though they hardly ever admit this. Popular writers often water down the Buddha's doctrine to homeopathic levels. "Nirvana" gets reduced to "happiness." The Buddha's take-home message gets summarized as "friendliness" and "altruism." His energetic drive for enlightenment is replaced by a kind of passive "presentism."

I'm not going to do anything like this. I think that it shows the Buddha far more respect to state his teaching and values as faithfully as possible, even if I (and you, my readers) vehemently disagree with him. The Buddha was a keen, systematic, and original thinker, and he deserves to be heard in his own tone of voice. Any human being, even a criminal in a law court, deserves this simple courtesy. I find it ironic that I probably explain his views more clearly than many of his most vocal supporters. I'm not a Buddhist, so I disagree with him in many respects, but I do admire him as a philosopher.

In this and later chapters I'll try to draw the demarcation lines as clearly as possible. It took me several years, but I now find it fairly easy to separate his mind-training methods from his beliefs and goals. I will particularly highlight where our paths and purposes diverge from his.

CONTINUOUS MINDFULNESS

The *Satipatthana Sutta* is a do-it-yourself training manual. It is designed to help an itinerant monk develop the habit of continuous self-observation in the pursuit of enlightenment. As is obvious in the *Sutta*, seated meditation was only part of his practice. The monk may have spent less than half his waking day sitting down. He didn't need to be "meditating" to be mindful. His real discipline was to focus inwardly and to cultivate his mind in every situation.

The Buddha divided the objects of attention into four general groups: the body, emotions, states of mind, and thought.

Each of these has subdivisions, and we could always add others if we wanted to, such as "mindfulness of action." Regardless of the object, the act of focusing always has a similar quality. We "hold the object in mind." We hold it "distinct" from related matters and potential distractions. When we focus well, something clicks into place. We know that we've got it. We sense the object of our attention in sufficient detail to evaluate it more accurately and confidently than we did at first.

All this is true whether the object remains in consciousness for a few seconds or an hour; whether it is something as exact as a thought or it is opaque like a mood; whether it is simple, such as a sound or an itch; or whether it is complex, such as a philosophical question or a life choice.

It takes years to become equally proficient across this vast range of mental objects. We may be skilled at focusing on the breath, but to accurately sense a mood or a problem is a different challenge altogether. Nonetheless, the gut feeling of getting a clear, uncluttered mental representation of something is much the same in all cases.

NAMING

In earlier chapters, I introduced an exercise called "Naming the Distraction." That was just one specific application of the way that "naming" is used in the *Sutta*. The Buddha said that we are mindful if we can hold any object "in mind" and describe it to ourselves (that is, "name" it). The gold standard of mindfulness is thus the ability to verbally identify the object. This ensures that there is nothing vague or approximate about being mindful. This deliberate use of language guarantees metacognitive awareness. The prominent use of naming (or labeling, or categorizing, or noting) throughout the *Sutta* also gives the lie to those writers who claim that mindfulness is a precognitive and nonverbal kind of perception.

Like the good teacher that he was, the Buddha gave many examples of naming. In the *Sutta*'s section on mindfulness of the body, for example, the Buddha says that when the monk is breathing in, he knows, "I am breathing in." When he is breathing out, he knows, "I am breathing out." When his body is calm, he knows, "This is a calm body." When he is walking, he knows, "I am walking." When he is eating, he knows, "I am eating."

In the section on mindfulness of emotion, the Buddha says that when the monk experiences a pleasant sensation he knows, "This is pleasant." When the monk experiences an unpleasant sensation he knows, "This is unpleasant." When he is angry he knows, "This is anger."

In the section titled "Mindfulness of States of Mind," the Buddha says that when the monk is energetic, he knows, "This is energy." When his energy is depleted, he knows, "This is lethargy." When his mind is tranquil, he knows, "This is tranquility."

The Buddha's examples of labeling are all short and simple. Naming something is not an invitation to speculate on it. Its purpose is to help "hold" the object for appraisal. When modern meditators name, they typically use just single words: "calm," "pleasant," "anger," "pain," "confusion." This categorizing captures the object for just long enough to evaluate it and choose a response. This is usually but not always a nonresponse (don't go there), or an acceptance of what can't be changed (stop fighting it). If the object is particularly useful in the context of your goals and values, you try to boost it. If it is useless or worse, you try to disengage from it.

Meditators nowadays tend to name an object only when they feel it is useful to do so. Naming is an excellent device for managing distractions, for example. However, the almost physical sense of "holding" an object in mind is more important than literally naming it. This ability to hold an object in mind is, paradoxically, reliant on also being firmly grounded in one's body. As the Buddha says, the monk "focuses on the breath in front of himself." The Buddha regarded body-mind stillness (*passaddhi*) as indispensable for steady attention and clear evaluation.

We can also hold an object in the form of an image or a feeling once we know how. Using language doesn't always help. For example, we can consciously grasp a musical phrase so vividly that it lodges in memory for several seconds thereafter, but there is no way to usefully name it.

As a technique, naming has considerable limitations. It is impossible to label more than a fraction of what arises in the mind. Many mental phenomena such as moods, intuitions, and reflections are far too subtle to be named. Naming doesn't help much with tranquility meditation, and some scholars argue that naming can obstruct other faculties such as absorption (*samadhi*).

However, the basic principle stands up very well. The gold standard for mindfulness is that you can briefly describe to yourself what you are doing, thinking, or feeling at any moment. You are mindful if you can "name" what is dominant in your mind.

In the *Sutta*, naming is used to evaluate an object prior to a response. Thus we do respond differently to stimuli according to their importance. We are not trying to freeze them all indiscriminately. We are looking for an appropriate response rather than none at all. For example, the sound of background traffic is easier to handle than a nagging problem with a child. Conversely we might need to sit with a mood of rising sadness or regret for several seconds before it "clicks" into place and we "know" it. Nor is there any need to ruthlessly disengage from an affectionate thought or a sudden memory that gives us pleasure. We can still focus well on the body and deepen our inner stillness throughout all of this gentle background activity.

In modern Vipassana practice under the influence of the reformer monk Mahasi Sayadaw, naming is used for a slightly different effect. Mahasi suggests "naming" (twice!) whatever arises at random in the mind as a continuous practice. A meditator might thus name hundreds of different objects in a single session.

This is not the nuanced "name, evaluate, and respond" method of the *Sutta*. It is to "name and dismiss" virtually everything equally, based on the presupposition that nothing at all will be worth attending to. It aims for a far more complete and uncompromising dismissal of cognitive activity and engagement with the world. It targets a universally passive, nonreactive, mirrorlike state of mind that is much closer to the Modern Mindfulness model than that of the *Sutta*.

The Mahasi, Modern Mindfulness, and Zen models usually posit a naive duality of mind and matter. In these approaches, the idea is that if we disengage from matter (that is, thoughts and sensations), we can return to some original state of pure consciousness (or bare attention, or emptiness). Our minds can then function like a mirror, seeing things "just as they are," uncontaminated by thought or feeling or memory. I think that this is a scientifically dubious idea and that when people practice this meditation they are actually doing something else altogether.

Nonetheless, both the Mahasi approach and that of the *Sutta* have the similar effect of slowing us down and discouraging action. Over time, experienced *satipatthana* meditators typically shift the bias of their response from overreactivity toward underreactivity, from overarousal to passivity. Through many hours of practice, they set a default of responding no more than necessary to any sensation, thought, emotion, or mood. This somewhat defensive but liberating stance is the mental equivalent of their physical immobility.

Within a meditation, this nonreactivity has an immediate payoff. It leads to a peaceful, detached disposition toward whatever arises in consciousness, and the body and mind can become exquisitely still. This body-mind stillness (*passaddhi*) is the basis for other ideal mind-states described in the *Sutta*. It supports the bliss of *piti*, and the contentment and acceptance of *sukha*. It contributes to states of flow and absorption (*samadhi*).

This inner stillness finally consolidates as *upekkha*: equanimity or serenity. This state of emotional detachment is idealized in Buddhism, and that attitude can trickle over into daily life. At its best, it manifests as a kind of calmness under fire, a relaxed, stoic tolerance of inner and outer stressors.

ARISING AND PASSING AWAY

An important refrain recurs throughout the *Sutta*: "He carefully observes how valences [sensations, or emotions, or states of mind, or thoughts] arise and how they pass away, and what causes them to do so. He observes this both in himself and in others." The Buddha believed that to calmly observe an unhelpful thought or behavior would diminish its power on the spot and help to eradicate it in the future. To amplify this effect, he further asks that we notice not just the object but also how it "arises and passes away."

For example, we shouldn't just notice "anger." We should also notice whether it is increasing or fading away, and store that episode in memory. Over time, this will help us understand the causal factors: what initiates anger and what helps it fade. Similarly, we see what contributes to healthy states of mind, and what helps sustain them.

Another aspect of the *Sutta* entails observing exactly the same phenomena in others: "He observes this both in himself and others." In other words, the Buddha was a people-watcher! We can learn about the birth and decay of sensations, thoughts, emotions, and behaviors by observing the process in others as well as ourselves. This is one reason we read stories, go to movies, and gossip: it is educational as well as fun.

A STAGE-BY-STAGE PATH

The Foundations of Mindfulness is based on two complementary skills. The first is a "procedural" skill, like riding a bicycle or learning a sport. This is the ability to relax quickly and be calm under all circumstances. This is the subject of the "mindfulness of the body" section of the *Sutta* and chapters 1–8 of this book.

The second skill is cognitive, namely "attention"— the concept we examined so thoroughly in chapter 14. *Sati-sampajjana* is the ability to consciously focus on and evaluate any body sensation, action, emotion, state of mind, or thought as it happens. The monk was encouraged to develop a keen sense of what was good or bad, healthy or unhealthy, "skillful" or "unskillful" in relation to all the objects of attention.

The four training foundations of the *Sutta* are like levels of a pyramid. An ascetic lifestyle supports a calm body, which supports a calm mind. This body-mind stillness supports the extinguishing of the emotions (equanimity), which supports the positive mental factors necessary for absorption states (*jhana*). With these foundations in place, the monk can aspire to deep, sustained thought and profound insight into the nature of life itself. This is why people hope for breakthroughs on retreats when they can become virtual monks for a while. As the first sentence of the *Sutta* says, the systematic cultivation of mindfulness throughout all four foundations is the *only* way to achieve nirvana.

We can read the *Sutta* in five minutes, but that would miss the point. It is a "how to do it" skill-training manual consisting of thirteen sequential exercises. They are based on abilities most adults already have. You and I can always notice and describe any strong sensation, emotion, or thought that captures our attention, but we rarely train that ability systematically. Consequently, we are unlikely to develop the broad-based, present-time, self-monitoring awareness that leads to a disciplined life and to the absorption states (*jhana*) that depend on this.

A monk of the Buddha's day, however, would have practiced most of those thirteen exercises thousands of times over months and years. He would have become expert in noticing his thoughts, emotions, and impulses as they arose on the spot, and thereby improving all his responses. We can do much the same if we want to. It just takes practice, but we shouldn't fool ourselves that focusing on the breath and watching thoughts dispassionately is all there is to know about mindfulness as presented in the *Sutta*. Those thirteen exercises are systematic and cumulative, and they need to be practiced individually for real accomplishment.

WHAT IS THIS PATH OF TRAINING FOR?

The *Sutta* has two goals. The first goal is *upekkha*—equanimity or tranquility—which involves a high degree of emotional and philosophic detachment from the world. Above all, it implies the end of suffering now and in the future. *Upekkha* is certainly attainable, and similar ideals are found throughout Western philosophy and early Christianity. Achieving this is the task of the first three foundations of mindfulness: mindfulness of body, emotion, and states of mind.

The second goal is nirvana, which is complete enlightenment. The monk can only achieve this through profound insight into the Buddha's theory of existence. This is the task of the fourth foundation of the *Sutta*: mindfulness of thought.

The Buddha's philosophy is encapsulated in two straightforward and logically sound formulae: the Four Noble Truths and the three characteristics of existence. The first of these is sufficient for equanimity. The second is the doorway into enlightenment.

The Four Noble Truths are as follows: (1) Life is suffering. (2) The cause of suffering is desire. (3) Desire can be extinguished. (4) The Eightfold Path of training extinguishes desire and leads to the end of suffering. The word "desire" in the context of the Four Noble Truths is also variously translated as delusion, craving, clinging, lust, attachment, or passion, all of which are canonically acceptable. This formula is often stripped down to "Nothing is worth clinging to."

The three characteristics of existence are much tougher nuts to crack. They are counterintuitive and pretty grim. The Buddha said we are deluded in thinking that we have individual personalities and that life is basically good, stable, and enjoyable. "That is not true," he said, "and it is no wonder that you suffer as a result of your delusions."

The three characteristics of existence are (1) impermanence (*anicca*), (2) suffering (*dukkha*), and (3) no-soul (*anatta*). The Buddha's argument about the nature of existence goes like this: All things are impermanent. Attachment to what is impermanent is the cause of all suffering. Above all, we suffer because of our attachment to our sense of self, which is also impermanent. The only solution is to renounce the world and our sense of self utterly. By doing so we can weed out the seeds of our actions—our evil karma—that would otherwise ripen as suffering in this and future lives.

It is hard for a modern practitioner to regard the three characteristics as a coherent argument. Above all, this philosophy requires a belief in karma and reincarnation to make any practical sense. If this is our only lifetime, there are far less draconian ways to avoid suffering. In modern Buddhism, the three characteristics operate more as a source of mystical ideas, philosophic speculation, and mind games than as a useful guide to behavior.

Although the Buddha's techniques are marvelous, it is obvious that his goals are not ours. He was an ascetic who despised all worldly pursuits. Doing nothing, resisting temptation, and watching without reacting might make us more peaceful, but they are hardly a recipe for an attractive life. Nor is nirvana, which entails extinguishing all affective responses to the world, a marketable prospect nowadays.

We are bound to use *sati* and moment-to-moment self-awareness for many purposes that the Buddha himself would despise. Our goals may include stress relief, better health and relationships, sensual enjoyment, clarity of thought, wealth, technical skills, better judgment and decision-making, social virtues such as empathy and love, the acquisition of knowledge or mastery, or the appreciation of beauty and the arts.

This means that our most highly cultivated mindful states may not feel or look particularly Buddhist. Quite the opposite in fact: they won't necessarily exhibit serenity, detachment, and stillness. Excellence in any field can only be achieved with strong, self-monitoring attentional skills. Athletes, judges, and connoisseurs all require well-trained, discriminating awareness to succeed in their endeavors. Of course they also make mistakes, but who doesn't? However, we can't say they're not mindful just because they don't meditate or profess sympathy for Buddhism.

The Buddha's techniques can teach us how to drive the vehicle of mindfulness, but we don't have to adopt his goals. We can go to destinations that are more important to us. Nearly everyone who practices mindfulness does this, whether they admit to it or not.

Chapters 1–8 described the first foundation of the *Sutta*, mindfulness of the body. In subsequent chapters I will describe the graduate levels of the *Sutta*: mindfulness of emotions, of states of mind, and of thought. When we look at the core of the *Sutta*, the Buddha's instructions are so lucid, it is easy to see where our uses branch out from his. For example, his systematic instructions for dissolving *destructive* emotions are quite superb, but he says almost nothing about the active cultivation of *good* emotions.

Nonetheless, we can easily use his techniques to amplify and refine emotion rather than extinguish it. His instructions are perfectly clear. Although he would be disgusted with our goals, we can easily use mindfulness to enhance and refine the pleasure we take, for example, in family life, music, or natural beauty. In the following chapters, I explain what he says about emotions, states of mind, and thought, and how we can tailor his techniques to our divergent purposes.

PART THREE

Other Foundations: Mindfulness of Emotion,
Mindfulness of States of Mind,
Mindfulness of Thought

16

Emotion at the Atomic Level

How does a monk observe the valences of phenomena? When he experiences a pleasant feeling, he knows: "This is pleasant." When he experiences an unpleasant feeling, he knows: "This is unpleasant." He also recognizes those valences that are neither pleasant nor unpleasant. Likewise, he is aware of the positive, negative, and neutral valences that accompany thoughts.
—SATIPATTHANA SUTTA

The field of emotion, or "affect," is notoriously difficult to analyze or classify. Cognitive scientists and psychologists have just as much trouble as a layperson does. The Buddha tackled this issue with great skill, and, in one case at least, his ancient terminology is actually *superior* to ours. The Buddha used the term *vedana* to talk about identifying emotions at the atomic level of our spontaneous likes and dislikes. This term has no equivalent in vernacular English, but psychologists, borrowing from the jargon of chemistry, refer to the phenomenon as "valence."

The Buddha recognized that nearly every perception that we notice, be it of a thought, sensation, emotion, or action, comes with an emotional charge that is either positive or negative. We either like or dislike the object to some degree, however small. We find it "pleasant" or "unpleasant." We have a subtle preference for or against it.

This for-or-against sensation is the *vedana*, or "valence," of an object. Psychologists also call this the "emotional charge" or "feeling tone" or "affective tone," but these terms lack the almost mathematical precision of "valence." A valence can be positive or negative, strong or weak. It can even be rated on a numerical 1-to-10 scale of positives and negatives. For example, a thought about "work" could be +3. A thought about "boyfriend" could be +6. A thought about "money" could be –2.

Valences are mostly subliminal. We rarely notice them against the prominence of the object, but they are usually not difficult to identify in any particular case. The effect of a valence may be tiny, but it is always there, subtly influencing our response to the object. The Buddha said that some perceptions can have a neutral affect (neither pleasant nor unpleasant), but this is quite rare in an ordinary active life. We are far more likely to notice those perceptions that come with an emotional charge.

We are always surrounded by thousands of possible stimuli. We can consciously notice only a tiny fraction of these. Our attention is always infinitely more selective than we realize, and it discriminates for a purpose. We scan for advantage or threat and ignore the rest. To notice any object at all implies that we have already attributed some value to it. (That is, we see it as potentially useful, painful, pretty, tasty, entertaining, repulsive, funny, uncomfortable, sexy, embarrassing, and so forth.) This positive or negative value is what gives the object its emotional charge.

Conversely, we are unlikely to notice anything that has a neutral charge, since such an object would be irrelevant to our well-being. Nor can we ever see a thing pure and naked, "just as it is," cut free from cognition, feeling, and memory—despite spiritual claims to the contrary. Even our slightest perceptions are valenced and purposeful. Each one is unique to us, enriched by years of our personal associations. No matter how pure each of our minds become, I will never see the same tree that you do.

The concept of valence explains why even the slightest perception (*sati*) is also an evaluation (*sampajjana*). This like-dislike response is a spontaneous, miniaturized judgment based on instinct, habit, and the memory of similar past experiences. A deeper part of our brain does a rough assessment of everything for us within milliseconds: "This object is promising or useless. Worth paying further attention to or worthless." All day long the valences of our perceptions steer us automatically toward profitable behavior and away from loss and threat.

ACTION TENDENCIES

So how does this dynamic work? Every valence induces what psychologists call an "action tendency." This is the *predisposition* to act, which precedes the act itself. The appropriate neurons in the premotor cortex will fuel up and prepare to fire, just in case they are needed. In Buddhism and yoga, these action tendencies are known as *sankharas,* or "volitions." We are prompted to move "toward" what we like and "away" from what we dislike. In psychology, these volitions are called "approach" and "withdrawal" action tendencies. We see; we like; we approach. We see; we don't like; we pull back.

The vast majority of action tendencies don't result in a whole-body action. We would be torn to pieces by competing valences if they did. When we do act, however, the dynamic goes like this: A perception triggers a valence, which triggers an action tendency in preparation for an actual movement. This whole process takes about a third of a second. In other words, it all happens *before* we are conscious of it. When we do finally notice something, a judgment, an action tendency, and a bottomless pit of past memory associations have already been woven into what seems like a simple perception.

This is the brain's super-fast, "quick and dirty" *automatic* process: the formula we described in chapter 6 as perception + evaluation + response. This process is perfect when we are faced with a danger that demands an instant response. Mindfulness, as the *conscious* perception and evaluation of something, covers the same ground but more slowly and accurately. It typically refines the automatic judgment that has already taken place and leads to a more considered response.

Because the words "valence" and "action tendency," *vedana* and *sankhara,* are not part of vernacular English, people often have difficulty understanding them. Nonetheless, it is quite easy to demonstrate their existence. I suggest you slowly read through the five words on the next page, and take a few seconds to imagine what each one represents. If you skim at usual reading speed, you will probably miss the valences. You are likely to find that some words have a positive valence and some have a negative one. You may also notice your body pulling back slightly or moving toward some of them (the action tendency).

peach   black   Marilyn   vomit   puppy

Did those words induce subtle affective and bodily responses in you? I hope so. If they didn't, try it again more slowly, and imagine physically touching each one.

Valences and action tendencies are the triggers for most of our instinctive behaviors, impulses, and mood swings. Although we usually notice only strong valences, even the weaker ones stimulate approach or withdrawal behavior to some degree. We get tugged in various directions just walking down a street. The Buddha saw valences as the enemy of stillness and peace.

Valences initiate most of our daily actions from below the conscious radar. We rely on them to make countless small and mostly adaptive judgments during the day. They are the thousands of tiny likes and dislikes that make us do this (grab some food, buy those socks) or stop doing that (the exercise, the office work) all day long. Valences also trigger our sudden shifts in mood. If you want to understand why you just did something unexpected, then look for the associated valence.

The object may literally be an object "out there" in the world, but the valence is always subjective. If we don't notice these subtle affective responses, our perceptions can be contaminated. We will mistakenly regard the valence as a quality of the object itself rather than our personal response to it. If we acknowledge our automatic response, however, we can usually modulate it if we want to.

The Buddha said that we're mindful of something if we can describe it to ourselves. To be mindful of a valence means that we can say, "I had a thought about my dog and it was pleasant," and recognize that as mild positive valence. Or "I had a thought about my neighbor and it was unpleasant," and note the presence of strong negative valence. This identification of valence can be important. A moment's reflection may tell us that our neighbor is not really as bad as Hitler, for example. Without this recognition, we may act toward him as if he were.

Once we recognize that valences are everywhere, it is surprisingly easy to notice them. The Buddha recommended identifying them as a meditation in itself. This simple practice alone is the second of his four foundations of mindfulness.

Once a valence becomes obvious, he said, we should name it as either "pleasant" or "unpleasant," "like" or "dislike," positive or negative. We could do this dozens of times a day whether meditating or not. To stop and hold a valence in this way also helps arrest its flow-on action tendency. Monitoring valence is a way of training ourselves to be less impulsive and reactive. In meditation, this restraint carries over in relation to even more subtle stimuli such as thoughts and moods. It supports the "watching without reacting" mode that is encouraged when we meditate.

We have four ways of identifying valence: strong or weak positive, or strong or weak negative. It is useful to recognize the positive or negative direction of a valence, but it is more important to notice its strength. We can easily cruise along with the mild positives and negatives, but a strong negative valence or a strong positive valence is each more likely to destabilize us than its weaker forms.

A person who is stressed doesn't need to analyze the bundle of emotions behind it. He simply needs to notice he is overreacting (strong negative valence) and adjust. Emotions can carry great visceral conviction, but they are often faulty. Anxiety is often patently irrational, and righteous anger can be little more than an adult temper tantrum, but we don't need to analyze these bundles of pain the way a psychologist might. The Buddha had faith that if we could "just see" the excessive strength of the valence, our response would start to self-correct naturally.

We can all notice our overreactions from time to time, but we hardly ever develop this ability as a conscious skill. We are novices not experts, Sunday golfers not pros. We typically notice our emotional responses only when they pass a certain threshold of intensity. This is often too late. It is better to stop the impulse before we hit the wall.

In the *Satipatthana Sutta*, the Buddha asked the monk to notice the valences of stimuli and their action tendencies hundreds of times a day, until the process became second nature. The monk was expected to name his transient valences in order to make them fully conscious. "Lunch: pleasant. Empty food bowl: unpleasant. Fatigue: unpleasant. Wind: pleasant. Bird noise: unpleasant. Girls singing: very pleasant, and dangerous. . . ." In this way, he could learn to recognize temptation, control his impulses, and arm himself in advance before a bad action tendency took hold.

The Buddha saw these subtle tendencies (*sankharas*) as the seeds of all our actions (karma) and thus the source of all present and future suffering. He warned that a simple sense perception can lead to feeling, to craving, to volitional activity, to clinging, to attachment, to disappointment, despair, regret, disgust, the whole mass of human suffering, and even rebirth itself. It all starts with a valence and an action tendency. This is why the Buddha saw "guarding the sense-doors" as so essential for inner peace.

Once we become mindful of a response, we can usually adjust its strength or intensity, but not its direction. We will still find an unpleasant object unpleasant, just less so. The girl is still pretty but not intoxicatingly so. We can't avoid judgment entirely and it would be silly to try. We would also have to eradicate all our affective responses to do this. In many cases this would be quite impossible. Try it out on the word "vomit" on page 183.

EQUANIMITY: "NEITHER PLEASANT NOR UNPLEASANT"

The Buddha, however, would disagree with me. He would say, quite correctly, that I had insufficient commitment to the path. If I really wanted to eradicate all affective responses and action tendencies, I could. Although the Buddha refused to define nirvana, the term does imply a state of perfect equanimity (*upekkha*). This in turn is defined as continuous neutrality of affect—feeling "neither pleasure nor pain." *Upekkha* is an invincible 24/7 serenity beyond any possible disturbance. It is a kind of total Zen cool, close to perfect indifference. In the Buddha's famous "Parable of the Saw" he says, "Don't be troubled even if bandits are hacking your limbs off with a saw."[1]

This equanimity, one of the highest goals in Buddhism, is difficult but not impossible to achieve. The monk strives toward equanimity by repeatedly—every minute of every day—trying to scale all his positive and negative valences back toward zero. Buddhaghosa says that equanimity "counteracts both the pleasant and the unpleasant . . . On seeing a visual object, the monk is neither glad nor sad. Rejecting both the attractive and the repulsive, he dwells in equanimity."[2]

This is the monk's spiritual training in the second of the four foundations of the *Sutta*. He tries to systematically neutralize all positive and negative valences, so he will no longer be as vulnerable to suffering or fate. He strives to minimize all his natural fears and desires, including his attachment to his body and to life itself. This ideal is not unfamiliar to us in the West. It is just an extreme form of Stoicism. It is often found in military circles, and it could partly explain the serenity of some old people.

To summarize: Every valence is a spontaneous, miniature judgment with a tendency to "approach or withdraw." The monk in training aims to reduce all these thousands of tiny judgments and their action tendencies toward zero. No judgment = no attachment to pleasant or unpleasant = no response = stillness, detachment, and tranquility. (Even if he is being hacked to death by bandits.)

IMPROVING OUR JUDGMENTS

To be mindful of a valence invariably leads to a reappraisal. This is the purpose of *sati* and of attention itself: to consciously perceive and evaluate something. As soon as we consciously recognize a valence, we will also know whether its embedded judgment is appropriate or not. This is an excellent way of noticing when we are overreacting. If so, we can peg back our response on the 1-to-10 scale from –7 to –4 for example.

But what if we're *not* overreacting? What if the judgment is perfectly accurate? Remember that we are making thousands of these tiny habitual judgments all day long, and they mostly work well. We tend to become mindful only of those few valences that are faulty. Is there any point in also noticing our ordinary, adaptive valences?

Absolutely. Valences initiate all our actions. No valence = no action. A valence is a judgment that leads to an action tendency: "This is worth doing" or "This isn't worth doing." If we can become mindful of a valence—if we can get a "clear and distinct image" of it—our awareness will lead to a more refined judgment and a more targeted response.

Making judgments is no picnic. It is not easy to make the hundreds of ordinary judgments we need to get through the day. We tend to blunder along, approximating our guesses, operating by rule of thumb and habit, and often making decisions without realizing it. Most of these decisions work out well enough. Some go weirdly wrong for no apparent reason. Some, with hindsight, seem utterly crazy ("What on earth was I thinking about!"). Some people make bold, blind, foolhardy decisions; others constantly mistrust and double-guess themselves, making important decisions days or months later than they should have.

Learning how to make good judgments in situations of uncertainty and inadequate information is a skill that takes decades to grasp. The Greek philosopher Aristotle regarded good judgment (*phronesis*) as one of the most important social skills or "virtues" of a mature human being. We never perfect it. We continue to learn. Rule books and maxims are far too crude for the complexity of even simple situations. One very good way to improve our daily judgments, however, is to notice the valences that initiate them.

A valence is an instantaneous judgment about how to act: "This is important—act now. This is not important—forget it. This would be bad—avoid it." If we can become fully mindful (*sati*) of the valence and the action tendency, we can evaluate (*sampajjana*) if it is accurate. A valence contains both a direction (toward or away, pleasant or unpleasant) and a degree of intensity (strong or weak). As noted before, the direction is easy to identify and usually can't be changed, but the intensity is what really matters. With a little practice it becomes easy to rate the intensity of most valences on a 1-to-10 scale. Once you notice that a particular impulse is a –7 or a +2, it is usually obvious whether it is appropriate or not.

Although we tend to notice only strong valences, it is also useful to notice the many smaller ones. They can go badly wrong also, and their effects can accumulate. Learning to make better judgments is just like any skill. We learn by making slight but frequent adjustments in the right direction over and over again, until the new skill is automated.

Do you want some practice? Can you pick the *intensity* on a scale of 1 to 10 of the objects represented in the block of words on the next page? The valence of each one is likely to be slightly or markedly different. I've actually placed similar objects together to make the exercise harder. Nonetheless, if you find that several adjacent words seem to have the same intensity, you probably haven't got it.

Remember to spend a few seconds with each word until both the valence *and* its intensity level become clear. If you move too quickly the valences will blur into one another. A valence involves a subtle body response that usually takes a few seconds to emerge in consciousness. Finally, can you confidently isolate the valence itself from any emotion that the object evokes? Don't be surprised if you find this exercise difficult to do. It is not how we usually operate.

Cake. Pork. Gin. Hotel. Home. Family. Father. Friend. Work. TV. Phone. Shakespeare. Hendrix. Mozart. God. Goddess. Ants. Meerkats. Moth. Buddha. Jesus. Hell. Reincarnation. Summer. Winter. Ethiopia. Brazil. Darwin. Dawkins. Dalai Lama. Prime minister. King. Dictator. Priest. The future. The past. Mortgage. Dying. Death. Spirituality. Football. Money. Bed.

THE VALENCE OF EMOTIONS

Although the valence is part of an emotional response, it is not the emotion itself. The valence gives us the volume but not the music. The brain regions responsible for valence (primarily the amygdala) can be quite distinct from those that represent anger or love or sorrow. The same valence can be the fuel behind many emotions. Moreover it is quite possible to be mindful of a valence—to feel its strength and direction—independent of the emotion driving it. Anger or sadness or fear or love can all have strong or weak valences, and each of them can be positive or negative according to circumstances.

In the next chapter, I'll present the Buddha's full repertoire of techniques for managing painful emotion, but since those techniques apply equally well to valences they are worth mentioning here. In the *Sutta*, the Buddha says that the monk should notice states of mind such as anger or sadness but also "how these states of mind arise and pass away." The emotion itself may not change from day to day, but its valence certainly will. A depressed or grieving or happy person may remain in that state for months, but the valence of those moods can fluctuate within a single day.

It is a big improvement for a depressed person to recognize "Yesterday I felt suicidal (strong negative valence) but today I just feel miserable (mild negative valence)." The intensity may have shifted from -9 to -4. If he observes this positive shift in the valence repeatedly and objectively, he will start to recognize what supports it. Exercise, social contact, doing something engaging, or being around an animal—all of these can reduce the severity of a bad mood, even if the mood itself still remains.

Likewise, anxious people have a strong bias toward highlighting what is painful and discounting what is good. Their days can be full of lovely events that they fail to notice. Psychologists and self-help books often encourage them to deliberately "savor" the enjoyable sensations of the present to counteract this tendency. This can be hard to do if you are racing and stressed. I would suggest something more practical. I call it "re-valencing." Every action has a valence that lingers a few seconds after it is over. If you're anxious, you are bound to undervalue most of what you do. You can change this habit by noticing the affective tone of simple actions.

How did it feel to put away the laundry? Deal with a difficult client or family member? Take the stairs instead of the elevator? Eat the sandwich instead of the cake? These are all good things, but did you actually register them? A valence is an automatic, heuristic judgment, and it may not be quite accurate. If you are mindful of it, you can re-valence it up or down to reflect its true value: "Yes, I am pleased that I did X. It was worth doing and I'm glad that I've done it."

The Buddha gave high priority to the conscious recognition and "naming" of valences because this is where all our actions start. Noticing valences is the second of the four foundations of mindfulness in the *Sutta*, but to most of us this practice will seem quite odd. Since "valence" is not part of vernacular English, we are not in the habit of noticing what it refers to. Nonetheless, if you wanted to adopt just one concept from the *Satipatthana Sutta*, you wouldn't go far wrong with "valence." If you want to understand and fine-tune your own emotions on a daily basis, it wouldn't hurt to start at the atomic level.

17

Painful Emotion

How does a monk contemplate his states of mind?
He recognizes the mind that is caught in desire and
the mind free of desire. He recognizes the mind that
is caught in anger and the mind free of anger. He
recognizes the mind that is caught in delusion and
the mind free of delusion....

He carefully observes how these states of mind arise
and pass away, and what causes them to do so.
He learns how to extinguish [bad states] when they
arise, and how to prevent them arising in the future.
—SATIPATTHANA SUTTA

The *Sutta* addresses what we would call "emotion" in both
its second and third sections. Probably because valences
are pivotal and relatively easy to recognize, they are included
as the lone subject of the small second section. The Buddha
deals with emotions proper in the much larger third part
of the *Sutta*: "Mindfulness of States of Mind." Before we

examine his methods, let's look at what cognitive science can now tell us about emotion.

Psychology, the study of the mind, is now profiting greatly from neuroscience, the study of the brain. For example, thanks to modern brain-scanning technology we can now link certain mental functions with activity in specific brain regions. This is starting to give psychology a scientific validity that it has previously lacked. The mapping of functions onto brain anatomy goes like this: Sensations are processed in the sensory cortex in the top, back, and sides of the brain. Emotions are processed in the limbic system in the center. Thoughts are processed in the prefrontal cortex in the front. Actions are initiated from the motor cortex, a strip across the top of the cerebral cortex.

Because the brain is modular, we could say that we each have at least four brains. We all have a sensory brain, an emotional brain, a thinking brain, and a motor—or physical action—brain. Likewise we can say that there are four main cognitive functions: sensing, emotion, thinking, and action.

These four brains work together for a common goal, which is some form of useful action. The sensory brain takes in information. The emotional brain evaluates it. The thinking brain considers strategies *if necessary*, and the motor brain initiates action. Notice that the thinking brain is an optional extra. Most mental activity is automatic or instinctive and doesn't require input from consciousness.

We can always pay good attention to any particular action, thought, body sensation, or emotion if we want to, but we can't focus on all of them at once. The mental stage is too small. Working memory has limited capacity, so we are forced to be choosy. We tend to give priority to our thoughts and actions, and barely notice our emotions.

We can usually describe in considerable detail what we've done in the course of a day. Because we always give a high percentage of our attention to our actions, they get embedded in memory. However, we may have virtually no memory of our changing emotions or body sensations during that day. If we didn't focus on them at the time, we won't remember them later.

Our daily actions are important in ways that emotion isn't. When driving a car we have to monitor what we are doing moment by moment to stay alive. Conversely, we only notice our emotions while driving if they become disruptive. As a result we can drive a car, or even manage a knife and fork, with far more sophistication than we can describe or recall our emotional states.

As we get older, we become more self-aware in roughly the following sequence: We become mindful of our actions first, then thoughts, then body sensations, and finally emotion (if at all). Some people don't get that far. A stressed person with a runaway mind may have virtually no awareness of his body or his emotions, apart from knowing that he feels really bad.

Yet neuroscience tells us that no brain function is capable of working on its own. Each part constantly talks to and argues with every other part via self-regulating feedback mechanisms. Emotions turn out to be crucial for making good judgments. Reason alone tends to be myopic and out of its depth in complex situations. Emotions power most of our judgments and our consequent behavior, for both good or bad—so it is worthwhile to become more aware of them.

So how does meditation help? A Standard Meditation Practice (see chapter 1) corrects our natural mental bias toward action and thought. *Sitting down* stops our habitual activity, and *focusing on the body* interrupts our habitual thoughts. This frees up our available attention to reorient itself toward our bodies and emotions, as it will naturally do. Whether we intend to or not, we invariably notice these with more subtlety than usual when we meditate. This somatic input is what makes us feel emotionally "grounded" and in touch with ourselves.

We eventually realize that body sensations and emotions are closely linked, and they collectively influence thought. Sadness and tiredness go together, for example. Anger, fear, lust, pride, and affection—all have obvious physiological effects. The American philosopher and psychologist William James even argued that emotions are bodily events that are only recognized by the mind afterward, if at all.

Nonetheless, emotions in themselves are far more difficult to grasp than are thoughts or body sensations or even valences. Emotions are usually subtle, fluid, complex, and pre-conscious. They can occur as impulses, likes and dislikes, body sensations, passions, or moods—and they can last for seconds or hours or a lifetime. We can discuss emotions in a generalized way, but in the flesh they are hard to identify. How would you describe your emotional state right now, for example?

MINDFULNESS AS THERAPY

In the third part of the *Sutta*, the Buddha tackles what we would call emotions and moods and does quite an acceptable job of it. What the Buddha calls "The Five Hindrances" is a short list of "bad" emotions: desire, anger, lethargy, anxiety, and despair. Any psychologist will recognize these as the primary culprits found in the pages of her professional bible: the *Diagnostic and Statistical Manual of Mental Disorders*.

The Buddha said, "I teach but two things: suffering and the end of suffering." His teaching thus has an affinity with the concerns of Western medicine and psychology in a way that other religions do not.

Mindfulness is a rather new therapy in psychology, but it is often presented as taking authority from the distant past. Mindfulness is commonly described as "a state of nonjudgmental acceptance" with the assumption that this is a fundamental Buddhist ideal. The list of the five hindrances shows how completely wrong this assumption is.

It is obvious that the Buddha doesn't want us to regard desire or anger in a nonjudgmental, open-hearted, and accepting manner. His own judgment is perfectly clear: Emotion is the root cause of all suffering. He argues that virtually all emotions, but especially desire or anger, are the original sources of all human misery and are the implacable enemies of inner peace and freedom.

Although the Buddha's hostility toward emotion is more extreme than ours, his approach toward it is still remarkably practical. He gives a detailed, step-by-step, psychologically acute strategy for diminishing those emotions that really are destructive.

The Buddha suggests that we name a painful emotion as the first step toward controlling it. As it says in the *Sutta*, when the monk is angry, he knows "this is anger." This implies that the monk has already arrested the tendency toward action, and he is not trying to "fix" the discomfort. He is trying to see that cluster of body sensations and turbulent thoughts as objectively as possible.

The *Sutta* goes on to say that the monk carefully observes how anger arises and how it passes away, and what causes it to do so. If the monk continues to observe his anger, he will find that it is bound to change. Emotions are like weather: they may fade quickly or slowly, but they can't maintain their initial intensity forever. The nonreactive watching mode also allows the monk to see how emotions naturally change: He observes how anger passes away. His blood pressure drops, his muscle tension fades, and he feels mildly embarrassed about getting so worked up.

If the monk notices this dynamic hundreds of times mindfully, it gets embedded in memory. (Remember that the etymological root of *sati* is "memory.") This inevitably predisposes him to be less vulnerable to similar aggravations in the future. He will remember that he just has to wait long enough, or preoccupy himself with something else, for a painful state of mind to fade.

This is a good result, but there is still far more to this therapy. The monk also trains himself to notice how anger *arises*. Through repeated acts of observation and memory, he gradually realizes what triggers his bad mental states: He observes how anger arises and how it passes away, *and what causes it to do so*. This will help him notice danger signs quickly and develop prophylactic habits in the future. In psychology, this is called the "early detection" of destructive tendencies.

The monk will eventually realize that certain things reduce his propensity to anger. These may include sufficient sleep, reflecting on his goals, being around supportive people, chanting the texts, and, above all, maintaining the habit of continual self-observation that is the *satipatthana* method.

The monk will also learn to recognize the mind that is "free of anger." Elsewhere in the Pali texts the Buddha asks the monk to notice a sign of his success that is actually a nonsign. This is when he *doesn't* get angry in situations when he did in the past. A psychologist would recognize this as "desensitization," or as the "extinction" of a habitual response.

Another instruction in the *Sutta* reinforces these insights: "He observes this both in himself and in others." As social animals we love to watch others, to speculate on motives, to try to read people's minds. In this way, we learn far more about human psychology than we could from navel-gazing alone. The Buddha encouraged the monk to learn about the universal nature of emotion in this way.

These methods of regulating emotion are also supported by a formulation called "the four efforts." This is nested away in the last section of the *Sutta*. It is the sixth part of the comprehensive path of training called the Eightfold Path. These "efforts" can be summarized as follows:

1. You know when a *bad* state of mind is present and how to abandon it.

2. You know how to prevent a *bad* state of mind from arising in the future.

3. You know when a *good* state of mind is present and how to strengthen it.

4. You know how to induce a *good* state of mind when it is not present.

The *Sutta* thus gives us a very thorough bundle of do-it-yourself techniques for disarming a foul emotion. They include stopping and naming the emotion; watching it fade; noticing what precedes it and understanding its causes; avoiding triggers and cultivating prophylactic habits; observing the whole dynamic in others; and constructing situations for positive states in the future. None of this is particularly "Buddhist." It is just common sense, but in the *Sutta* it is meticulously mapped out. Many psychologists have been using variants of these techniques for decades, and we find them throughout Western philosophy.

It is good to have techniques to reduce excessive emotionality, but it is important to remember that this actually wasn't the Buddha's goal. He wanted to extinguish emotion completely. He taught that even pleasant emotions would lead to the whole miserable cycle of desire, attachment, disappointment, and despair. His whole teaching is often crystallized in the aphorism "Desire is the cause of suffering."

The Buddha typically equates desire, the first of the five hindrances, with craving, clinging, greed, lust, attachment, and bondage. Even aspects of desire that we would find positive, such as love, affection, familial ties, sensory pleasure, and the appreciation of beauty, are swept up into this negative categorization. Verse 212 of the important text called the *Dhammapada* states it bluntly: "Anyone who loves is bound to suffer."[1] These antagonistic attitudes toward the passions and normal human affections seem extreme, but we forget that they were once commonplace in many parts of the Christian world as well.

There was nothing easygoing about the Buddha. He never held political power, but, in his own zone of control, he created just as tight and regulated a monastic order as did Saint Bene-dict, the founder of Christian monasticism. The original Bud-dhist order had 227 rules for monks and 311 rules for nuns. (A senior Theravadin monk once told me that, with all their subdivisions, these rules now exceed 10,000.)

It is not at all surprising that we prefer our mythical mix-and-match image of the Buddha to the historical one. Our make-it-up-as-you-go Buddhism is far more palatable (and useful) than what he originally taught. His strategies regarding destructive emotions are excellent, but his hos-tility toward our most common positive emotions is hard to reconcile with a modern sensibility. I doubt if any layperson applies the Buddha's methods now without drastically adapt-ing them to twenty-first-century values.

Fortunately, in the West we have another tradition of emo-tional management—namely, that of the Greek and Roman philosophers. This approach is also based on careful self-observation, and I'll examine it in chapter 19. It is quite easy to incorporate the Buddha's strategies into their more tolerant, humane, and practical philosophies.

18

States of Mind

He lives observing The Seven Factors of Enlightenment. *When he is Mindful, he knows it. When he is not Mindful, he knows it. He carefully observes how mindfulness comes and goes, and what causes it to do so....*

Likewise, he contemplates the other Factors of Enlightenment. *He carefully observes how Investigation, Energy, Bliss, Stillness, Absorption, and Equanimity arise and pass away, and what causes them to do so. He learns how to strengthen each one of these qualities when it is present, and how to bring it forth when it is not present.*

—**Satipatthana Sutta**

All meditation practices have strategies for coping with runaway thought, some better than others. Ignore it. Shut it out. Focus harder. Let it pass through. Watch without reacting. Put it in a box. And so on. However, the mind can be a monster, and mental chaos is not a problem that can be so readily solved.

Naming thoughts to control them is a useful technique, but it often misses the target. The actual content of the thoughts may be irrelevant. The real problem may be the underlying emotion or state of mind. If we are anxious, every issue is drastic. If we are angry, everyone is against us. If we are despondent, every venture is hopeless.

There are also poor states of mind that are not directly attributable to any emotion. A disorderly state of mind will stuff up anything we try to do. We may be distracted, scattered, obsessed, tired, hyperactive, fed up, worn out, or capable of nothing. It is better to think of these as states of mind rather than emotions. In the *Sutta* the Buddha describes these states of mind in a similar fashion: "the shrunken mind and the distracted mind . . . the restless mind and the settled mind," and so on.

The Buddha suggested that we learn to repeatedly identify the state or quality of our mind at any time. With practice we can isolate the *quality* of our mind from the *contents* (the thoughts) and from the dominant *emotion*. For example, we should be able to say to ourselves, "I'm thinking about Miranda (mindfulness of thought). I'm obsessing about her (mindfulness of a state of mind), and I hate her (mindfulness of emotion)." This is what it means to be fully mindful according to the *satipatthana* method.

As usual, the Buddha asks that we name a state of mind to get a good grasp of it. Even if we can't shift it, we will at least know what we are dealing with. Our terms don't need to be fancy. They just have to be words that feel right, that seem to click. Any psychologist will recognize the therapeutic value of descriptive words and the importance of having appropriate language for self-analysis. A client who can recognize "I'm ruminating again" or "I'm catastrophizing again" is taking a huge step toward self-control.

Most of our bad states of mind will be familiar visitors. If we can be mindful of them, however—if we can learn to hold them in mind and appraise them consciously—we will discover something intriguing. The state of mind may be familiar, but the *valence* will vary from day to day. Some days the anxiety is raging. At other times it just grumbles in the background. If we see this fact repeatedly, and store that in memory (the etymological root of *sati*), we will eventually become much more attuned to triggers, to causes, and also to solutions.

Here are some kinds of faulty cognition that we are likely to recognize if we look for them:

- Overthinking: due to worry or perfectionism.

- Obsession: fixating on one issue to the exclusion of all others.

- Scattered thought: the tendency to jump too quickly from one issue to another due to anxiety.

- Distraction: being unable to pay attention due to boredom, disinterest, or escapism

- Rumination: aimless, chaotic, low-level, mental mumbling.

- Dullness: due to fatigue, sickness, disappointment, or depression.

Many of these states of mind will be familiar to you, but can you distinguish them? If you can say, "Right now I'm obsessing" or "Right now I'm scattered," then you would be mindful of your present-moment state of mind. It is this kind of refinement that the Buddha was recommending.

Among the dozens of different states of mind, the one every meditator needs to be able to recognize is attention. She needs to know when she's focused and when she's not; when she's mentally in control and when she's not; when she's on track and when she's lost it; when she's doing what she intended to do (for instance, focusing on the body), and when she's wandered off. Similarly, no meditator will achieve anything much until she can recognize the opposite state that the Buddha called "the distracted mind."

All of the Buddha's strategies for managing emotions apply equally well to states of mind. The teaching is as follows: Name the state of mind. Notice how it arises and passes away. Notice what precedes it and understand its causes. Observe the whole dynamic in others. Avoid triggers and cultivate prophylactic habits. Construct situations that support positive states in the future.

All these strategies can help stop us from drifting into bad states in the future and help us gradually dissolve them when we do. They also helps us boost the good states when they are present and helps keep them around longer than usual. This sequence corresponds to the four efforts that I described in the last chapter (page 199).

If we check our states of mind regularly, we will find that we're rarely at our cognitive best all day long. We often have to cruise on automatic. We find that good, self-monitoring thought is hard to maintain and it decays rapidly under less-than-optimal conditions. Here are some causal factors that the Buddha would want us to recognize.

Our capacity to think clearly suffers if we are *stressed*; if we are *overemotional* for any reason; if our brains are *overloaded* with more information than they can comfortably handle; if we have made too many decisions in the preceding hours (*decision fatigue*); or if we are physically *tired*.

If we are mindful of these states of physical or mental depletion, we will also see what helps and what doesn't. Pushing on regardless or having another cup of coffee are usually dodgy strategies. If we are too tired to think straight, we should just stop trying. It is far more sensible to leave the issue till later, potter around with trivia, do some brainless housework, watch TV, or just go to bed.

States of mind often have a bodily inertia that makes them much harder to modify than thoughts or valences. Being aware of them, however, enables us to sensibly adjust to the real-life circumstances that induce those states of mind. The second-century BCE Stoic Epictetus said, "Know what you can control and what you can't control." The corollary is "Don't stress out about what you can't control. Learn to cheerfully accept it." It is often futile to struggle against a state of mind. This is when the modern idea of mindfulness as "a state of nonjudgmental acceptance" may be perfectly appropriate.

THE IDEAL MEDITATIVE STATES OF MIND

The Buddha regarded the five hindrances, the painful emotions discussed in the previous chapter, as being the negative states of mind. The seven factors of enlightenment (which will be discussed one by one in the next section of this chapter) are the countervailing positive states of mind. These are not "good" emotions or moral qualities such as compassion, honesty, or justice. (The *Sutta* was composed for solitary monks who don't interact with other people in those ways.[1]) Rather, the seven factors are the ideal states of mind that are essential for the most profound states of meditation (*jhana*). This, in turn, is the basis for the intuitive thought and insight (*vipassana*) that lead to full awakening. This is why they were called the seven factors of enlightenment.

Perfect meditation states are rare, but they really do occur—even for beginners. Most religious traditions recognize and try to describe them. They are quite organic and intrinsic to consciousness. The literature acknowledges that countless people achieve them with little or no instruction. We are guided to them by our natural homeostatic instincts for body-mind equilibrium.

In Buddhism, these states are called absorptions—in Pali, *jhana*. There are said to be four (or eight) *jhana* of increasing subtlety and depth. The commentaries analyze and argue about the distinguishing characteristics of each *jhana* in enormous detail. Much ink has been spilled and hot air released over this. One teacher refers to this as "the *jhana* wars."

In the Pali texts, there is a lot of overlap between the descriptions of the four *jhanas* and the seven factors. Moreover they both converge on the ideal mental state of equanimity (*upekkha*).

The *jhanas* are meditation states and are therefore transient, but their effects are expected to trickle back into ordinary life. Over time, a good practitioner will be peaceful under all circumstances, not just when she has withdrawn from the world to meditate. This cyclic model of attainment is common in many spiritual practices. It involves a repeated retreat or withdrawal from the mundane, to allow time and space for ascent into perfection, followed by a return to ordinary life until the ideal mental qualities are well expressed in both.

The *jhanas* and the seven factors of enlightenment can be interpreted broadly or narrowly. Monks have traditionally insisted that only they can achieve even the first of the *jhanas*. The impure, sensual, and money-grubbing lives of laypeople were said to preclude all but the most modest meditative attainments. That was the usual hardline interpretation when I was training.

In 1986 I did an eleven-week solitary retreat at Wat Buddha Dhamma in the forest north of Sydney, Australia. The abbott was Phra Khantipalo, one of the most senior Western monks in the world. When I said I seemed to be entering the first of the *jhanas* he politely but firmly dissuaded me. That was quite impossible, he said. I had a girlfriend. Even though I hadn't seen her for months, just the thought of sensuality would undermine my spiritual attainments. Phra Khantipalo has since disrobed and married (and separated) and may well have changed his opinion on this matter.

In the West, a broad, liberal interpretation of the *jhanas* now prevails. It seems obvious that laymen and -women achieve these meditation states regularly, despite what the monks used to claim. Most regular meditators will have seconds or minutes here and there when they are experiencing at least the first, second, or third *jhanas*. These may not be particularly strong or durable, but they are genuine.

The Buddha's training algorithm applies just as much to the seven factors as to any other object of consciousness. Identify the state of mind. Notice how it comes and goes. Understand its causes and its enemies. Embed that understanding in memory. This body of hard-won direct knowledge will inevitably strengthen those good states when they appear in the future. Work hard and repeat the procedure until awakening.

THE FACTORS, ONE BY ONE

The seven factors of enlightenment divide into three active mental qualities—investigation, energy, and bliss—and three passive mental qualities—body-mind stillness, absorption, and equanimity—governed by *sati*, which partakes of both. *Sati*, or mindfulness, has a metacognitive, monitoring function over the other six factors. It is said to refine each state of mind and balance them against each other, so you don't get too much of any one good thing.

Investigation (*dhamma-vicaya*) is the first of the active factors. A perfect example of this is the gentle but persistent investigation of fine sensory detail that accompanies body scan meditations. In the *Sutta*, the Buddha is also asking us to examine our *mental* processes in similar detail. Without the quality of investigation, we may become tranquil through meditation, but no great insights will occur. *Dhamma-vicaya* loosely correlates with the much weaker term from Modern Mindfulness, "curiosity."

The second active factor is energy (*viriya*), which means drive, will, and determination. *Viriya* is related to the English word "virile." It suggests the physical and mental strength of a warrior. The quality of *viriya* is similar to *atapi* (persistent effort), which we talked about in chapter 14 as being an integral quality of *sati*. U Pandita says that *viraya* is "an enduring patience in the face of suffering or difficulty. Effort is the ability to see to the end no matter what, even if one has to grit one's teeth."[2]

The third active factor is bliss (*piti*), the sense of vitality and delight in the body that was described in chapter 7. Buddhaghosa is quite graphic in describing the five kinds of *piti*: "Minor happiness, momentary happiness, showering happiness, uplifting happiness, rapturous happiness. These arise in the monk, pervading his whole body."[3] Without this inner exuberance and sense of reward, a meditator can easily slide into depression, and many do so.

Piti is frequently linked with *sukha* as a one-two sequence. After *piti* comes *sukha*, which is usually translated most inadequately as "contentment." This is a state of being utterly at peace with the present moment, just as it is. It implies such a deep acceptance of the inevitable pains and discomforts of life that they cease to be a problem. *Sukha* didn't make it into the list of the seven factors, but it is integral to the four absorption states (*jhana*) that cover exactly the same territory. We can regard it as an honorary factor of enlightenment.

Investigation (*dhamma-vicaya*), energy (*viriya*), and bliss (*piti*) are more dynamic than we might expect as ideal meditative qualities of mind—hence the characterization of them as "active" factors within the seven factors of enlightenment. There was certainly nothing indolent about the Buddha's approach. The style of the *Sutta* is very much about body-mind transformation and purposeful effort toward an ultimate goal.

The goal and the final stages toward it *are* tranquil, however. They are much more what we think of as meditation. The final three mental qualities are body-mind stillness (*passaddhi*), absorption (*samadhi*), and equanimity (*upekkha*). Remember that the perfection of each of these states is mostly likely to occur first in deep sitting meditation. To a spectator, it might seem as if nothing is happening at all.

The first of the passive factors, body-mind stillness (*passaddhi*), is a state in which the body becomes perfectly still and the mind is silent for long periods (as described in chapter 1). This state is described as being the antidote to the fourth of the five hindrances—namely, anxiety. The onomatopoeic Pali term for anxiety, *uddhacca-kukkucca*, is commonly translated as "agitation and worry." In *passaddhi*, this vanishes completely.

The second passive factor builds on the stillness of *passaddhi*. This is absorption (*samadhi*), also called one-pointedness (*ekagatta*). *Samadhi* is a kind of enthralling tunnel vision or positive obsession that loses sight of everything else, even the body itself. There are no distractions to contend with in this state, and *samadhi* is often used as a synonym for profound tranquility. *Samadhi* sets up a self-sustaining feedback loop of bliss that paradoxically occurs within a body that is utterly still.

The last passive factor and the concluding point of the seven factors is equanimity (*upekkha*), or serenity. In this state, the awareness of having a body has almost vanished. All activity, thought, and emotion have shrunk to the minimum possible while remaining alive. No body sensation + no thought + no emotion = no sense of personal self. As the Zen texts say, "Body and mind drop away." The residual consciousness is sometimes described as boundless space or emptiness. The Beat poets called it "big mind" or "big sky mind."

EQUANIMITY: THE ULTIMATE GOAL

Upekkha is also the dominant state of mind in the fourth and final *jhana*. It is said to be the launch pad for the intuitive thought that breaks through to nirvana. In fact, *upekkha* is much more likely to be the final stage altogether for any practitioner.

Nirvana is almost impossible to comprehend or describe. It is a spiritual term beyond the realm of reason that seems to mean everything and nothing simultaneously. In fact, nirvana literally means "extinction." It refers to the extinguishing of the life force that drives the cycle of births and deaths. Modern writers play philosophic mind games with this concept but don't pursue it seriously. As a basic precondition, the path toward nirvana demands celibacy and extreme social isolation, and few Westerners are willing to go that far. (For one thing, it would require disconnecting from the internet.) Nirvana has receded into myth, and only historical figures are said to have attained it. Contemporary Buddhism has many spiritual leaders, but only devotees would regard any of them as enlightened. I frequently ask Buddhists to name a current enlightened master, and their eyes glaze over. No one fits the bill.

Upekkha, however, *is* attainable, and the stages on the path from normal human misery toward some degree of philosophic detachment are easy to imagine. Both the Buddha and modern psychologists aim to alleviate suffering, and improvement doesn't need to be perfect to be worthwhile. The

Buddha and modern psychologists even recommend similar strategies. Learn to calm down, control impulses, wind back emotion, detach from useless thought and activity, and automate all of these strategies so that they become habitual.

The word *upekkha* correlates well with our word "equanimity" and has similar ethical connotations. Wikipedia says that equanimity is "a state of psychological stability and composure which is undisturbed by experience of or exposure to emotions, pain, or other phenomena that may cause others to lose the balance of their mind."

A more extreme form of equanimity is reflected in the Buddhist concept of emptiness (*sunyata*). As the Buddhist scholar B. Alan Wallace bluntly describes it, "Let the space of your mind be emotionally neutral, like physical space, which could not care less whether bullets or hummingbirds streak through it."[4] This metaphor suggests an almost dehumanized state of mind, and this is no mistake. Wallace, a considerable scholar, really does know what "emptiness" means in the Tibetan and Zen scriptures. "Could not care less" is a reasonably good description of the emotional neutrality of *upekkha* as it appears in the texts.

The pursuit of equanimity has a long history in Western philosophy. Aristotle saw a good life (*eudaimonia*) as demanding an appropriate balance between the excess and deficit of emotional expression. Although it took skill and self-awareness to get that balance right, he felt there really was an appropriate degree of anger, love, pride, or pleasure to be found in any particular situation.

In contrast, the Roman Stoics tried to eradicate all emotional responses—at least, toward that which was beyond their control. The Stoic ideal state of dispassion (*apatheia*) included a cheerful acceptance of fate that still allowed them to enjoy the pleasures of the day. The ideal of their philosophical counterparts, the Epicureans, was similar. The Epicurean ideal, *ataraxia*, referred to a mental state free from worry and emotional disturbance, compatible with ordinary human pleasure. These ideals of philosophic detachment—but without the pleasure—can also be found in early Christian thought.

The Buddha's approach was at the extreme end of this spectrum. He aimed to eradicate emotion completely. The Buddha said that even the least desires lead to attachment and suffering. He taught that there is no "good" or "safe" level of desire, any more than there are tolerable levels of airborne asbestos. In general, he said, we should regard desire as we would a poisonous tree. We should cut it down. Dig out the roots. Sift the soil for root hairs. Burn the lot. Sift the ashes. Burn again. And throw what remains into a river.[5] He was adamant that eradicating desire was the only way to finally attain freedom from samsara—the cycle of suffering, birth, and death.

The meditative practice to achieve this starts at the atomic level of emotion on valences, as discussed in chapter 16. We have been discussing *upekkha* as a state that is "neither pleasant nor unpleasant." The monk identifies the affective tones, or valences, of literally everything that arises in his mind and strives to reduce them all to neutral. This is what the Buddha meant by digging out the root hairs of the poisonous tree and burning them.

This occurs through the process that psychologists call "extinction." In meditation language, it is "just watching without reacting," or nonjudgmental acceptance. If we repeatedly inhibit our tendency to respond to a stimulus, its positive or negative valence will get weaker over time until it finally induces no response in us at all.

All this is to say, the nonreactive, neutral, "impartial" state of *upekkha* neither suppresses nor engages with what arises. It is free from desires and aversions—a virtue proclaimed in the opening section of the *Sutta*. *Upekkha* is easiest to cultivate in meditation or in retreat, but this equanimous state of mind is expected to trickle back into daily life. A good practitioner will become calmer, more detached, less troubled, less responsive, and less engaged. He will also be more cool, rational, adult, and philosophic about life and fortune in general. This is *upekkha*. It is not quite nirvana, but it about as close as anyone is likely to get nowadays.

19

Optimizing Emotion

The selective reduction of emotion is just as prejudicial for rationality as excessive emotion.
—ANTONIO DAMASIO

Uncontrolled emotion is truly a horror. It has been responsible for the slaughter of millions throughout history. Even in peacetime, fear, anger, and greed contaminate many lives and devastate others. Fear emerges as chronic anxiety; anger as impotent rage or resentment; greed as the compulsive pursuit of excess. Many psychologists battle all their professional lives to help repair the effects of fear, anger, and greed—unregulated emotion—in their clients.

Psychology and the mindfulness movement have enlisted the Buddha in this war against excessive emotion. To "sit, stop, and look" combats impulsive behavior. To "calm down" reduces inflammatory arousal. To "accept whatever is happening" reduces pointless struggle. To achieve a state of thoughtless silence, however short, can give a breathing space for a more considered response.

Meditation promotes the ideal of inner stillness and non-reactivity, at least while meditating. With practice, this effect can trickle back into the world of activity as a kind of inner reserve and resilience. This simple technique, done well, can have remarkable effects. Perhaps it really can help free us from the crippling, addictive, distorting, humiliating effects of malignant emotion and make us more "happy."

Psychologists have to help client after client "down-regulate" their emotions. The Buddha in his search for serenity tried to extinguish emotion altogether. Overall, it seems, psychologists, meditators, and writers on mindfulness tend to unthinkingly regard emotion, per se, as the enemy of mental health. In the mindfulness literature, it is almost impossible to find any positive reference to normal human emotion. There are some small exceptions to this. Compassion, loving-kindness, gratitude, and moderate sensory enjoyment are usually permissible, but these are rather tepid and smack of Sunday school, in contrast to the true primal passions.

Since 1952 the bible of psychology has been the *Diagnostic and Statistical Manual of Mental Disorders*. Compiled by hundreds of writers, and revised and augmented every few years, the *DSM* is a true masterpiece of collective analysis and description. Every possible example of mental discontent, however slight, is described with the precision of great novelists. Its purpose is to give accurate and quantifiable descriptions of mental disorders as a basis for targeted treatment. As the Buddha recognized with his emphasis on naming, good terminology is an extremely useful tool all in itself.

The descriptive achievements of the *DSM* are remarkable and unique, but the manual also lays itself wide open to attack.

A description of symptoms is not the same as a diagnosis. It wouldn't serve to identify syphilis or typhoid, for example. Nor would the most exquisite description help in the absence of a cure. Most psychological therapies and pharmacological treatments are blunt instruments at best. It does seem that most benefits in psychotherapy come from the human element: the interaction of a sympathetic counselor and the client.

Unfortunately, the *DSM* approach seems to have the effect of pathologizing almost every aspect of emotional life. It turns shyness, sadness, worry, exuberance, restlessness, self-criticism, laziness, lust, greed, boredom, neediness, resentment, and "feeling off" into pathologies that need to be addressed and corrected, primarily through medication. One excellent book critical of the *DSM* approach alludes to this drift toward mass insanity through its title: *How Everyone Became Depressed.*[1]

The fifth edition of the *DSM* (*DSM-5*) has been spectacularly ridiculed for its pathologizing tendencies, not least by Allen Frances, the chairman of the previous edition, *DSM-IV.* In the introduction to his 2013 book, *Saving Normal*, Frances said, "The road to Hell is paved with good intentions and unexpected consequences." He continued, "Despite our efforts to tame excessive diagnostic exuberance, *DSM-IV* had since been misused to blow up the diagnostic bubble and create 'false epidemics.'"[2] He also said that *DSM-5* was likely to tip tens of millions more people from "normal" into "sick."

When he was at a party with the *DSM-5* writers, Frances writes, he realized that he personally qualified for many of the new disorders that appeared in the new book: "My gorging on the delectable shrimp and ribs was *DSM-5* 'binge eating disorder.' My worries and sadness were going to be 'mixed anxiety/depressive disorder.' The grief I felt when my wife died was 'major depressive disorder.' My well-known hyperactivity and distractibility were clear signs of 'adult attention deficit disorder.' And let's not forget my twin grandsons—their temper tantrums were no longer just annoying: they had 'temper disregulation disorder.'"[3]

The *DSM* approach can seem extreme to the point of Monty Pythonesque absurdity, but it is not without precedent in history. The search for emotional purity knows no bounds. Medieval monks were expected to exert continual vigilance over their wicked minds. Paranoid totalitarian states such as Russia and China demanded an impossible degree of self-criticism from their citizens. Psychology and pharmacology both have a history of inventing diseases they claim to cure. And we see this distrust of normal emotion prominently in Buddhism.

Because the Buddha regarded stillness and serenity as the highest good, he saw every emotion as potentially painful, a sliding away from equilibrium. The word "emotion" is based in the French and Latin that literally means "movement out." Emotions are ultimately prompts for action. They take us out of stillness.

But is it really fair to stigmatize emotions this much? Are they always inherently destructive, interfering with the smooth working of the rational mind, or is the problem only one of excess or deficit? Do emotions *always* create a cognitive bias that prejudices clear sight, as some psychologists suggest? Are fear and anger always negative, or can they be rational and adaptive? Surely we can make a distinction between the toxic fear of chronic anxiety and an appropriate, optimal level of concern regarding the future and one's health. Nor is the complete absence of fear desirable. The joyful and foolhardy behavior of teenage party animals suggests otherwise. Many die from a deficit of fear.

EMOTION IS NECESSARY FOR GOOD JUDGMENT

The Western philosophic tradition takes a more nuanced approach to emotion than did the Buddha. Despite the difficulties inherent in researching emotions, many cognitive scientists now argue that they are crucial for a well-functioning mind. Above all, emotions are necessary for intelligent, adaptive *thought*.

Emotions do several things: (1) They make us move. No emotion, no valence or action tendency = no action. (2) Emotions contribute to our ability to evaluate the importance of things and determine our choices. A judgment devoid of emotional input is emasculated and adrift. (3) Emotions are the source of every kind of pleasure and satisfaction, from the simplest to the most complex.

Western philosophy has always tended to value reason over passion, but not exclusively so. Aristotle was a great believer in an active, well-directed life, but in the *Nicomachean Ethics*, he also recognized that "intellect itself moves nothing; choice is the efficient cause of action." He saw choice based on desire as the source of all behavior for good or bad. The Enlightenment philosopher David Hume seconded this point in *A Treatise of Human Nature* (1739-1740), saying, "Reason is, and ought only to be the slave of the passions, and can never pretend to any other office than to serve and obey them."

The great neurologist Antonio Damasio (born 1944) has convincingly argued that emotion is essential for good judgment (and for the optimal biological state of homeostasis, and for our fundamental sense of self). His insights stem from the clinical study of brain lesions in patients unable to make good decisions because their emotions were impaired but whose reason was otherwise unaffected.

In his 1994 book, *Descartes' Error*, Damasio describes his landmark case study: a patient named Elliot, a highly intelligent man who turned out to be "an exceptionally pure version of this condition." The removal of a brain tumor left Elliot emotionally inert, although his reasoning powers were undamaged. His IQ remained superior. "His knowledge of the business realm he had worked in remained strong," says Damasio. "His skills were unchanged and he still had a flawless memory."[4]

Elliot's loss of emotion, however, meant that his capacity for judgment vanished overnight. He lost all instinct for what needed to be done or what was worth doing at all, and he deliberated endlessly over the tiniest decision. He eventually lost his job, his wife, and his second wife, and went bankrupt through absurd speculations. He finished up living in the care of a sibling.

Damasio argues, "Emotion is integral to the process of reasoning, for better or worse." He adds: "Selective reduction of emotion is just as prejudicial for rationality as excessive emotion."[5] In other words, *too little* emotion is just as destructive of clear thinking as *too much* emotion. This conclusion mirrors Aristotle's belief that the intelligent citizen should aim for an ideal state of *optimal* emotionality: the "mean" between excess and deficit. Damasio did the research for an idea that Aristotle only theorized, but they came to the same conclusion. Please read Damasio's elegant and masterly books for a full explanation of why emotion is essential for rational thought, but here is one simple reason.

Conscious thought has limited capacity. It can see with great precision, but it can process only two or three aspects of a situation at once. It can't see the forest for the trees. It is too narrowly focused, too dominated by language, and too disembodied to evaluate a complex issue, unless emotion is guiding its deliberations.

Emotion, on the other hand, draws on a truly colossal library of memories, somatic behaviors, and habitual responses. Its database is much vaster than what conscious thought can call on. It doesn't present an argument, however. It presents a conviction and an opinion: This is how I *feel* about X.

This emotional response may not be perfectly accurate. It is likely to be heuristic and approximate. It relies on pattern recognition and memory, both of which can be faulty. But its tone is likely to be basically right. The emotional networks in our brains know how we've responded to similar situations in the past and what happened thereafter, and they can print all that out as an emotion. The purpose of being *mindful* of an emotion is to fine-tune this initial judgment.

The language of valences—positive or negative, strong or weak—is not that sophisticated. The valence just suggests what to do: it works at the level of immediate action. Emotion goes a lot further. Like a valence, an emotion is also a value judgment, but it is profoundly anchored in our bodies, our life histories, and our sense of identity. If we have to make a hard decision, recognizing the underlying emotions and their accompanying stories will give us a perspective that reason or the valence alone cannot. The valence tells us what to do and how important it seems to be. The emotion tells us why.

OPTIMAL EMOTIONALITY

Many writers and moralists blithely talk about "negative emotions," of which anger is the poster boy. The new science of evolutionary psychology has seriously challenged this view. It argues that any emotion that was truly maladaptive would have been selected out of us over time. The men or women who expressed it would be handicapped in the race to breed, and that trait would die with them.

Evolutionary psychology argues that there are no inherently negative emotions. What has survived the evolutionary winnowing process is basically good. The immense problems that the passions cause come from excess or deficit, or expression at the wrong time. Even the most unpleasant emotion can be adaptive if it is optimally expressed in the appropriate situation. A single eruption of berserk rage at the right time could save your life or someone else's. If you are being attacked by drug-crazed thugs, you want Rambo at your side, not the Dalai Lama. With this in mind, we can start to see the potentially positive value in any emotion.

For example, anger is essential for defense, attack, and the fight against personal and political injustice. Fear is an appropriate response to danger, uncertainty, sickness, and aging. Sadness tells us when to give up on a futile or lost hope, and it is a very appropriate response to global warming. Jealousy defends against threats to the family and holds relationships together. Envy can prompt the competitive spirit that leads to extra effort. Shame is crucial for recognizing social norms. Disgust and self-disgust is the basis of many moral judgments. Pride is an immense boost to confidence and further effort. And where would our familial and social networks be without at least some lust? Where would the world economy itself be without greed? Trade in unnecessary luxury items has fueled the growth of civilizations for thousands of years.

It is hard to imagine getting through life at all without this bundle of sharp-eyed instincts guiding us along. Every one of these emotions can be positive, adaptive, and productive. Nor should they be any more unpleasant than a pain such as childbirth or physical training that leads to a good outcome. Productive emotions above all are *rational*. They determine the judgments that lead to our best and most adaptive actions. They lead us to a good life.

Aristotle gives us what is still the subtlest interpretation of emotion. He took the Greek and Roman motto "Nothing in excess" very seriously. An appropriate emotion was the "mean" between extremes. There was an optimal level of emotionality in any situation. Too much courage was foolhardiness. Too little courage was cowardly. Nor was this a universal fixed norm for everyone. What was optimal for a strong young man would be excessive for an older, weaker man. In the *Nicomachean Ethics*, he says, "Anyone can get angry. That is easy. But to get angry to the right degree, at the right time, with the right person and for the right outcome, that is not easy."

And he went on. Too much pride was arrogance, but too little was false modesty. Too much generosity was profligate, but too little was miserly. Too much self-control is rigidity, but too little is incontinence. Too much sensual enjoyment was debasing, but too little was prudish. Too much conversational wit was buffoonery, but a deficit was boorish. A well-bred man could and should express emotion intelligently. A few centuries later, the emotional repertoire of the well-rounded Renaissance man also required that you could talk well, sing well, fight well, and know how to entertain the ladies.

Aristotle said that a satisfying, well-directed life (*eudaimonia*) was not a passive possession. He said that you couldn't develop the mind without actually using it in practical situations: "A man becomes just by doing just things." We develop our compassion only by actively helping others. *Eudaimonia* depended on continual training, on seeking excellence in those social and intellectual skills that make us human. In practice, it meant seeking the appropriate level of emotional expression in *this* situation, *today*, for *us*, until we die. As Aristotle said, "This is not easy." Despite this, he knew that well-expressed emotion would give us a richer and more rational life than trying to eradicate the passions entirely.

In this context, the Buddhist ideal of tranquility under all circumstances looks rather shallow and antisocial. I imagine that Aristotle would regard it as boorish and uncivilized, and certainly of no use in ancient Athens. Even the modern positive psychology movement, which is often linked with both Buddhism and mindfulness, seems selective and moralistic in the virtues it promotes. Happiness, compassion, self-control, and resilience are certainly valuable, but they are a pale shadow of our full emotional range.

IS SADNESS ALWAYS BAD?

According to some media reports, a quarter to a half of all Westerners are staring depression in the face. This is ridiculous, of course, but should we always regard sadness, melancholy, grief, regret, shame, and despair as psychological toxins to be purged? Are they incompatible with the ideal of mental health, or are they just an unavoidable part of being a feeling human being?

In the Bible, the author of Ecclesiastes, said to be the high priest of Jerusalem sometime around the third century BCE, memorably expressed nearly every one of the painful emotions in the paragraph above. Despite his thoroughgoing pessimism, he still proclaimed what Friedrich Nietzsche would have called "a joyful wisdom": "A man has no better thing under the sun, than to eat, and to drink, and to be merry."

Although he was a Jew, the author of Ecclesiastes was certainly aware of the Greek ideal of the "mean," and he probably knew his Aristotle. In Ecclesiastes, chapter 3, we read: "To everything there is a season. . . . A time to be born, and a time to die. . . . A time to kill, and a time to heal. . . . A time to weep, and a time to laugh. . . . A time to love, and a time to hate; a time of war, and a time of peace" (Eccles. 3:1–8). He also said, "Sorrow is better than laughter: for by the sadness of the countenance, the heart is made better. The heart of the wise is in the house of mourning; but the heart of fools is in the house of mirth" (Eccles. 7:3–4).

The controversial twentieth-century guru Bhagwan Shree Rajneesh had an almost identical opinion. "Sadness has something of depth in it which no happiness can ever have. If you want to be happy always, you will become a shallow person, a superficial person." Rajneesh may in fact have been consciously paraphrasing Ecclesiastes. Many religious teachers know little beyond the scriptures of their sects, but Rajneesh had an encyclopedic knowledge of the world's spiritual literature.

The literary critic Harold Bloom makes the bold claim in his 1998 book that Shakespeare invented the modern human mind. In act 4, scene 3, of *Macbeth*, Shakespeare vividly expresses our modern, post-Stoic, non-Buddhist sensibilities. When the nobleman MacDuff is told, "Your wife and babes are savagely slaughtered," he is struck dumb. When encouraged to speak, his tenderness floods out: "All my pretty ones? Did you say all? What, all my pretty chickens and their dam at one fell swoop?"

Macbeth's challenger, Malcolm, trots out the standard Stoic line, "Dispute it like a man," and MacDuff responds: "I shall do so; / But I must also *feel* it as a man. I cannot but remember such things were that were most precious to me." Malcolm then encourages MacDuff: "Be this the whetstone of your sword. Let grief convert to anger; blunt not the heart, enrage it." Soon afterward MacDuff takes his revenge, kills Macbeth, and restores peace to Scotland, all through the driving forces of love, grief, and anger. He chooses to be a man of feeling rather than a Stoic, and is nobler for it.

EMOTION AND CULTURE

Stories and plays like *Macbeth* give us approximate guidelines for social behavior. As Aristotle understood, these dramas enable us to experience and try out for size a huge range of emotions in a contained "virtual" way. Stories explore nearly every emotionally charged situation, but love, power, and death are particularly appealing. Many great nations have a foundation myth of warfare and would not be nations without it. For the Greeks, the foundation story was the *Iliad*, which starts on the very first page with the wounded pride and rage of Achilles. Any educated Greek boy of twenty-five hundred years ago would know how to act well in war because of his knowledge of the legends.

A child brought up on stories is doing a simulated exploration of emotions he or she will face in later life. The Greek and Indian myths, the biblical histories, the Grimm Brothers' fairy tales—all are educational as well as entertaining. In Victorian England, the novels of writers such as Charles Dickens were felt to be so edifying for the masses that they could largely replace the moral strictures of moribund Christianity. The millions who wept over the fate of Little Nell in *The Old Curiosity Shop* were learning how to weep and what to say as they wept, according to the culture of the day. These are good Christian virtues of empathy and caring, but taught and refined through fiction. (Oscar Wilde famously provided the intellectual counterview: "One must have a heart of stone to read the death of Little Nell without laughing.")

We love stories, movies, novels, and histories so much because they are literally mind-expanding. We can explore whole psychic universes via the rocket fuel of simulated emotion. But perhaps the finest training in emotion comes from music. The love songs that we hear in our teenage years often shape us for life.

I had a strange but fortunate musical upbringing. When I was ten I came across a huge cache of classical records that

I was free to borrow. My parents had just bought a record player, and I was able to stumble my way through Stravinsky, Bartok, Mahler, Schoenberg, Strauss, and Bach. As a kid I loved bizarre rhythms, loud noise, vivid color, and over-the-top emotionality. I had the luxury of entering the mind of a Russian aristocrat in Paris (Stravinsky), and the mind of a Bohemian Jew in Vienna (Mahler). I would never have developed that range of human sympathy through sitting alone and meditating.

Music also inoculated me against Buddhism. When I signed up for my first Vipassana retreat, I had a flash of insight. I thought: "If I find out that there is no place for Jimi Hendrix in this system, it's not for me." Hendrix at that time was my symbol of the god-intoxicated musician.

And of course, there isn't. The Buddha hated all sensory pleasures. He would also have told Aristotle, Galileo, Shakespeare, Newton, Bach, Beethoven, Darwin, Einstein, Joyce, and Picasso to stop wasting their lives in trivial pursuits. Nor did he have any sense, as the Jesuit poet Gerard Manley Hopkins did, that "the world is charged with the grandeur of God." It is perhaps anachronistic to expect the Buddha to see Nature as a source of wonder and delight, but many people in antiquity did. He said nothing to encourage any kind of engagement with the world or with aesthetic beauty. His values were utterly alien to mine. His arguments were sound, but I knew his conclusions were wrong.

EMOTION AND VALUES

An emotion is essentially a deep, intuitive value judgment about something. Emotions are the source of nearly all our personal values, and yet we hardly ever consider them in isolation or even know what they are. Emotions tend to be subliminal, automatic, habitual, and instinctive. Although they drive our behavior, we are far more likely to give our available attention to the actions they initiate.

To be mindful of an emotion means holding it in mind distinct from what usually surrounds it. To stop and look at an emotion typically puts the brakes on it, which is a desirable outcome both for the Buddha and for most psychologists. However, seeing an emotion clearly can also tell us how much we value something and why. When we do this, the *sati-sampajjana* formula kicks in. The clear perception of something (*sati*) leads to a more accurate evaluation (*sampajjana*) and a better outcome.

Since the purpose of emotion is to drive behavior, we can uncover our core values by looking at how we choose to spend our time and energy. These are the biological equivalents of hard cash. They tell us how much we think something is worth. We can reverse engineer from our actions back to the emotions behind them.

So how many hours a week do you spend on the following: Work? Social relationships? Entertainment? Exercise? Information gathering? Deliberate learning? Eating? Distraction? Rest? Does the balance feel right, or at least good enough? Once you know how you spend your time and energy, you can then look at the emotion and valence and ask, "Why?"

In each case, it could be any one or combination of the following emotions and motivators: pleasure, fear, love, ambition, desire, excitement, duty, shame, empathy, escapism, fantasy, self-pity, pride, habit, guilt, boredom, or fatigue. Once we can hold a particular emotion in mind (*sati*), the evaluation (*sampajjana*) is bound to arise: "Is this optimal? Is this too much or too little? Should I give this more energy or less?" We could scale it down or scale it up, or shift it sideways to include another emotion, or target it for a more rewarding outcome. It is not at all easy to isolate, hold, and evaluate an emotion (*sati-sampajjana*), but it can be very satisfying when we do.

To summarize, the Buddha and many mindfulness writers tend to pathologize emotion in pursuit of a tranquil mind. They attempt to *minimize* emotion—in contrast to Aristotle, who preferred to *optimize* it. They seek to control and reduce it rather than develop it.

In fact, there are many good reasons for cultivating emotion. These include the following: (1) Emotion is essential for rationality and good judgment. (2) Emotion powers all our actions for good or bad. Every emotion can be adaptive if expressed optimally at the right time. (3) Emotions and their valences are the source of our core personal and social values. (4) Emotional intelligence is essential for free and satisfying social intercourse. (6) Emotion as expressed through story and music trains us in cultural sophistication and empathy with others. We can use mindfulness to cultivate all of these aspects of our humanity, but the results will not look particularly Buddhist.

20

Embodied Thought

Meditation is commonly seen and promoted as a way of escaping the tyranny of runaway thought. Many mindfulness writers go further and seem to regard cognition itself, like emotion, as a kind of pathology. They certainly feel it is antagonistic to meditation, and hardly ever have a good word to say about it. As Paul R. Fulton and Ronald D. Siegel write in the anthology *Mindfulness and Psychotherapy*, "Mindfulness meditation is distinguished from other [psychotherapeutic]) traditions by its near total abandonment of thinking.... When we are hijacked by discursive thinking about the past or future, we have left the domain of mindfulness."[1]

Mindfulness writers often attack thoughts by denying their reality. For instance, in their bestselling book *Mindfulness: An Eight-Week Plan for Finding Peace in a Frantic World*, Mark Williams and Danny Penman say, "Mindfulness meditation teaches you to recognize memories and damaging thoughts as they arise.... They are like propaganda. *They are not real.* They are not *you*."[2] And in another essay from

Mindfulness and Psychotherapy, Paul Fulton suggests, "By learning to see thoughts as events with no special reality, we come to appreciate our mind's incessant tendency to build imaginary scenarios that we inhabit as if they are real."[3]

As Kabat-Zinn has said, "Our thoughts may have a degree of relevance and accuracy at times, but often they are at least somewhat distorted by our self-centered and self-serving inclinations."[4] Elsewhere he argues that while we meditate we should deliberately note our thoughts one by one, and return to the breath as quickly as possible. "During meditation, we intentionally treat all our thoughts as if they are of equal value. . . . we intentionally practice letting go of each thought that attracts our attention, whether it seems important and insightful or unimportant and trivial."[5] To see all thoughts as "of equal value," whatever their contents, and to let them all go, implies that they are all worthless.

Psychologists and mindfulness writers like to appear calm and objective, but you can feel the invective behind the words they use to describe thinking: discursive, unreal, biased, hijacked, transient, propaganda, deceptive, distorted, self-centered, self-serving, imaginary, incessant, trivial, and so on. These terms would be often appropriate, but the total absence of any *positive* descriptors is telling. I assume these writers do know the value of cognition, but they obviously regard it as antagonistic to the mindful state itself. They seem to feel that thinking should only occur *before* or *after* being mindful, but never during it.

These writers seem to be taking their inspiration from Zen, and in particular Dogen, whom you might remember from chapter 8. Dogen said of the practice of *shikantaza*: "Sit firmly, and think of not-thinking. How you think of not-thinking? By not thinking! This is the essence of *zazen*." In the "Fukanzazengi," Dogen instructs: "Cast aside all involvements and cease all affairs. Do not think good or bad. Do not administer pros and cons. Cease all the movements of the conscious mind, gauging of all thoughts and views."[6] Earlierin the same text, he recommends: "Cease from practice based on intellectual understanding, pursuing words and following after speech, and learn the backward step that turns your light inward."[7] Elsewhere he says, "Non-thinking must become the eye through which you view phenomena."[8]

This mystical, antithought tendency runs deep in Buddhism, but, strange to say, it doesn't come from the Buddha! The Modern Mindfulness movement is frequently criticized by orthodox Buddhist authorities, teachers, and scholars for so blithely dismissing the philosophic aspects of the tradition.

The Buddha himself valued analytic, goal-directed thought very highly indeed. The four training disciplines of the *Sutta* all converge on mindfulness of thought, which is the apex of the mind-training pyramid. The purpose of the training is to develop a mind capable of sustained, penetrating insight (*vipassana*) into the nature of reality itself. Or to put it more simply, the purpose of mindfulness *according to the Buddha* is productive, goal-directed thought, not the absence of thought.

Buddhism is the most philosophically structured of all great religions. The doctrine is presented as a series of rational, step-by-step arguments that converge on the truth from different angles. If you accept its premises, it presents a logical and coherent analysis of suffering, its causes, and the ultimate escape from suffering and rebirth.

Every Buddhist school has a tradition of philosophy around this cluster of arguments, which is usually regarded as the peak of the spiritual path. None of these traditions is truly philosophic in the Western sense of open-ended dialectic and skeptical enquiry. Nor are they scientific or empirical as is frequently claimed by modern enthusiasts. They still require a high degree of unquestioning faith, and they all focus narrowly on their own hypotheses. However, they do present alternative modes of thought that we can usefully apply today.

Nor is there just one approach. Each of the three major forms of Buddhism dominant in the West has its own in-house style. We can call them "embodied thought" (the Buddha's original formula); "contemplative thought" (in Tibetan Buddhism); and "intuitive thought" (in Zen).

CONTEMPLATIVE THOUGHT

Let's start with contemplative thought. Most religions have practices in which we are asked to contemplate various spiritual and moral ideas. In the Dalai Lama's lineage, the "Lamrim" is the equivalent of the Catholic catechism, but much larger. It is a training discipline with a long list of themes that the monk or keen practitioner was encouraged to meditate on for years.

These themes are regarded as the summation of the whole teaching according to Tibetan Buddhism. Studying formally, the practitioner would spend days or weeks on each one, complete with visualizations, prayers, purification rituals, and a rote learning of all the arguments, and he may repeat this cycle indefinitely throughout his life.

The Lamrim includes themes such as the imminence of death; the dangers of material existence; the danger of falling into lower rebirths; the horrors of the hell realms; the peerless value of the teaching; the great good fortune of having a guru; overcoming "self-cherishing" and attachment to self; taking refuge in the Buddha, in the dogma, and in the clergy; the moral mechanics of karma; suffering and the end of suffering; the aspiration for enlightenment; cultivating universal goodwill; emptiness; and so on.

This is contemplative thought. It has every right to be regarded as "meditation," although it bears little resemblance to what I've described in this book. There is no focus on the body, emotions, states of mind, or present-moment experience. Religious contemplations typically expect you to overcome your natural doubts and argue your way toward final, fixed answers and beliefs.

Contemplative thought can work well, however, if we choose *our own* subjects and are encouraged to find *our own* answers. We find this practice throughout Western philosophy. Well-bred Greek or Roman students would reflect on and discuss certain universal subjects at depth for years at a time. Classical themes included the nature of the good life; old age, sickness, and death; the inevitability of loss and the fickleness of fortune; the nature of the cosmos and our place in it; controlling the passions; the qualities of a good citizen; the relative values of fame, wealth, sensual enjoyment, and power; and so on.

There is no correct, final answer to these questions, but reflecting upon them is invaluable for shaping character and in helping us find our way through the particular world and society we happen to be in. Nor does this kind of contemplation require faith in authorities. It is the classical Greco-Roman path of spiritual development through open-ended inquiry. And although contemplation is a kind of deep, feeling thought, it is still fundamentally rational, and it actually thrives on argument.

INTUITIVE THOUGHT

Intuitive thought is the dominant house style of Zen, and it is not rational at all. It is certainly a kind of thought, but it takes pride in being obtuse, confrontational, and immune to argument. Buddhism, like Christianity, has a huge tradition of exegesis and commentary by scholar monks. Zen, however, is a late reform movement. It defines itself as being "a teaching outside the scriptures," and its past masters habitually ridiculed the study and learning developed in rival schools.

The Zen theory of mind is nonetheless simple and intuitive. We are all enlightened but we don't yet know it. We all have a pure buddhamind within us. This is our "original face." By sitting very still and not thinking for a long enough time, the tangle of our thoughts and conditioning will gradually disintegrate, and the mirrorlike buddhamind will shine forth. By sitting in *zazen*, perfectly balanced, focused, and alert, we literally become the Buddha. In a flash, when the circumstances are right, "body and mind drop away," and we finally recognize that we are already enlightened.

Zen is still a kind of thinking, but it has a very simple form. The practitioner "holds in mind" an idea without actively thinking about it. That idea is "emptiness" or "non-self" or "buddhamind," or one of its other expressions. It becomes the framework around which the practitioner's nonthinking revolves, and the reference point for whatever experiences arise in *zazen*. It still requires faith in the idea of enlightenment and in the efficacy of the practice. The Zen master Hakuun Yasutani says, "To do shikantaza one must have a firm faith in the fact that all beings are fundamentally buddhas.... If one's faith in that fact is shaky, one's shikantaza is also shaky."[9]

I came across essentially the same technique and doctrine when I was exploring Tibetan Buddhism. It was framed like this: The body is corrupt and subject to death, but the mind is always pure and deathless. The mind is the immortal diamond in the mortal lotus (living matter). This is a classical Indian concept: The individual soul (atman) is identical to the world soul (Brahman). Freedom comes by liberating mind from matter, by achieving non-self and emptiness (*sunyata*).

In the Tibetan practice of Dzogchen (Sanskrit: *Mahamudra*), every kind of striving is seen as counterproductive. It is argued that you can't possibly achieve awakening if you anxiously hanker after it. Nonetheless, you still vigilantly protect yourself against thoughts until their insubstantiality becomes nakedly obvious. By systematically killing off your engagement with thought and action, and by doing literally nothing for as long as possible, your natural, strong, empty, luminous, incorruptible, primordial, eternal, timeless, clear-seeing, all-pervading, wish-fulfilling original mind will eventually emerge.

By meditating we seek our own buddhamind (*bodhicitta*), which is identical with the Buddha's. By seeking our own truth, we approach Ultimate Truth. When young, I found this very encouraging, even if I didn't quite believe it. It gave tremendous sanction to intuition, and obviated any need for study, knowledge, or even much life experience.

This appealed to my somewhat lazy and reclusive temperament. It implied that I could understand the essence of Buddhism and the universe by navel-gazing alone. If I stayed on retreat for long enough, I would bring forth the *bodhicitta*, know everything that was worth knowing, and also become an instant authority on Buddhism itself. Unfortunately, the more I meditated and saw how my mind actually worked, the more childish and faith based this idea seemed to me.

EMBODIED THOUGHT

Although contemplation and intuitive thought are genuine meditation practices, both are remote from what the Buddha originally taught. The Tibetan contemplations seek to inculcate beliefs such as karma and reincarnation, and Zen tends to valorize buddhamind or a state of transcendent emptiness. Neither give any serious attention to body sensations, emotions, states of mind, or present-moment experience as recommended in the *Satipatthana Sutta*, except to dismiss them as secondary to mind itself.

A term from cognitive philosophy is useful in order to explain the Buddha's approach: "embodied cognition," or embodied thought. It indicates a way of thinking "through" the body, or thinking while remaining fully aware of present-moment body sensations. The cognitive process operates as it usually does, but the process is heavily influenced by input from the body.

The Buddha described how to integrate this active, investigative thought into a standard meditation in a text we mentioned in chapter 3 called *Mindfulness of the Breath*.[10] In this text, he explains how a monk can contemplate "impermanence" (*anicca*) while still focusing on the breath. We can regard "impermanence" as a placeholder for any worthwhile thought.

Mindfulness of the Breath asks the monk to silently say, "in . . . out . . ." repeatedly as he breathes. Done conscientiously, this simple repetition keeps him on track, enhances focus, and protects him from mental wandering. To make this a contemplation, the monk simply adds an extra word: "Contemplating impermanence, I breathe in. Contemplating impermanence, I breathe out." In practice, he would strip this down to "*Anicca* in, *anicca* out." In this way, the monk could split his attention more or less equally between body awareness and thinking.

He wouldn't need to flick his attention from one to the other. He can attend to both at once with a fifty-fifty split. He would be monitoring the ever-changing, real-time, proprioceptive, and visceral sensations of his body while simultaneously speculating about impermanence. Despite the huge difference between these two objects of focus, a trained mind can handle this quite easily. Body awareness and directed thought can fit together surprisingly well, and I'm sure neuroscientists have some explanation for this.

In practice, meditators more frequently contemplate what is most important at that moment in their lives, rather than elements of Buddhist dogma. Experienced meditators often do a considerable amount of productive thinking when they practice, whether they admit it or not. No one goes on a ten-day retreat just to feel peaceful.

In another text mentioned in chapter 3, *Mindfulness of the Body*, the Buddha gives a metaphor to describe this kind of embodied thought.[11] He says that the mind is like a chariot harnessed to thoroughbred horses at the crossroads, and the monk is the skilled charioteer. He can drive out and back by any road whenever he likes.

This implies that the monk can follow any train of thought (or "road") safely because he knows how to steer his attention (the "horses"). He knows when to let his horses run (goal-directed thought), when to bring them to a halt (stop a thought), and when to change direction (switch to another thought). He can return to body-mind stillness and mental silence (the crossroads) whenever he wants to. These are metaphors for the kind of expert attentional control that we will discuss in the next chapter.

Embodied thought has some huge advantages over normal thought. To control the tendency of thought to run riot, we need a place to escape from thought. This sanctuary is the body, or the sensory present (or both). Being grounded in the body enables us to readily slow down or stop or abandon any thought.

Embodied thought means that we can also "hold a thought in mind" *without* actively processing it. When we do this, we will find that lateral associations and insights are more likely to spontaneously appear. The brain naturally recruits memories associated with any object we focus on. By holding the thought still, we can see it in a broader context than if we were just driving it forward.

Being grounded in the body also makes us more conscious of the valence and emotion of any thought. (Remember that emotions appear first in the body and are only later recognized by the mind.) The valence tells us how important a thought seems to be. The emotion gives us the reasons why.

Being more conscious of our *actual state of mind* can also tell us when we are deceiving ourselves. We can recognize from simple body signals when we are playing out a fantasy or denying a reality, hoping for a quick fix, or trying to boost our ego. It can also tell us when we are simply too anxious, scattered, dull, or obsessed to deal with the matter at all at that time.

Embodied thought is also excellent for catching those bright ideas that are called "insights" in Buddhism. Because we are calmer when we meditate, we are more able to extract an especially useful thought from the background noise. We can prevent an insight from being overrun by relentless inner chatter. When we think, we can deliberately catch, hold, elaborate on, and remember the genuine insights that arise.

SHALL I BECOME A MONK?

Let me give you an example of how this all works. When I was on retreat, I had to deal with several issues that had no obvious solution. What shall I do with my life? Shall I stay with my girlfriend? Shall I return to my home in the country? Shall I become a monk? By thinking through the body, I was able to process these very thoroughly, without getting caught in the runaround of useless overthinking. I could actually meditate on them.

I did so by breaking each issue down into its component parts and looking at each from the perspective of thought + valence + emotion + state of mind + body sensations. I isolated and nonverbally evaluated each aspect of the issue, as much as I could, while staying grounded in my body. This is what kept me calm and grounded and enabled me to consciously direct my thoughts.

So I would think, "Shall I become a monk?" and consider in compact form the thoughts relating to that. Then I would notice the valence: How strong or weak, positive or negative, was this option? In other words, *how important* did it seem to be? I would then notice the emotion, or cluster of emotions, behind it. *Why* did this issue seem important?

It was like laying out all the ingredients of that issue in front on me on a table. Thought + valence + emotion + state of mind + body sensations: The separation was critical. I was aiming to get a clear and distinct image of each one without trying to prematurely force them to a conclusion. Throughout all this, I would still be monitoring the real-time body sensations and my state of mind.

The next day, I would do it again: thought + valence + emotion + state of mind + body sensations. The thoughts about becoming a monk frequently remained the same. Thoughts often have this unconvincing, cracked-record quality, but the associated valence would almost certainly have changed. The prospect would seem more or less attractive than the day before. Similarly, the dominant emotion might have changed, or if it hadn't, different secondary emotions may have emerged.

On the retreat, I discovered something quite remarkable. The issue would *always* look different at different times of day. The morning thoughts were commonly enthusiastic and positive. The afternoon thoughts were more cautious and considered. The midnight thoughts often had a sublime confidence that rarely survived into the morning. So which was the correct answer?

Over the weeks, the process of *sati-sampajjana*, the conscious perception and evaluation of things, really showed its strength. Each time I was able to hold and assess an individual thought, valence, emotion, state of mind, or associated body sensation, it became fractionally clearer. When I let it go, I was then sending better quality information into the black box of the mind. Much of the processing was happening in sleep, so the next time I reviewed that issue, the different ingredients would have become more congruent and harmonized.

It was like counting up the votes. At a certain point, it became crystal clear what the electorate wanted. I can still remember the actual time (late morning) and the place (about two hundred yards from my hut) when I knew for certain that I would never, never, never become a monk. That question dropped off the mental list and has never reappeared since, even for a moment. Embodied thought combines the advantages of both contemplation and intuition while being anchored in the present-moment reality of the body. When we come to a conclusion, we will have a certainty about it—an insight—that doesn't come from reason, prejudice, passion, or the clever mind alone.

The Buddha said that this is the masterly quality of cognition we should be aiming for. He said that we achieve enlightenment only through deep insight into the nature of existence, as he understood it, but this is where we tend to part company with the Buddha. The Buddhist path starts with the renunciation of all sensory pleasures and the extinguishing of all emotion, and few Westerners are prepared to entertain that.

Nonetheless, it is easy to extricate the Buddha's mind-training methods from his goals. We can use those methods for any purpose that we choose. The Buddha's methods are sophisticated and elegant. They are based on constant cross-referencing and feedback mechanisms using all parts of the body and brain. Over time, they can enable us to bootstrap ourselves out of our blind instincts and habits into something resembling wisdom.

Embodied thought as described in the *Sutta*—allowing the body to be part of the process of cognition—is a powerful skill. It enables us to follow a thought at length without getting distracted; to return to silence at will; to stop a thought and see it in its broader context; to see the valence of a thought; to see the emotions around it; to assess the state of mind in which the thought is being processed; to catch and remember any insight that arises; to compare the value of one train of thought against another; and finally to walk away from the thought-world completely when the mind needs to rest and digest.

21

Attention

The Buddha said, "The systematic four-stage training in attention is the only way to enlightenment." My students quickly realize that the main skill I want them to learn is attention, and that relaxation and mental calm are just spin-off benefits that arise from focusing on the body.

Attention is an underrated, neglected, and misunderstood function, except perhaps in the field of education, where the effects of its deficiency are painfully obvious. We tend to assume that we can always pay attention when we want to, or that we could always focus better if we tried. Psychologists often disparage attention as being irrelevant to mindfulness. Meditators see it as a chore, and few people develop it as a skill unless they have to. Nonetheless this book is all about attention, so it is worth examining it in more technical detail.

Let's start at the cellular level. The overriding purpose of the nervous system throughout the animal kingdom is to initiate movement in response to stimuli. This is why animals have a nervous system and plants don't. Plants are fixed in place, but animals constantly have to move toward reward and away from danger.

Evolution tends to conserve primitive functions, so the brain still does the same task as much simpler nerve circuitry: It initiates action. The great pioneer of research on the frontal lobes of the brain, Joaquin Fuster, categorically defines the purpose of the prefrontal cortex as "goal-directed activity." We evolved rational, thinking minds to make decisions in situations that are too complex for instinct and habit to deal with. To quote Fuster more fully: "The entirety of the frontal cortex . . . is devoted to action of one kind or another, whether it is skeletal movement, ocular movement, the expression of emotion, speech, or visceral control. The action can even be mental and internal, such as reasoning. The frontal cortex is therefore 'doer' cortex, much as the posterior cortex is 'sensor' cortex."[1]

The nervous system operates according to what neurologists call a "perception-action cycle." Nerve cells divide into "afferent" sensory neurons that allow for perception, taking in information, and "efferent" motor neurons that initiate action on the basis of that information. However, that is not the whole story. Between the input and output comes evaluation. Although the input may be simple and the output is usually a single action, the evaluative process in between is phenomenally complex.

The act of perception doesn't copy an external object like a camera does. Every sense perception is shredded into hundreds of tiny components in specially designated regions of the cortex. This information is then reassembled in parallel with other sensory, emotive, and memory data in so-called "association areas." This is how the brain recognizes an object and attributes value to it prior to a response. For each sensory neuron, there can be *thousands* of "interneurons" doing this evaluative work. That's how important it is. Making good perception-response decisions determines happiness or misery for most humans, and life or death for animals.

The cycle of perception + evaluation + action (or inaction) goes like this. You touch a hot stove (perception). You evaluate it (bad). You pull back (action). We also met this dynamic in chapter 16, on emotion at the atomic level: perception + valence + action tendency. Simple information is processed quickly. The perception-action cycle will happen in a nanosecond within a cell—the speed at which enzymes switch on and off. The process is much slower when consciousness is involved. It might take five seconds to decide which breakfast food to buy. It might take thirty seconds to choose the best route to drive across town.

The perception-action cycle at every level of the biological hierarchy is self-regulating and continuous. Each action instantly changes the local situation, which leads to new evaluations, and so on, resulting in a nonstop negative feedback loop that balances out the activity for optimal results. These feedback loops maintain homeostatic balance throughout the body, and the same is true within the brain. The constant backchat between thought, emotion, memory, and bodily sensations optimizes our behavior. It is the preconscious foundation of our intelligence.

AUTOMATIC AND CONSCIOUS THINKING

Do you assume, like Descartes, that thinking is always conscious and always reliant on language? Many scientists now believe that a lot of *high-quality* thought occurs just below consciousness and that it doesn't need language. This dual-processing theory argues that cognition ("mental processing," or "thinking") has two operational modes: "automatic" and "conscious"—or intuitive and rational. Some scientists prefer more neutral terms: system 1 and system 2. In other words, we have both an automatic system for perceiving, evaluating, and responding to inputs (system 1), and a conscious system (system 2).

The automatic system is primary. It operates continuously and on parallel tracks day and night. We make most decisions without reflecting on what we do. Our brains make literally thousands of evaluations and choices each day. Shall I put on the left sock before the right sock? Cross the road now or wait? Continue doing this or switch to that? This "see-evaluate-do" nervous-system processing is based on a colossal repertoire of learned behaviors called "action schemas" that no longer require much conscious thought.

We can get dressed, drive, eat, work, shop, talk to colleagues and family, answer the phone—all on automatic pilot. These action schemas take years to learn. A successful life largely depends on developing ever more sophisticated action schemas, routines, habits, flow-on sequences, protocols, algorithms, and see-do responses. What we do on automatic pilot can be very clever indeed. The automatic system should never be disparaged.

Brilliant as it is, the automatic system has limits. It relies totally on pattern recognition and learned skills. It can manage yes-no options but not either-or. It can't make side-by-side comparisons. It is hopeless at mathematics. It is oriented to instant gratification and has no sense of future planning. Above all, it can't manage novel situations.

Fortunately, the automatic system does know its limitations. It includes a sort of radar function designed to detect errors, internal conflicts, and shortcomings. The command center seems to be in the anterior cingulate cortex in the forebrain, where signals from consciousness, emotion, and the body all meet. This self-monitoring is a paradoxical kind of *automatic* metacognition. When it realizes it can't cope, the automatic system bumps the problem upstairs. It calls on the conscious system to get involved. This is when we start to *deliberately* pay attention. This is when we become mindful.

The conscious system sees consequences and options that the automatic system can't imagine. It is more cool, rational, and farsighted, but at the price of being considerably slower. It makes its more informed decisions long after the automatic system has initiated the first response, so it has to play catch-up. It will typically overrule or modify the "quick and dirty" rule-of-thumb evaluations of the automatic system. Once everything is back on track, it lets the automatic system take over again.

We invariably regard attention as a fully conscious function, but this neglects its automatic dimensions. It is better to think of attention as the way we distribute our cognitive and metabolic resources across the whole spectrum of mental activity. Attention is like a paymaster handing out money (that is, glucose and oxygen) for work to be done. It does this by activating particular neural networks at the expense of others (selection) according to what seems most salient at the time (evaluation).

However, the paymaster is nothing like a CEO making top-down decisions. The many competing demands from the organism, thousands every second, are processed according to feedback mechanisms. This activity is too complex and chaotic for consciousness to handle. It is collective, local-level decision-making on an unimaginably vast scale. This is why it is so hard to "control" our attention. The boss can't make every decision in the factory.

Returning to our metaphor, "paying" attention is, in fact, just like spending money. We first have to pay for food, shelter, and clothing, and with luck we have some money left over for discretional spending. Similarly, most of our attention and cognitive resources go to keeping us alive, safe, and well. Only the remainder is available for conscious attention. Fortunately, automatic processes are fast and economical, and they do most of the work.

Conscious attention is slower and more expensive. It activates the specific network of brain cells that supports the mental representation of an object, and it massively increases their energy consumption. This takes effort and so comes with a high price tag. Conscious attention operates serially rather than in parallel. It is more precise than the automatic system, but it can only do one thing at a time. It also tends to be a "stop, look, and evaluate" mechanism that can interrupt our natural flow.

Over time, this is even *physically* exhausting. The Swedish psychologist Anders Ericsson, famous for his research on the kind of intensive training necessary for exceptional musical ability, argues that even the best of us can only manage five or six hours a day of conscious attention. Whenever possible we will save energy, avoid hard thought, and operate on automatic pilot instead.

BOTTOM-UP AND TOP-DOWN ATTENTION

In his 1890 classic, *The Principles of Psychology*, William James said, "Attention is the taking possession in clear and vivid form of one of several simultaneously possible objects or trains of thought." In other words, attention is always "selective." We select one thought at the expense of competing thoughts–saying "yes" to this and "no" to everything else. This involves "taking possession" or "holding something in mind." Furthermore, we do so because it makes that object or thought "clear and vivid." Paying attention to something massively enhances detail and recruits the emotional tone of related memories to help evaluate it.

Yet we do seem to pay attention all day long to what we are doing without much effort. It's not hard to watch TV, then have a conversation, and then engage in some task. Even when doing nothing, we naturally focus on whatever thought or sensation "catches our attention." This is what psychologists call "bottom-up," or "reactive," attention. It is our natural, involuntary instinct to respond to what is in front of us. If the things that grab our attention are mostly worthwhile–work, people, knowledge–then bottom-up, reactive attention can guide us through a very good life indeed. But we shouldn't count on life being that simple.

In complex situations we need to switch to "top-down," goal-directed, discriminating, "selective" attention instead. This enables us to make calculated choices, defer gratification, resist distractions, and plan a few steps ahead, even when we really don't feel like it. Top-down attention fine-tunes the way we move toward goals that are not immediately present. This is much harder to maintain than bottom-up attention.

We can usually focus well against competing alternatives only when the issue is important (meet the deadline, feed the child) or if the matter contains some inherent satisfaction or intermediate reward (sweating at the gym, posting the letter). But how do we stay focused on a remote but important matter when the option of watching TV and eating junk food beckons? Research now indicates that willpower, like muscle strength, is a limited resource that is readily depleted. When we are suffering "decision fatigue," we need a more subtle strategy than "trying harder." Sustained, top-down attention is a skill that can be strengthened just as muscles can. It takes many repetitions (like "reps" at the gym), corrective feedback, good habits, and sufficient motivation.

Fortunately, the act of focusing has one excellent ally: dopamine. If we *feel* what we are doing is worthwhile, the reward circuitry of the brain steps in to support our efforts. The neurotransmitter dopamine drip-feeds us regular small doses of enthusiasm to keep us focused. We can magnify this effect if we consciously notice our satisfaction, be it physical or mental, in what we are doing. We need dopamine as a cheerleader for demanding tasks.

But if that gut feeling of value is lacking, then focusing becomes a real chore. People often give up on meditating because it doesn't *feel* worth the time it takes. The rewards seem too small. Nor are meditators much encouraged to be mindful of the physical benefits and pleasures. For many people, being inactive, sitting still, and "just watching" don't seem to be strong enough reasons to continue.

IT TAKES TIME TO FOCUS

Researchers have discovered that we can't focus instantly on any new object. It takes time. They propose that the process has three stages: (1) We disconnect from our previous thoughts, (2) we orient toward the new object, and (3) we finally "lock on" to that object. These last two stages are the equivalents of the stages called *vitakka* and *vicara* in Pali (we touched on *vitakka-vicara* as an aspect of mindfulness in chapters 7 and 14).

To focus means activating the neural networks relating to a new object while simultaneously cutting off supply to the old ones. No matter how resolutely we try to abandon a previous thought, it will still take a few seconds to vacate the mental stage and fade into the wings. Until that disturbance goes, we can't focus well on anything new. As a rule of thumb, the shift of energy supply from the old object to the new takes about ten to twenty seconds.

At a certain point, we manage to lock on to the new object. We make contact with it and we know it. We hold it firmly in our grasp. We establish it as the prima donna on the mental stage. It is now in the foreground, in the spotlight. We zoom in on it. These are all metaphors that cognitive psychology uses to illustrate this state of good focus.

The act of focusing commonly has a binocular, staring-straight-ahead feeling that comes from the region above the eyes (the orbitofrontal cortex). Focusing induces the calm, single-minded, subject-object gaze of a predator. We "grasp" the object or "take possession of it," as William James said, in a way that is distinctly physical. As the Buddha suggests, we "hold the breath in front of us." We don't want the object to escape because we get distracted.

Even when we do "make contact" with an object, we can still readily lose it. The next stage is to "sustain contact" over time. This is why meditators commonly count their breaths. They can tell when they are getting lost because they lose the count. Or they scan through the body, using it like a roadmap to resist going off on sidetracks.

Deep sustained focus results in an acute perception of detail. We feel each ripple of the out-breath, and the space before the new in-breath starts seems to last forever. If we listen to music, we catch the exact beginning and end of a phrase and feel each nuance of the orchestral color. If we examine an idea, we feel its full resonance within our bodies and minds.

If we are paying attention to an *action*, we move with the optimal levels of muscle tone, arousal, and coordination. In sports this equilibrium is called a state of "dynamic balance" (as discussed in chapter 8), and many athletes report that everything moves in slow motion when they are "in the zone." Sustained attention takes time to establish, but it can exponentially improve the quality of anything we do.

SWITCHING AND SPLITTING ATTENTION

At any moment in our brains, dozens of thoughts will be competing for their time under the spotlight: The Nobel laureate Gerald Edelman called the phenomenon of selecting from among thoughts at the cellular level "neural Darwinism." This competition is particularly true with our normal, undisciplined, bottom-up style of attention. Philosophers from the time of Ecclesiastes onward have lamented that there is no end to the weariness of thought. So many actors! Such a small stage!

Maintaining focus on any one object of attention is hard enough, but being able to let go of an object and switch to something else—dis-focusing and re-focusing—is just as important. We rarely find this easy to do. It can be most unpleasant to get interrupted when we're fully engaged in something, and our resistance to switching can be visceral. Nonetheless, being able to smoothly switch our attention as required is a critical cognitive skill. If we can't do it, we get caught in the painful habit of useless, exhausting overthinking. Most of us suffer from this at least occasionally, and some have their lives devastated by it.

Even more subtle than switching attention is "splitting" attention. In general when we focus, we try to give all our free attention to just one thing. This is so hard to do that we are pleased when we seem to achieve it. In reality, our attention is always split whether we realize it or not. Attention always involves both "focusing" and "monitoring." Our cognitive resources are always divided between what is onstage and what is in the wings, between the object in the foreground and the peripheral mental activity in the background, between conscious thought and automatic thought.

Researchers have shown that even with strong mental focus there is still some processing of what they call the "unattended data." This is how it should be. Complete tunnel vision would be disastrous. If we were meditating well, for example, we wouldn't notice the house burning down around us. It is usually best to do one thing at a time as much as possible. It allows for a detailed, unobstructed representation in the mind, leading to a clear evaluation and response. However, to hold two things simultaneously in the mind is occasionally better than a strong single focus.

For example, we usually make either-or choices sequentially. We do a virtual simulation of option 1. Then we stop and do a virtual simulation of option 2. We then toggle between them until one option finally claims us. This approach has its shortcomings. If at all possible, it is sometimes better to hold two options side by side on the mental stage and *feel* the tension between their respective values.

SHARP FOCUS AND SOFT FOCUS

Recognizing the quality of our focus is an essential part of what the Buddha calls "being mindful of our state of mind." The quality of our attention can vary enormously from second to second, day to day, and from activity to activity. It can be deep or shallow, sustained or intermittent, clear or dull, strained or effortless. It often fluctuates according to events within our bodies and the environment that we can be quite unaware of. Even when we focus well, our attention still tends to fluctuate on a bright-dim continuum. I suspect this is due to the subtle oscillation in energy supply between the focusing and monitoring functions. I'm sure that scientists will eventually be able to measure this.

Whenever we meditate, we could be more or less alert, or more or less relaxed. We may notice the object in detail and know exactly what is happening in the moment: This is sharp focus. Or we may be gliding along with minimal effort: This is soft focus. So long as we remain on track, doing what we intended to do, both extremes are perfectly fine, and each has its own benefits.

Alertness gives us sharp focus and often a sense of mental pleasure and control. The longer we focus, the more resources and memories we bring to that object, and the more the peripheral interference fades. We often feel a dopamine-rich sense of engagement and intimacy with it. At that time, everything else is temporarily "de-selected."

Strong sustained focus is like a telephoto or zoom lens. It can be as sharp as a diamond, as penetrating as a microscope. It can split time into leisurely, radiant nanoseconds. Its emotional tone is one of reward-driven enthusiasm. Strong focus is essential for the states of bliss that meditators occasionally experience. It is also perfect for listening to music or enjoying any sensory pleasure.

Of course strong focus is not always good. It can easily get too close to the action and lose the bigger picture, resulting in obsession. Strong focus is a hallmark of compulsive, repetitive behavior and addictions, and a single-minded fixation on the bad is typical of depression. Even strong focus on what is good can destabilize other aspects of our minds and lives.

Soft focus, on the other hand, usually means that we are staying focused on the body or the breath but only just. This sleepy, dark, inward-looking, and almost unconscious state is very restful if we can remain in control. It allows the homeostatic processes of the body to restore balance in much the same way that sleep does. The low-frequency theta brainwaves and fragmentary dream images that occur in stage 1 sleep are often present in this threshold state.

Soft focus is more like a wide-angle lens. It is more broadly inclusive than sharp focus, but definition is fuzzy. It can be good at peripheral monitoring, "watching with detachment," and indeed it may do little else. Its emotional tone is one of relaxation and contentment. Mindfulness as "nonjudgmental acceptance" is squarely in the soft-focus camp.

It is a different matter if our focus gets even looser. This often results in a state of mind that is drowsy, rambling, uncontrolled, vulnerable to any troublesome thought, and somewhat depressed. We may still be physically relaxed, but if we're not tired enough to fall asleep, it is a kind of pointless, low-level chaos. It lacks the sense of direction and value that is essential for a good mood.

We can't entirely control our level of alertness, but we can turn it up or down to some degree. The Buddha used the metaphor of tuning a lyre. The music sounds best when the strings are neither too tight nor too loose. This means that we should recognize when our attention is too brittle and edgy and deliberately soften it. More commonly, we should recognize when we are becoming too vague and dreamy, and wake ourselves up.

Throughout this chapter, my descriptions betray the prejudices of the English language. It is very hard to avoid the assumption that conscious is better than automatic; that "selective attention" implies a free, autonomous choice; that focusing is intellectually noble; that strong focus is better than soft focus; and that the peripheral data is bad, nothing but a source of distractions and temptations.

In fact, the brain is not designed to work in full sunlight alone. The mental processes that happen in the shadows are equally important. The fully conscious mind is a pinnacle of evolution, but it still relies on our rich substrata of automatic and unconscious behaviors to function well.

Many researchers recognize that the benefits of mindfulness are largely due to attentional training. It is unfortunate that few people who actually teach meditation take this seriously. Relaxation and emotional detachment always seem to be more important and immediate goals than mental control. Even when paying attention is encouraged, the emphasis on being "nonjudgmental" at the same time severely undercuts the evaluative and regulatory function of attention. "Paying attention" is often reduced to little more than the instructions "When your mind wanders, return to the breath." This is quite inadequate if we want to actually *train* our attention, as the Buddha recommended.

22

Good Judgment

Mindfulness is often described as a nonreactive, passive, just-watching state of "bare attention" that enables us to see things "just as they are" without verbal elaboration or associations from memory. This attitude also tends to assume that nonaction (what Taoists call *wu-wei*) and not-thinking are superior to any kind of deliberate action or thought, and it adopts an ethically neutral stance toward whatever happens (nonjudgmental acceptance). This approach is embodied in the Buddhist slogan "Nothing is worth clinging to"—or in more modern language, "Nothing is worth reacting to." (Shakespeare satirized this idea in *Hamlet*: "Nothing is either good or bad, but thinking makes it so.") While this attitude certainly supports the meditative ideal of stillness and inner peace, it was not how the Buddha understood mindfulness.

The term *sampajjana* means "good judgment" or "evaluation." *Sati* is so closely linked to *sampajjana* in the *Sutta* that they are frequently combined into the phrase *sati-sampajjana*. Even when *sati* is used on its own, *sampajjana* is always implied. *Sampajjana* literally means the "accurate understanding" or "clear comprehension" of something. According to Analayo, *sampajjana* "can range from basic forms of knowing to deep discriminative understanding."[1]

Above all, *sati-sampajjana* is not at all ethically neutral. Because the *Sutta* is intended as a practical, self-guided manual for the journey to enlightenment, *sampajjana* is better translated as "evaluation" or "good judgment" rather than "clear understanding." It is not knowledge for knowledge's sake. Nor is it a way of "savoring" our present-moment experience "just as it is." *Sampajjana* is instrumental. It means understanding that a particular thought, sensation, or action will either help or hinder our movement toward immediate and long-term goals.

For the monk, *sampajjana* meant recognizing what was good and bad, useful or useless, in even the smallest matters, so he could control his behavior and eventually become enlightened. If he saw an attractive girl, he had to evaluate what she meant for him and how he should respond. She wasn't bad or evil in herself, but further acquaintance with her would be bad for *him* if he wanted to awaken. He couldn't make any kind of progress without making functional yes-no, right-wrong, good-bad judgment calls every step of the way.

This is probably true for any great achievement in life. To stay solidly on track toward any distant goal, we have to be able to say "no," most of the time at least, to the potential distractions along the way. We may have different goals from monks, but the same principle of discriminating attention applies to us. Cheesecake, as a dense form of the sugars and fats that our bodies need, would undoubtedly have been seen as "good" throughout most of human existence. Our instincts tell us that it is good. It certainly *tastes* good. If we are diabetic, however, or if we need to lose weight, cheesecake is definitely bad for us, and we need to act as if that is the truth.

Ultimately, an elite monk would see into the deep nature of existence itself and evaluate it as "suffering, impermanent and devoid of self." This is the classical "road to Damascus" insight in Buddhism. This insight is said to result in profound disgust and a resolution to abandon the world, and it is the precursor to full awakening. I give this example not to suggest that the Buddha's opinion about the world was right, but to illustrate how integral good judgment was to his concept of mindfulness.

Another primary meaning of *sati* is "memory." In the texts, this is described as constantly holding our ultimate goals in mind. This is actually very hard to do. We are hardwired to discount future benefits against immediate pleasures. Nonetheless, these long-term goals should ideally determine our judgments in the present. But before I explain further how mindfulness contributes to good judgment, let's explore another facet of what *sati* itself implies.

SATI: TO HOLD SOMETHING IN MIND

Sati means "to pay attention to" or "to focus on" something. It is a transitive verb, not a noun. It is not a "thing." It is something that we *do*. This means it is always oriented toward an object. To "be mindful" is to "hold in mind" anything that the mind is capable of conceiving. Above all, *sati* is "selective, sustained attention." You say "yes" to this, and "no" to everything else. You orient toward an object (*vitakka*) and lock on to it (*vicara*).

To be mindful also means holding the object metaphorically in front of you. This suggests objectivity and clarity of vision. This mental space is what Descartes, in his *Meditations*, called "the stage of the mind." Cognitive psychology calls it "working memory." Descartes said this enables you to get a "clear and distinct" image of the object. You see it accurately, and you understand its true value and significance for you.

To hold something in mind also means holding it *still*. You see it but don't deliberately think about it. This suggests a non-reactive, clear-seeing quality of attention. Vipassana, Zen, and mindfulness-based stress reduction generally aim to globally devalue thoughts, per se, and to down-regulate emotions in the interests of tranquility. The Buddha's approach, on the other hand, seeks to understand thoughts. This understanding is what *vipassana*, or "insight," entails.

The Buddha's term *dhamma-vicaya*, as the second of the seven factors of enlightenment, means the "investigation of phenomena." When we hold an object still, without thinking about it, this places it within its broader context of associated memories. Paradoxically, this enables us, if we choose to do so, to go on processing the object, but in a lateral, nonlinear, intuitive way. This is how "just watching" can lead to a deeper, gut understanding of the object than just talking to ourselves about it.

This feeling of holding something calmly in the spotlight, holding it distinct from everything else, and carefully examining it, is quite unmistakable once you get it. Something clicks into place. You feel face-to-face with the object. This is true whether the object is vast or tiny, trivial or profound, momentary or enduring. To be calm, alert, undistracted, and fully focused on something is a marvelous mental state. As the

Buddha said, you are like a charioteer in full control of your team of fine horses, able to direct and stop and switch your train of thought as you wish. This is high-quality *sati*.

MAKING JUDGMENTS WHILE WE MEDITATE

When we meditate, our attention is always split between the focusing and monitoring functions. We choose to focus on the body as much as we can, but we can't avoid noticing the other "not-body" phenomena that also arise in the mind. At first, most of our efforts have to go into focusing on the body or the meditation collapses. Later, when we attain a good degree of stillness and mental control, we can devote more of our cognitive capacity to processing and evaluating the peripheral data. I would guess that many if not most meditations eventually gravitate toward some kind of Open Monitoring practice.

Over the years, an immense array of thoughts, sensations, emotions, memories, impulses, stories, images, and fantasies will arise in the mind, as they should. This is what gives us the full picture of who we are. It is the raw material of our self-understanding. Let's call all this the "stream of consciousness" for short. New meditators are often astonished by the vast inner library they uncover when they sit. This also explains why they can meditate for years without getting bored. The big question is, how do we relate to all of this? There are many possible strategies, and they all imply some kind of screening or selection, evaluation, or preference.

We make thousands of judgments every day, but they are mostly subliminal or automatic. We can easily flush our automatic judgments to the surface, however, by noticing where our attention goes. Attention is the currency of the brain. It streamlines oxygen and glucose toward the network of cells that support the mental representation of an object. This typically leads on into the kind of "approach or withdraw" reaction described in chapter 16. You intuitively choose to give more attention to something, or you dump it, or you switch to something more promising.

Notice that as we distribute our energy moment by moment, anything we choose to focus on or do is at the expense of the alternatives. We read the paper rather than go for a walk. We think about a celebrity rather than focus on the breath. Endlessly surfing the web has its reward (that is, it can feel "good" to do), but it can also be "bad" because it takes time you need to spend elsewhere. To stay with any thought or sensation or activity is to implicitly decide "This seems to be more important than anything else just now." You can even measure how valuable you judge it to be by noticing the amount of time you spend on it.

When we meditate, we are making a strong judgment that this activity deserves twenty minutes of our time. Our basic preference is obvious: We orient toward the body and away from thought; toward the sensory present and away from past and future; toward stillness and away from stimulation. We relax the body and calm the mind, and gravitate toward an ideal homeostatic state of body-mind stillness.

In Zen, this is *shikantaza* (just sitting, not thinking). In Vipassana, it is *jhana* (absorption). Done well, this can induce a timeless, thought-free state of inner peace that is so satisfying that many meditators regard as the highest good of all. Unfortunately, these states take long or repeated sittings to achieve, and they dissolve once you stop meditating. This is where Open Monitoring meditations come in.

When you have a good degree of body-mind stillness, you no longer need to see the stream of consciousness as the enemy. You can divide your attention equally between inner and outer. Without losing focus on the body, you can also choose to examine any peripheral thought, sensation, memory, emotion, or problem that arises. You simply ask: "What is this? What is happening now? Is this worth any further attention or not?"

Frequently it is. As we do the Open Monitoring practice, we also make small, subtle, wide-ranging reappraisals and micro-judgments about the peripheral thoughts and emotions that arise. We can hold each one clearly in the mind and choose our response. Over time, we sense how we stand in relation to the complexity of our present experience. *Sati-sampajjana*, the calm, conscious perception and evaluation of phenomena, is sensitively realigning us toward the raw data of our inner lives, without our getting caught in runaway thought. We remain calm and centered, but we also "see" exactly what is happening for us in the moment. We know who we are.

MEDITATING ON A DECISION

And there is more. While meditating, you can simultaneously reflect on a problem. If you have to make a financial decision— such as to buy or sell shares or trade in a car—you would normally think at length before deciding. By meditating, however, you can take a different approach: You can deconstruct the issue and see it in a broader perspective.

When your mind is relatively calm and still, you can split your attention equally between the body and the problem. In other words, you continue to scan the body or track the breaths while you break the issue down into its component parts, following the format of the *Sutta*, in order to see each part as accurately as possible.

Those parts are the thoughts themselves; their affective charge or valence; the underlying emotion; the state or quality of mind; and the body sensations that occur during the process. In reality, these all interpenetrate, but with practice you can provisionally separate them out. You can see each one—thoughts + valence + emotion + state of mind + body sensations—relatively clearly and distinctly on the stage of the mind, and hold it still.

Let's go through this process in more detail. To start, you hold the issue in mind. You ask: "What is this?" and you name the issue in as few words as possible, such as "buying shares" or "buying a car." Then you ask: "What is the *valence* around this issue?" Is it strong or weak, positive or negative? In other words, how important does this issue seem to be for your well-being? Once you can see the valence, you don't need to do anything else for the moment. Your mind will tend to automatically reappraise it up or down as appropriate.

Then you can ask: "What is the underlying *emotion*?" Is it excitement or fear of missing out or dread or desire? Then you ask: "What is my *state of mind*?" If you recognize that you are agitated or exhausted or anxious, you will see that you are in no fit state to make any decision, no matter how convincing the arguments. Conversely, you will also recognize when it is exactly the right time to act.

By consciously focusing on your body throughout, you can remain calm and centered, with no physiological urge to make an immediate decision. A clear sign that you are truly in control is that you can freely abandon the issue and give full attention to your Standard Meditation Practice. Alternatively, you can switch to another problem on your mental list.

Mindfulness can also help make judgments that are more emotionally complex. Issues around work, relationships, health, identity, and satisfaction are truly vast, and the rational mind has its limits. When I was young, I eventually realized that a sexual relationship is too complicated to ever fully comprehend. Even when a relationship was going well, I never really understood what was happening. So how can you make a decision to stay or go, for example, or to speak or be silent, without making a complete mess of it?

The best meditative strategy is still to deconstruct the issue into its component parts—thoughts, valence, emotion, state of mind, body sensations—as in the example of buying shares or buying a car. But this is not enough on its own. We can't complete this process in just one or two meditations. We need to do it repeatedly, *and* at different times of day, *and* we can't just do it while we're meditating. We have to be able to identify those components in the live situations during the day. It is amazing how wise you can seem to be when sitting, and how confused you become when you return to the world.

At a certain point, however, the answer will be perfectly obvious. You finally know exactly what to do. Alternatively, you may wake up one morning to find that the process of deliberation is over. The last votes were counted overnight. You then find yourself acting as if a decision has already been made.

COMPARATIVE EVALUATION

Yes-or-no decisions are hard enough, but either-or decisions place even greater demands on our cognitive capacity. At any time, we are likely to have the problem of competing good things in our lives. We all have primary life goals that are hard-wired into us. At the most basic level, we have a will to live and thrive. It is very hard to overrule that, as people who try to commit suicide often discover.

Moreover, we all need money or some form of support; we all need some social recognition or love; we want good health; and we want to enjoy our lives. We can't opt out of these high-value goals and choose to simply drift along, accepting whatever happens. They all take continual effort. We instinctively line up our actions against these ethical yardsticks every day and make our judgments accordingly. If we try to ignore those inbuilt goals, the result is poverty, isolation, sickness, misery, and an early death.

Money, love, health, and enjoyment are all worth pursuing. However, it is almost impossible for any of us to achieve excellence in all of them at once. They compete against each other for our limited resources of energy, time, interest, and money. Every decision we make will be a trade-off against those natural goals. We might wish for a vantage point from which we could have an overview to put everything in perspective, but at that height we wouldn't be able to imagine how the detail would work out on the ground.

In these situations, we can use a judgment strategy that I call "comparative evaluation." Both A and B may be good. They both have high positive valences, and both may be necessary, but how do they compare against each other? How should we best distribute our energy between them? How can we compare, for example, the issues around work versus family life? Career versus health? Education versus adventure?

Having a baby versus a career? Spending versus saving? Leisure versus achievement?

These issues are too big to compare rationally, but you can evaluate them through embodied cognition. By thinking through the body, and becoming fully conscious of the valence and emotions around an issue, you can gradually construct an integrated body-mind image of it that isn't solely reliant on words. You can start to think of "work" as a relatively stable, muscular, visceral, gut feeling within you, rather than a riot of words and behaviors. If you do the same with, for example, "family life" or "health" you will get an entirely different image. Every issue is likely to have its own unique configuration of muscle tone, arousal, affect, and mood. It has its own body-mind image or signature.

Once an embodied image becomes coherent and stable and familiar, you can compare it with another. You can place them both on the mental stage and turn your attention slowly from one to the other. How does "work" make you feel? Give it a minute or two to become vivid. Now switch to "family life." How does that make you feel? You can let the thoughts and emotion and colors of each one emerge as you do so, but you try not to verbally elaborate on them.

Ultimately, you are trying to sense their respective weights and emotional tone. Both may be good, but which of the two feels more substantial and worthy, at least in this moment? Are you undervaluing or overvaluing one over the other? This is usually not a winner-takes-all situation. You have to choose how best to distribute or sequence your energy between them.

If you want to be thorough, you do this repeatedly, both in meditation and out. I also suggest you get into the habit of comparing the relative value of *all* the big goals in your life, and even the little ones as well—A versus B, A versus C, A versus D, then B versus C, B versus D, and so on—in order to discover what is truly important to you. When you make decisions, you will be working from judgments that are closer to the substrata of your primary values.

INSIGHT

Most of our thinking is routine, pedestrian, and workmanlike at best, but occasionally we have a truly brilliant thought. We call this an "insight." The skies open up. The problem is perfectly illuminated. The answer comes with effortless conviction. The *Sutta* is a training manual designed to produce just this kind of brilliant thought. I gave the classic example of the monk's preawakening insight near the start of this chapter. In fact, the term *vipassana*, which literally means "repeated deep seeing," is usually translated as "insight."

The author Arthur Koestler (1905–1983) proposed four stages of creativity or insight: preparation, incubation, the flash of insight itself, and the subsequent verification. The first stage, preparation—brooding over an idea, collecting data and hypotheses—is completely rational. For instance, Alfred Russell Wallace (1823–1913), the cofounder of evolutionary theory, spent years looking for an explanation for the diversity of species. When Isaac Newton (1643–1727) was asked about how he achieved his miraculous year of scientific and mathematical discoveries in 1666, he said he thought about nothing else for months at a time.

Koestler's second stage, incubation, loosely correlates to what we have called embodied thought. Wallace lay for weeks in a fever before his insight into evolution through natural selection dawned upon him. For Newton, the moment of insight is captured in the legend of the falling apple. For both these scientists, however, years of verification and testing had to follow. You can't automatically trust an insight! Intuitions are frequently wrong.

The Buddha certainly understood this process. The *Sutta* is a systematic training of the mind in preparation for deep thought, and for the flashes of insight that knit it all together. Sitting meditation is the *first* part of the *first* of the four foundations of mindfulness. The pursuit of insight, on the other hand, is the *last* part of the *last* of the four foundations. Another Pali text describes the process: "When his concentrated mind is thus purified, bright, unblemished, malleable and steady, the monk devotes himself to investigating the Buddha's dogma."[2] For example, in the *Sutta*: "The monk reflects on the Four Noble Truths that lead to nirvana. He understands by direct experience that: Life is suffering. The cause of suffering is desire. Desire can be extinguished. The Eightfold Path of training extinguishes desire and leads to the end of suffering."

In other words, the Buddha is asking the monk to think in depth about the nature of life. The Buddha was a much more rational, nonmystical thinker than we give him credit for. In the texts, he repeatedly sets up his premises and argues his point from many different angles on concepts such as interdependent origination, the three characteristics of existence, the five aggregates, the six sense bases, and so on. It is fair to say that he regarded at least some degree of rational analysis as a crucial prerequisite to awakening.

He still knew that thought alone was not enough. We can easily give our assent to a philosophy without a deep conviction that it is true. The Zen student knows that she is already enlightened, but she doesn't quite believe it. We know that overeating is bad for us, but it doesn't feel that way.

Insights, however, are more potent and embodied. They go deep and carry a lot of weight. A bright idea or a breakthrough insight typically consolidates much of the rational analysis that has preceded it. It can irreversibly shift the thinker's internal orientation to that issue, or it may simply be a big step along the way. Afterward, an insight can seem blindingly obvious, and easy to take as a given. (When Darwin's colleague T. H. Huxley read Darwin's foundational text on evolutionary theory in 1859, he exclaimed, "How extremely stupid not to have thought of it!")

Nonetheless, insights don't have to be earth-shattering to qualify as such. We can regard an insight as any bright or potent idea that stands out from the usual run of mental chatter. They are the best part of your mental activity, so it is useful to be mindful of them. If you have an insight, I suggest you do the following:

Stop your mental flow and hold the insight in mind. Hold it still and feel it. How true or deep does it seem to be? Is it going to hold up in different circumstances? Evaluate it and remember it. I frequently go for long philosophic walks. At the end I typically ask myself, "What were the best three or four ideas?" Other people might write them down. I deliberately lodge them in memory.

Making big decisions is a lonely activity. The rule books usually don't work, and simple nostrums are deceitful. As the journalist and satirist H. L. Mencken famously put it, "For every complex problem, there is an answer that is clear, simple, and wrong." Aristotle regarded "practical wisdom" (*phronesis*) as the ability to make good judgments in situations of uncertainty and inadequate information. He saw this as one of the fundamental skills of a mature adult.

The Western term "enlightenment" means being able to think and determine the truth for yourself, based on the evidence, without reliance on political or religious authorities. The *Sutta* is a comprehensive mind-training discipline that aims at just this kind of self-reliance and mental vigor.

The Buddha's methods for improving our judgments are sophisticated and thorough. Meditation grounds us, and embodied thought is a type of cognition based on constant cross-referencing and feedback mechanisms using all parts of the body and brain. Over time, this can lead us out of childish, habitual, "confirmation bias" thinking toward a more intelligent and open-ended way of relating to the world. By clarifying our everyday decisions, mindfulness can help us become insightful, independent thinkers. It can make us enlightened, in the Western sense of the word.

In this book we have now traversed from sitting meditation, which is the *first* part of the *first* foundation, to embodied thought and insight, which is the *last* part of the *last* foundation. This chapter marks the end of my analysis of the *Sutta*. The remaining four chapters discuss the modern understanding and applications of mindfulness.

PART FOUR

Modern Applications of Mindfulness

23

The Scientific Evidence

Tens of thousands of studies on mindfulness and meditation have appeared since I started teaching in 1987. Many of these are of questionable quality, but the general drift is clear. Mindfulness seems to have positive effects for people suffering from anxiety, depression, pain, stress, insomnia, substance abuse, and eating disorders. It helps with medical conditions such as cancer, hypertension, postoperative recovery, diabetes, irritable bowel syndrome, fibromyalgia, skin conditions, and poor immune function. It seems to work in all populations, from children to the elderly, and across a great variety of occupations.

Mindfulness has gone from strength to strength in recent years, but the research is still struggling to describe how it achieves the results that it does. Let's look at some of the most plausible hypotheses: namely, relaxation, enhanced body awareness, attention and thought control, and emotional regulation.

RELAXATION

Most people would describe relaxation as a major reason for meditating. The most uncontroversial aspect of the research is that meditation enhances parasympathetic activity (the so-called relaxation response described on page 50). This alone is enough to explain its beneficial effects on heart rate, blood pressure, immune function, digestion, pain tolerance, and sleep quality. Learning to relax quickly and frequently during the day has the potential to permanently lower baseline levels of arousal and stress.

So is relaxation part of the answer to alleviating mental distress? Not at all, according to some psychologists. From the start, the psychological literature has devalued the idea that relaxation could be useful as part of a treatment strategy. The pioneering writers constantly downplay its potential as an agent of change and describe it as a pleasant side effect at best. They say this despite the fact that some degree of physical relaxation is virtually guaranteed in any meditation, while achieving a state of nonjudgmental acceptance is far less certain or measurable, even subjectively. I have yet to see any study that attempts to assess mindfulness in isolation from the confounding influence of relaxation. I'm sure it would be easy to design.

Psychology has a long tradition of devaluing what happens in the body in favor of purely mental dynamics. I won't argue the obvious—that being able to consciously relax is crucial, and that doing so is both pleasant and good for you—but I suggest that you keep in mind the prejudice against the value of relaxation in the psychological literature. You can easily read dozens of scientific reports and not find a single reference to relaxation as a possible causative factor.

ENHANCED BODY AWARENESS

Meditation invariably enhances body awareness (and induces relaxation), whether that is the intention or not. This has many well-documented advantages. Enhanced body awareness leads to a conscious awareness of one's emotions. It acts as an early warning device to pick up signals of overreactivity. It helps us to recognize our biological needs and limits long before crisis point. It seems to enhance our ability to accommodate unpleasant moods and sensations. It has the potential to increase empathy through the recognition of the body signals of others.

Enhanced body awareness also alters the way that we think of ourselves. Our sense of self-identity operates through two distinct systems. The "narrative" system relies on language, memory, and a sense of purpose. This is "doing" mode: "This is me, my history, and what I do." The "experiential" system relies on nonverbal, immediate interoception, and our sense of location in space. This is "being" mode: "This is how I feel in this moment."

Meditation strengthens this bodily sense of self at the expense of the narrative sense, and it consequently weakens excessive thought. If we feel grounded in our body, we are more able to see a thought as being "out there," outside the body. Each time we do so we implicitly give more value to embodiment and less to mental chatter. Doing this thousands of times can train us to automate the response, and so reduce the tendency toward rumination and self-referential verbal narratives.

ATTENTION AND THOUGHT CONTROL

Attention is the essential skill in meditation, and it consists of a variety of sub-skills. Learning to focus and *sustain* attention on the body is the antidote to the jumpy, anxious, scattered mind. Learning to *switch* attention away from a thought or behavior ("Let go and focus on the breath") breaks the opposite tendency to fixate and ruminate. Learning to *split* attention appropriately increases mental efficiency and coping skills.

Anchoring the mind in the body helps inhibit the secondary elaborative processing of the thoughts, sensations, and emotions that arise while we meditate. Learning to "name" or "label" thoughts guarantees metacognitive awareness and is so beneficial that we find it in many therapies. The emphasis that mindfulness-based stress reduction places on devaluing thoughts indiscriminately undoubtedly helps many patients also. This ability to take a more detached stance in relation to one's thoughts and feelings is called "decentering" or "defusing" or "reperceiving" in the psychological literature.

These terms all suggest a general tendency to devalue thoughts per se. This is a common meditative strategy, but I prefer the Buddha's approach. *Sati-sampajjana* is "the conscious perception and evaluation" of something. Being conscious, it evaluates a thought *accurately*, as it deserves, rather than automatically downgrading it. This is closer to the older cognitive behavioral therapy term "reappraisal" than to "defusing" or "decentering." This may be the most important mindfulness skill in managing anxiety and depression.

The research also suggests that even a very brief mindfulness intervention can enhance our sense of self-control and discrimination. The reappraisal of any thought or impulse doesn't even need to be conscious. A two-second "stop and look" pause is enough time for an implicit reappraisal.

EMOTIONAL REGULATION

Meditation lowers physiological arousal. This contributes to lower heart rate, blood pressure, and cortisol and adrenaline secretions while you are meditating. This may not change your underlying emotion, but it definitely turns down the volume. Meditation also weakens thought, thereby reducing the verbal amplification of any situation. It also requires that we sit still for several minutes, which means that we inevitably disarm our musculature and are less primed to act impulsively. This non-action is a profound signal from the body to the mind. It says, "No great urgency. No need to act right now." It undermines the primary role of emotion, which is to initiate some kind of physical action.

Psychologists speculate that poor emotional regulation is a primary driver of anxiety and depression. Conversely, they see a strong correlation between self-reported mindfulness and good emotional control strategies. Mindfulness seems to help through mechanisms such as early intervention, reappraisal, exposure, and the extinction of habitual responses. Paradoxically, trying to see things nonjudgmentally invariably results in a reevaluation of the object. Most commonly we down-regulate its emotional charge. We see it as less important and therefore requiring little or no response. Some researchers now see positive reappraisal, not acceptance, as the key mediator of therapeutic change.

The pioneering mindfulness writer John Teasdale explains how even a few seconds of *conscious* perception are bound to result in an *automatic* reappraisal. To be mindful holds an object in working memory for long enough to recontextualize it. Just a second or two of mindful attention to an emotional situation gives plenty of time for memories of similar past situations to arise. Since the mind automatically evaluates any new information and updates its assessments within milliseconds, being mindful of something will invariably modify the initial rule-of-thumb judgment about it.

Good meditators gradually learn to automate a more tolerant approach toward unpleasant stimuli, so they no longer need to cognitively control the process. Mindfulness thus contributes to our largely automatic reappraisals of moment-by-moment experience. Practiced regularly, this produces a stable, dispositional tendency to be mindful.

Finally meditation enhances emotional control through brain mechanisms that are now well understood. Focusing and language are left-lateralized prefrontal cortex functions. Meditation thus results in front-back, left-right, "reason-emotion" inhibitions. Although both hemispheres always work together, focusing enhances left-hemisphere dominance over the right. The left hemisphere is analytical and rational and is associated with self-control and "positive" emotions. Conversely, the right hemisphere is more inclusive but is also more vulnerable to emotional confusion. Dampening the right hemisphere thus improves mood and a sense of control.

A front-back inhibition also occurs. The "rational" pre-frontal cortex inhibits the "emotional" limbic system deep in the brain. The orbitofrontal cortex (the region above the eyes) is highly active when we focus and use language, and the "naming" function in meditation enhances this effect. Scans using fMRI technology show that naming unpleasant emotional states results in a down-regulation of the amygdala. This means that even a few seconds of mindfulness ("Stop, look, and evaluate") can speed up a return to emotional baseline after an overreaction. Over time and with training, this return to baseline can become an automatic response, requiring little cognitive intervention.

So far, I haven't presented any substantial proof that meditation works. I've just presented some of the theories by which it *could* work. Let's now look at what the researchers, as opposed to the popular writers, are saying.

HOW GOOD IS THE SCIENCE?

There is a "widespread belief that meditation practice is scientifically certified to be good for just about everything," according to Linda Heuman in her recent 2014 article in the Buddhist magazine *Tricycle*.[1] Mindfulness has gained respectability from the simple fact that so much research is being done on it, but how good is the science? Has journalistic and researcher exaggeration and hype inflated the public perception of mindfulness?

Many scientists think so. An eleven-author team writing in the journal *Clinical Psychology: Science and Practice* quotes the researcher Scott Bishop, who argued that the popularity of mindfulness-based stress reduction has grown "in the absence of rigorous evaluation."[2] Willoughby Britton is a clinical psychologist and neurologist in the field. When interviewed by Heuman for *Tricycle*, she said, "The public perception of where the research is at is way higher than the actual level."

Most mindfulness research shares some common problems: the small size of studies; the lack of replication or peer review; the lack of double blinding; the selection criteria; the questions of dosage, durability, and size of effect; the exclusion of confounding effects (such as relaxation); overreliance on self-reporting questionnaires; poor monitoring of participant adherence to practice protocols; the confirmation bias tendencies of researchers; and, finally, the lack of comparisons with other treatments. An enthusiastic new report in the media about the promise of mindfulness could have ignored or trivialized all of the issues in this paragraph.

Fortunately, we can trust some scientists to evaluate the science itself. We can't ever take the results from a single paper at face value, but the meta-analyses that summarize the conclusions from hundreds or thousands of papers are far more reliable. One of these meta-analyses reviewed nearly twenty thousand research papers. Published in a 2014 issue of *JAMA Internal Medicine*, the study (Goyal et al.) has given us the best positive evidence yet for mindfulness.

The study's fifteen authors concluded, "Mindfulness meditation programs had moderate evidence of improved anxiety … depression … and pain" but "low evidence of improved stress/distress and mental health-related quality of life."[3] The results are hardly resounding, but they do seem to be reliable, and they suggest that mindfulness is promising as a mental health treatment for perhaps 10 to 20 percent of the population. They also match my experience as a teacher. I find that mindfulness works well for anxiety, depression, pain, and insomnia. I also tell people with medical problems that mindfulness will be most useful in reducing the anxiety that accompanies health issues, but that a cure is unlikely.

My experience also suggests that mindfulness can have superb results for people who are temperamentally suited to it but only mediocre or nil results for those who are not. This is why the discretion of a doctor or a psychologist in recommending mindfulness to a patient is so important. Mindfulness training could be next to worthless if it is given indiscriminately to a particular population. In fact, the averaging-out effect of studies probably gives a misleading impression of the usefulness of mindfulness training: Some participants could have spectacular results, while those who are ill suited to the practice could drag the statistics down.

In 2007 the University of Alberta's Evidence-Based Practice Center in Canada published a meta-analysis of the best 813 studies available at that time. It concluded that none of them achieved the standard of good research, but it did identify two issues that explained why. It argued that two issues would have to be clarified if mindfulness is ever to deserve scientific respect: (1) There are no generally accepted definitions of meditation. (2) There are no good hypotheses about how it works.

The abstract to another meta-analysis, by Peter Sedlmeier et al. (a seven-person team at the Chemnitz University of Technology in Germany) put it this way: "We conclude that to arrive at a comprehensive understanding of why and how meditation works, emphasis should be placed on the development of more precise theories and measurement devices."[4] If mindfulness is to gain credibility, it will need to trim itself down to a workable definition and a hypothesis capable of being tested. Above all, it needs good technical terms free of ambiguities and contradictions. At some point, I think researchers will also need to differentiate between mindfulness as a cognitive function (attention) and mindfulness as an ideal state of mind (nonjudgmental acceptance). These two interpretations are not compatible with one another. They are not even two poles of a sliding scale. One is a measurable, down-to-earth, cognitive function. The other is a poorly defined psychological or spiritual ideal.

In practice, the question finally comes down to what degree of proof we personally find acceptable. Do we have a high standard for proof or a low one? For reasons of professional integrity, I demand a high standard of proof. I admit that I am more difficult to please than most. Despite being a mindfulness teacher, I do not want to be seen as another New Age enthusiast who will believe anything!

Whenever I find scientific claims in popular books or the media, I try to trace them back to their original sources in the research literature. I usually find that the claims are based on single trials that use far more nuanced expressions such as "a small but statistically significant increase." I've now read hundreds of the scientific papers. As a nonprofessional, I still find it hard to objectively evaluate any of the claims beyond the abstract on the first page.

I have my own rough standards for interpreting scientific claims about mindfulness. First, don't believe anything that comes from a single study. There is no possible way that all design faults could be eliminated—that only comes from multiple trials. Second, don't trust any claim that does not refer to a traceable study. Third, don't trust grapevine generalizations such as, "Researchers now believe that . . ." Far too many researchers are willing to give credence to poor-quality studies.

Finally, don't trust claims based on popular opinion or even widespread usage. Science is about proof, not popularity or placebo. The histories of medicine and psychology are full of fads. The resounding popularity of bloodletting over millennia was never a proof of its efficacy. If Google, Monsanto, and the US military have big mindfulness programs, this doesn't prove anything in a scientific sense.

24

The Story of
Modern Mindfulness

What I refer to as Modern Mindfulness has been around for decades now, and tens of thousands of people are working in the field. Popular interest in mindfulness dates from 1979 when the American biologist Jon Kabat-Zinn developed his mindfulness-based stress reduction program. This program started life as a treatment for relief of chronic pain, and uptake into the wider culture was modest until psychologists started to experiment with it.

MBSR has now been adapted for anxiety, depression, and many other psychological disorders. Two other therapies that use mindfulness as components in their broader approaches developed about the same time: dialectical behavior therapy and acceptance and commitment therapy. Most mindfulness research, however, has been done on the MBSR model. As a one-technique therapy, it is the industry standard.

Until MBSR appeared, meditation had remained firmly within the grip of Buddhist, yogic, Christian, and New Age groups. I had been peripherally involved in some of these groups for years and became increasingly disgusted by their childish level of thought, lack of imagination, and reliance on authority. With such poor advocates it was hardly surprising that meditation had failed to thrive in the secular West.

Out of this unpromising background, Kabat-Zinn and his colleagues managed a minor miracle. They have firmly established a place for standard meditation practice in mainstream psychology and spearheaded its general acceptance in Western culture. This wasn't at all easy to do. The Transcendental Meditation (TM) movement had tried to become similarly established for decades and had largely failed. We talked briefly about Kabat-Zinn's own sources in the introduction to this book, but now let me explain the background to MBSR in a bit more detail.

For twenty-five hundred years, Buddhist meditation was largely an in-house doctrine. It was only taught by monks to monks. Laypeople were generally regarded as incapable of either practicing or teaching meditation because their impure lives precluded it. In reality very few monks practiced meditation, either. Traditional Buddhist monks mostly train in chanting, ceremonial, and magical skills, and they have surprisingly little interest in what we would call meditation.

Early in the twentieth century, however, a back-to-the-roots revival of Buddhist meditation emerged in Burma (today's Myanmar) based on the *Satipatthana Sutta*. Ledi Sayadaw, U Narada, and Mahasi Sayadaw were the most prominent monks, but laypeople were also involved to an unprecedented degree. U Ba Khin, a charismatic bureaucrat and politician, led retreats for laypeople and founded the

International Meditation Centre in Rangoon in 1952. This established the formula of ten-day Vipassana retreats that went on to sweep the world.

These retreats retained many Buddhist values, but they were commonly described as "pure meditation, not Buddhism." And in fact, U Ba Khin authorized several Burmese and Western laypeople to teach them. This was the spark that ignited a wildfire. For the first time in its twenty-five-hundred-year history, Buddhist meditation was being taught on a large scale by laymen, and even women, to other laypeople, many of whom had no Buddhist allegiances at all.

Thousands of backpackers, hippies, and other seekers attended Vipassana retreats in the 1960s and 1970s, and hundreds became monks or nuns for a while. Within a decade, dozens of Westerners including myself were teaching ten-day retreats far removed from the original Buddhist goals. I taught about forty retreats of three to ten days' duration until I stopped over duty-of-care concerns.

In 1975 a group of young Western teachers acquired a large property in Massachusetts where they established the Insight Meditation Society (IMS). Most Western Buddhist groups are overseen by an Asian monk of a particular lineage, but IMS didn't take that path. Almost by default this enabled it to become the umbrella group for a wide range of nonmonastic Western teachers throughout the world. IMS is very much the spiritual anchor for modern Western Vipassana. Many if not most of its founding teachers and writers will have practiced and taught there.

Jon Kabat-Zinn was not originally involved in Vipassana, but he had been heavily interested in Zen for many years.

When he attended IMS he saw the potential for a different kind of meditation. With understandable caution he adapted the standard ten-day Vipassana retreat format of breath and body scan meditations into an eight-week program for pain relief.

Mindfulness-based stress reduction requires participants to dedicate a total time of about sixty to seventy hours to this program. This involves participation in a class as well as daily home practice using guided meditation CDs. Seventy hours is close to the amount of time a ten-day retreatant would spend in formal meditation, and the usual session is forty minutes long. MBSR is thus a faithful adaptation of a formal retreat into a household setting. These demands of time and commitment mean that MBSR is certainly not a quick-fix, pop-psychology technique. It places the same high value on inactivity and withdrawal from the world that Buddhism itself does.

Because the MBSR training is so demanding, it is commonly abbreviated to fit the requirements of time-poor people. The eight-week program becomes six weeks or four weeks. The standard one-day workshop is omitted. The yoga sessions are dropped. The forty-minute meditations become twenty minutes and so on. I'm sure that many of these modifications improve the program. I have taught thirty thousand people since 1987, and I find the law of diminishing returns usually sets in after twenty to twenty-five minutes of meditation. However, MBSR is surprisingly accommodating in another respect.

Ten-day Vipassana retreats emphasize strong self-discipline and attentional training. The retreats come with many variants, but they typically involve seven to ten hours a day of sitting on the floor, with no talking and no reading for the whole ten days. It is understandable that Kabat-Zinn wanted MBSR to have a more accommodating approach for his target group of people in chronic pain. So he took the word "mindfulness" and gave it an entirely new meaning.

For the Buddha, to be mindful (*sati*) means to pay attention, or to consciously perceive and *evaluate* something, such as a body sensation, emotion, state of mind, thought, or action. Similarly, Rhys Davids, the *Satipatthana Sutta*'s nineteenth-century translator, probably chose the archaic word "mindfulness" as a translation of *sati* because of its strong moral tone. It implies a sense of careful self-observation and judgment.

In the century between Rhys Davids and Kabat-Zinn, the word "mindfulness" was almost exclusively used as a description of Vipassana meditation practice. It is hard to imagine this now, but "mindfulness" as a noun did not enter common usage until this century. Even as a professional meditation teacher, I hardly ever heard the word used outside the Buddhist context before about 2002.

Soto Zen meditators, by contrast, do quite a different practice from the *Satipatthana Sutta*. They try to achieve a state of "emptiness," or *sunyata*, through "just sitting, not thinking." This is an *unfocused*, passive, and undiscriminating state, "open" to passing sensory experience. The Zen teacher Dan Leighton describes it as an "objectless" meditation "that does not grasp at any of the highly subtle distinctions to which our familiar mental workings are prone."[1] For the Buddha, mindfulness (*sati*) correlates with attention. For Kabat-Zinn, however, mindfulness (*sati*) correlates much more strongly to *sunyata* (emptiness).

Presumably because this spiritual terminology was unsuitable for MBSR, and because his therapy did take its outer form from ten-day Vipassana retreats, Kabat-Zinn used the (then-underutilized) word "mindfulness" to describe this ideal state. His definition of mindfulness as "a state of nonjudgmental acceptance" is a remarkably good, secular description of *sunyata*.

Redefining mindfulness, and orienting it toward "emptiness" was a bold move, but at that time, no one cared what he was doing. Few people practiced Vipassana, and the mindfulness boom had not yet started. I have searched the commentarial literature in vain for any use of the word "nonjudgmental" prior to Kabat-Zinn. There are related terms—nonreactivity, the watching mind, bare attention, and choiceless awareness—but these are all modern. So where does "nonjudgmental" come from?

It seems to come from the second-century Indian philosopher Nagarjuna, considered by some to be the most important figure in Buddhist thought after the Buddha himself. The Buddhist doctrine of *sunyata* was formulated by Nagarjuna about seven hundred years after the Buddha's death. In Nagarjuna's philosophy of "nonduality," all distinctions of right and wrong, good or bad, future or past, large and small, enlightened or ignorant, are seen as ultimately false. They should be abandoned in favor of the mystical vision of Oneness. Nondualism is the idea out of which Dogen, the founder of Soto Zen, like thousands of Chinese and Tibetan teachers before him, recommended the ultimate transcending of all judgments ("zazen has nothing to do with right or wrong"). However, Dogen wasn't talking about *sati*. He was referring to *sunyata*.

Kabat-Zinn, however, seems to be the first person to use the word "nonjudgmental" as a defining characteristic of *sati*. This descriptor of mindfulness starts with him. It only goes back forty years. It doesn't derive from the Buddha or from any Theravadin source that I know of.

Kabat-Zinn's claim that he is authentically translating *sati* and original Buddhist principles has been taken at face value by most modern writers ever since. No psychologist or researcher of that time knew enough about meditation to know any better. He was criticized by scholars, but their voice is rarely heard in the popular literature. The *Sutta* was virtually unknown except as the iconic source. No one was checking what the Buddha actually said. Through viral replication in the years since, "nonjudgmental" is now embedded in modern consciousness as a defining, nonnegotiable quality of mindfulness.

MINDFULNESS IN THERAPY

So does it matter? Maybe not. There is no doubt that Kabat-Zinn's new definition, by importing a Zen perspective, has vastly expanded the use of meditation as therapy. The emphasis that Modern Mindfulness places on nonjudgmental self-acceptance has some huge therapeutic advantages. It makes meditation far more acceptable to a psychologist's usual clientele. Tens of thousands of people have now benefited from the Modern Mindfulness approach who would never have otherwise considered meditation.

Anxious and depressed people tend to be overly self-criti-cal and dread the idea of further failure. In contrast, the Mod-ern Mindfulness version of mindfulness is often described as being so easy that it is almost impossible to fail. As the bestselling mindfulness author Daniel Siegel says, "There is no particular goal, no effort to 'get rid of' something, just the intention to experience being in the moment."[2]

The emphasis on acceptance also allows mindfulness-based stress reduction to offer a new way of monitoring the peripheral thoughts and sensations that invariably arise in meditation. Unlike classical practices, MBSR is quite tol-erant of the mind's tendency to wander. When meditating, we are bound to periodically lose focus on the body and get distracted by thoughts, emotions, daydreams, sleepiness, impulses, and pains. This can make practitioners very frus-trated, and it often prompts them to abandon the meditation altogether.

MBSR treats this common situation with sympathy and even indulgence. It regards peripheral thoughts, sensations and emotions, good or bad, as integral components of any meditation (which they are). It recommends that we treat these potential distractions "kindly," like visitors who come and go. We are allowed to identify or mentally "note" them, as long as we don't engage with them as much as usual. We are encouraged to regard them as transient mental events of little intrinsic value.

John Daido Loori describes the related Zen practice: "When you're doing shikantaza you don't try to focus on anything specifically, or to make thoughts go away. You sim-ply allow everything to be just the way it is. Thoughts come, thoughts go, and you simply watch them, you keep your awareness on them. It takes a lot of energy and persistence to sit shikantaza, to not get caught up in daydreaming. But little by little, thoughts begin to slow down, and finally they cease to arise."[3] Psychologists will recognize this as the process of extinction: The repeated reduction of a response eventually leads to no response.

Meditators often achieve good states of body-mind stillness through a perpetual, persistent, and ever-more-subtle "letting go" of physical tension and arousal. A meditator who is well embodied will also notice how certain thoughts and emotional responses make her tense up, and so impede her drift toward stillness. This will prompt her to gradually abandon those thoughts and responses as well. This effort to universally "let go" of everything doesn't involve much focused attention, but it can still lead to excellent results.

Some writers even claim that whatever attentional training occurs in MBSR is irrelevant. When meditating, it is still necessary for a practitioner to maintain some degree of focus on the body, but MBSR even discourages this cognitive effort. After "letting go" of a distracting thought, the meditator is instructed to "place" or "rest" the mind gently back on the breath or the body. MBSR promotes a soft form of attention that is supposed to feel almost effortless. This correlates with the important Taoist idea of *wu-wei* (literally, "no-action"). This concept argues that all striving is counterproductive since it would disturb the natural spontaneous purity of the mind.

In MBSR therapy, this passive, nonstriving stance is labeled "acceptance." Acceptance is a useful concept that is rarely emphasized in traditional meditation. Students are encouraged to notice unpleasant sensations and thoughts without resisting them. They are to be reframed as "just" sensations, not requiring a response. Students thus learn to relax despite pain or a bad mood, increasing their capacity to tolerate discomfort and emotional distress. In psychology, this is called "negative affect tolerance" or "pain tolerance."

Trying to forcibly change or get rid of a stubborn pain or mood can be very frustrating for a meditator—or anyone. Strategies to avoid pain by ignoring it have been repeatedly demonstrated to be counterproductive. They actually *increase* arousal and mental agitation. To become more accepting of what can't be changed counteracts our natural tendency toward denial, suppression, and "experiential avoidance" and actually reduces the physiological markers of stress. The "just watching," "open" stance recommended by MBSR thus sits in the zone of neutral affect between reacting to discomfort or suppressing it. This is one of the most positive outcomes of the MBSR method.

Nonetheless, a state of pure nonjudgmental acceptance is still quite hard to achieve. It is more of a spiritual ideal (*sunyata*) to aspire to than a concrete reality. (This also explains why it is so difficult to do research on.) No matter how hard we try to "just watch what happens" we will invariably make appraisals and readjustments along the way. Furthermore, the instructions on MBSR's guided meditation CDs gently encourage these micro-judgments and reappraisals. The students do want to relax and calm their minds, and the instructors want to help them do so.

If we notice that a muscle is unnecessarily tense, we release it. If we notice an emotional overreaction as such, we downgrade it. If we notice an obsessive thought, we discount it as "not worth thinking about" and refocus on the body. The instructions frequently refer to cutting off, "defusing," objectifying, "letting go," "decentering," and generally devaluing unwanted thought and emotion. Does all this really qualify as being a "nonjudgmental" attitude toward whatever happens?

Through the practice of MBSR, the client can learn how to relax his body, tolerate negative mood, and become less reactive and better able to control his thoughts and impulses. There would be no point in doing the lengthy training otherwise. So how can we reconcile all this positive, goal-directed change with the definition of mindfulness as "nonjudgmental acceptance of present-moment experience" or "just watching what happens without reacting"? That's a problem that researchers are now trying to sort out.

25

The Modern Definition

*Although the contemporary view of the concept
"mindfulness" is increasingly becoming part of
popular culture, there remains no single "correct" or
"authoritative definition" of mindfulness and the
concept is often trivialized and conflated with many
common interpretations.*

—DAVID VAGO AND DAVID SILBERSWEIG[1]

The word "mindful" as an adjective dates from the fourteenth century. It means to pay attention, or to take care to avoid mistakes and improve performance. That definition still works equally well today. In 1881, however, T. W. Rhys Davids chose to resuscitate "mindfulness," an archaic noun form of the word, to translate *sati* (attention). By shifting the concept of "mindful" from an adjective to a noun, and strongly associating it with Buddhism, he inadvertently opened up the floodgates for new possible usages.

"Mindfulness" as a noun now represents a diverse range of "things" in a way that the word "attention" could never do.

Mindfulness can now be a meditation practice (Vipassana), a therapy (mindfulness-based cognitive therapy), an ideal state of mind (nonjudgmental acceptance), a way of life ("be here now"), a cognitive function (attention), a popular movement, and the essence of Buddhism itself. This is the protean bundle of phenomena that for convenience I refer to as Modern Mindfulness.

When Kabat-Zinn chose to give a Zen interpretation to mindfulness, he virtually had a clean slate to work with. In 1979 there were no more than two or three readily available books on the *Satipatthana Sutta*. I assume he knew Nyanaponika's *The Heart of Buddhist Meditation* (1962). He may also have read Soma Thera's *The Way of Mindfulness* (1949), which was the book that I started with in 1975. However, the field of English-language literature on early Buddhism is still tiny even now, and there is very little dialogue between the players. Modern scholarship has a more accurate understanding of the past, but it seems to operate in a different universe from meditators, monks, psychologists, and popular writers.

In the East, the teaching of Buddhism remains an oral tradition. The original texts are in languages (Pali and Sanskrit) that are just as dead as Latin. Senior monks have absolute freedom to interpret the texts as they wish. In a similar way, Kabat-Zinn's new definition of mindfulness undoubtedly arose in the informal oral context of meditation instruction. It is quite loose—more descriptive and allusive than definitive—and he frequently rephrases it to suit his purposes in talks and books and articles. But what works perfectly well in an oral context is often too indeterminate for scientific application. Researchers struggle to make Kabat-Zinn's definition of mindfulness work, and some have questioned whether it can be regarded as a definition at all.

AN EVOLVING DEFINITION

So what is mindfulness? A commonsense answer would be that it is a standard meditation practice, as in chapter 1. Focusing on the body for relaxation and mental calm is certainly a necessary, if not sufficient, requirement. Few people think of mindfulness as being anything other than a meditation practice, but it is rarely defined this way.

In his 1994 bestseller, *Wherever You Go, There You Are*, Kabat-Zinn defined mindfulness as "paying attention in a particular way: on purpose, in the present moment, and nonjudgmentally."[2] Although this states that mindfulness has a purpose, Kabat-Zinn doesn't spell out what that is. This places tremendous weight on the concluding word "nonjudgmentally." By default, it seems that the purpose of mindfulness is to achieve a state free of all judgments.

In 2003, however, Kabat-Zinn presented a revised "working definition" in a paper for the journal *Clinical Psychology: Science and Practice*, in which he defined mindfulness as "the awareness that emerges through paying attention on purpose, in the present moment, and nonjudgmentally to the unfolding of experience."[3]

The difference between these two definitions is significant. In the science journal, mindfulness is no longer described as a form of attention. It is identified as the emergent quality of "awareness" *that arises from* paying attention. This suggests that you would start a meditation in a non-mindful state and gradually achieve mindfulness as you approach some degree of body-mind stillness (*passaddhi*) or equanimity or emptiness (*sunyata*). This new definition reorients Modern Mindfulness further away from "attention," which is a perpetually volatile cognitive function, toward a relatively stable and ideal "state of mind."

The word "nonjudgmental" is still important, but it remains problematic. A definition built on a negative is difficult to grasp, so other descriptors are frequently included. For example, in the 2003 paper Kabat-Zinn added: "The words for heart and mind are the same in Asian languages; thus 'mindfulness' includes an affectionate, compassionate quality within the attending; a sense of open-hearted friendly presence and interest."[4] (See Thanissaro's criticisms that follow.) These new descriptors all incidentally tend to push the meaning of mindfulness even further from "attention" and more toward "an ideal state of mind."

When I was a young meditator in the Tibetan tradition, I was encouraged to look into my heart and listen to "the Buddha within" (the *bodhicitta*). This approach effectively sidelines the historical Buddha and even the whole Theravada tradition, but it is a common strategy in Tibetan and Zen Buddhism. It is a large part of the Mahayana's polemic dismissal of original Buddhism and the Pali Canon.

This belief that intuition alone is an infallible guide to truth is also a strong part of the American psyche. The New England transcendentalist Ralph Waldo Emerson's great essay *On Self-Reliance* (1841) argues that a firm intuition is always superior to learning, cultural knowledge, the dictates of authorities, and even the apparent facts of a given matter. Jon Kabat-Zinn's efforts to intuit and describe the ideal meditative state of mind are in keeping with this approach. It may be no coincidence that Emerson lived and worked only twenty miles away from Boston, where Kabat-Zinn developed MBSR. It seems that Emerson had a big aura. This faith in the reliability of intuition and personal interpretation saturates the popular literature about mindfulness. In the absence of any doctrinal guidelines, any journalist or popular writer can have a go at defining mindfulness with little fear of criticism.

WHAT DO THE SCHOLARS SAY?

Buddhist scholars, however, are much more concerned with the historic facts and the literal meaning of words. So how do modern definitions of mindfulness compare with *sati* as I described it in chapter 14? First, Modern Mindfulness is a more complicated construction. It contains more essential adjectives and qualifiers than *sati*. Second, *sati* refers to a cognitive function (attention), whereas Modern Mindfulness refers to an ideal meditative state of mind. Third, the purpose of *sati* (the conscious perception and evaluation of something) is to make good judgments prior to a response, whereas Modern Mindfulness is invariably described as a passive and nonjudgmental state. Buddhists and scholars have repeatedly criticized Modern Mindfulness on this last point, but their pop-guns have had no effect on the Modern Mindfulness juggernaut.

In 2004 Scott Bishop et al. cleverly converted Kabat-Zinn's term into academic language. Mindfulness, they wrote, "has been described as a kind of nonelaborative, nonjudgmental, present-centered awareness in which each thought, feeling, or sensation that arises in the attentional field is acknowledged and accepted as it is."[5] This definition, however, is clearly out of line with the traditional model, according to the Buddhist scholar B. Alan Wallace. In his 2006 book, *The Attention Revolution: Unlocking the Power of the Focused Mind*, Wallace says that "the modern understanding departs significantly from the Buddha's own account of sati and those of the most authoritative commentators in the Theravada and Indian Mahayana traditions."[6]

Wallace supports his point by quoting from an early text called the *Milandapanha*, an early Buddhist attempt to explain the nature of *sati*, which says that *sati* "calls to mind wholesome and unwholesome tendencies."[7] *Sati* sees ahead to the outcomes of these tendencies, explains Wallace: It identifies particular tendencies as either beneficial or unbeneficial, helpful or not helpful. Wallace goes on to say, "Rather than refraining from categorizing experiences in a nonjudgmental fashion . . . sati is said to distinguish between wholesome and unwholesome, beneficial and unbeneficial tendencies. The contrast between ancient and modern accounts is striking."[8]

In sum, there is no mystery in scholarly terms about what *sati* means, or at least what it is not. It has been exhaustively analyzed in the traditional commentaries. It would be fair to say that no serious Buddhist scholar would agree with the Modern Mindfulness definition of *sati* as "nonjudgmental." It is completely unsupported. Not a shred of evidence exists for such a meaning in the original texts, and there is a mountain of evidence to the contrary.

So how did *sati* come to be associated with qualities such as nonjudgment, acceptance, and even compassion? In his thoughtful article "Mindfulness Defined," Thanissaro

Bhikkhu makes a perceptive observation. Each of those terms is found in the original texts, but they don't apply to *sati*!

Thanissaro points out that the word "nonjudgmental" correlates much better with the Buddhist term *upekkha* than with *sati*. *Upekkha* is that state of stillness and detachment in which all one's affective responses to the world have vanished. The absence of liking or disliking means the absence of any "approach or withdraw" tendency. This also implies no judgment and therefore no decision to act in any way.

Thanissaro also comments that the word "acceptance" is much closer to the Buddhist term *sukha* (contentment) than to *sati*. *Sukha* is a kind of deep unshakeable happiness independent of circumstances. According to Thanissaro, it includes the sense of present-moment enjoyment: "Appreciating the moment for all the little pleasures it can offer: the taste of a raisin, the feel of a cup in your hands."[9]

He goes on to say, "I've heard mindfulness described as 'affectionate attention' or 'compassionate attention,' but affection and compassion aren't the same as mindfulness. They're separate things."[10] ("Compassion" equates loosely to the Pali words *metta* and *karuna*, but it is quite unrelated to *sati*.)

Thanissaro continues: "Popular books offer a lot of other definitions of mindfulness, a lot of other duties it's supposed to fulfill, so many that the poor word gets totally stretched out of shape. It even gets defined as Awakening, as in the phrase—a moment of mindfulness is a moment of Awakening—something the Buddha would never say."[11]

Thanissaro's conclusion is very sensible: "It's best not to load the word mindfulness with too many meanings or to assign it too many functions."[12] Pali and Sanskrit, the two languages of ancient Buddhist texts, are both capable of highly refined psychological distinctions. This subtlety is destroyed when one word is expected to serve a range of often contradictory meanings.

Thanissaro's analysis also explains why the modern definitions of mindfulness have failed to gel. *Sati* means attention. This is a single unified function: the perception and evaluation of something prior to a response. Modern Mindfulness, however, is an umbrella term, covering ideas of mindfulness as attention (*sati*) + being nonjudgmental (*upekkha*) + acceptance (*sukha*) + compassion (*metta*) + body-mind stillness (*passaddhi*) + openness (*sunyata*). It is also regarded as a therapy, a meditation practice, a way of life, and the essence of Buddhism itself. It would be fair to say that mindfulness as described in the psychological literature is not a unified concept at all. Let's hope that the researchers will eventually disambiguate it back into its component parts, and assess their relative importance. My guess is that attention (*sati*) is probably more valuable than the rest of the mindfulness bundle combined.

IS MINDFULNESS MORE MORAL THAN ATTENTION?

Sati is a Buddhist word but not a Buddhist concept. Attention is a universal and ubiquitous cognitive function, and it is not even moral. The Buddha said, as is obvious, that *sati* can be used equally well for good or bad purposes. For example, soldiers need to focus well to kill. The Buddha even had terms that highlighted this. He talked about "right" mindfulness (*samma-sati*) and "wrong" mindfulness (*miccha-sati*). However, this doesn't sit well with psychologists or modern Buddhists or popular writers, all of whom would prefer a more elevated description of *sati*.

Nyanaponika proposed a solution in his 1962 book that is now commonly adopted by all. He spent two pages brilliantly describing *sati* as attention, "the cardinal function of consciousness." He links it to memory, heightened perception, associative and abstract thinking, and the research work of the scientist and philosopher.

Finally he makes a distinction between "attention" (*sati*) and "*right* attention" (*samma-sati*). This latter term is the seventh stage in the Eightfold Path of training contained in the Four Noble Truths. Nyanaponika argued that the word "mindfulness" should only be used for "*right* mindfulness." It should only refer to that kind of attention that is directed toward moral goals in the Buddhist context. Otherwise, it is just mundane, everyday "attention."[13] Ever since Nyanaponika's proposal, "mindfulness" has carried some kind of moral quality, however ill defined that might be.

When Buddhist writers discuss mindfulness, then, they particularly identify it with *samma-sati* rather than just *sati*. For non-Buddhists, mindfulness is less specific, but it still suggests a Buddhist-flavored, compassionate, friendly, passive kind of attention. Of course, this complicates the term enormously. Mindfulness becomes the kind of attention that a good Buddhist would approve of, but how would you scientifically describe that? Nonetheless, the psychologists' claims to authority based on Buddhist sources do have some validity. They have mistranslated *sati*, but, perhaps in compensation, they have embellished it with other elements of Buddhist morality.

26

Using the Language

Scientists and psychologists routinely take words from common English and redefine them as technical terms. If a word has two or three separate meanings, we will still tend to assume that they are all *essentially* the same. Our habitual laziness alone guarantees this blurring of distinctions and the blunting of our mental tools. The field of mindfulness is particularly vulnerable to this cognitive confusion.

If a word has multiple meanings, we need to know which one we are using in any context. A psychologist recently contacted me with a problem. She was contracted to teach mindfulness to improve work safety on a mining site, but she couldn't see how developing a state of nonjudgmental acceptance would help. Of course it can't. She needed to teach mindfulness in its sense of "paying attention to avoid mistakes."

It makes a huge difference whether we see mindfulness as a discriminating, choice-making function or as a passive, meditative state of mind. There are strange consequences if we take the Modern Mindfulness definition of nonjudgmental acceptance seriously. We need to make judgments continuously all day long. We have to be mindful to care for a child, to handle machinery, or to shop for food. We couldn't cross a road safely in a state of nonjudgmental acceptance. Nor if we tried and got hit by a car is nonjudgmental acceptance the best response to a broken leg. Modern Mindfulness would be entirely counterproductive in these situations.

Defining Modern Mindfulness as an ideal state of mind limits it enormously. It locks up mindfulness with the monastic virtues of inactivity, emotional detachment, and withdrawal. Unfortunately, this is a tiny part of our daily experience. It seems that we can be mindful in the modern sense only when no response is required—for example, when we are meditating, or in a therapy session, or on a retreat. Whenever we had to make a judgment or choose between options, we would actually have to *stop* being mindful to do so. Nor could we mindfully think about the past or future.

Of course this is quite absurd. No one goes that far, but this is the problem with the Modern Mindfulness definition. If taken literally the way technical terms should be, it can only apply within meditation, or when no action is required, or when it is best to temporarily suspend action. On the other hand, the definition of *sati* as attention (which is naturally evaluative), does not suffer from this limitation. It is applicable all day long and clearly improves the quality of our actions.

I've discussed this paradox with psychologists. As a writer I'm prone to be pedantic about the accurate use of words. I've found that psychologists are likely to be more pragmatic. In mental health therapy, "nonjudgmental" usually means being *less* judgmental, or less reactive, or temporarily suspending judgment, or improving a judgment, or being less self-critical, or seeing something "objectively," or even making a correct judgment. But it hardly ever means making no judgment at all.

NONJUDGMENTAL

If people associate any one word with mindfulness, it is Kabat-Zinn's "nonjudgmental." In his 1990 book on stress and self-care, *Full Catastrophe Living*, Kabat-Zinn says that our automatic tendency to evaluate our experience as either "good" or bad" prevents us from seeing things "as they actually are." "This habit of categorizing and judging our experience locks us into automatic reactions ... that often have no objective basis at all. ... When practicing mindfulness it is important to recognize this judging quality of mind when it appears and assume a broader perspective by intentionally suspending judgment and assuming a stance of impartiality."[1] In other words, "being nonjudgmental" means the *suspension* of judgment, and "impartiality" means making no response either way—no "approach or withdrawal tendency."

Since every perception comes with an inbuilt judgment or valence, to be mindful means temporarily suspending that judgment and asking, "Is this accurate or not?" In this way, we can create a gap between stimulus and response for a better judgment to arise. The usual outcome is to down-regulate an emotion, or reappraise a thought. The reappraisal doesn't even need to be conscious. Most commonly a *conscious* perception leads to an *automatic* reappraisal anyway.

In the therapy context, "nonjudgmental" usually means being *less* judgmental than usual. Or it is about *improving* a judgment rather than abandoning it altogether. Modern Mindfulness writers often distinguish between what they consider to be automatic, thoughtless judgments (the bad ones) and conscious, considered ones (the good ones).

"Being nonjudgmental" can also be used to mean seeing something "objectively," as if from the outside. If we are able to see the pain of cancer as "just sensation," we apparently feel less judgmental about it. We no longer evaluate the pain as "bad." Similarly, if we are able to see a suicidal thought as "just a thought," we have essentially neutralized it. We no longer see it as a dangerous thought that requires some response.

"Being nonjudgmental" in a therapy setting often means little more than refraining from harsh judgments about oneself. It means not giving in to negative self-talk and self-criticism. One writer glosses it as not criticizing oneself "for having irrational or inappropriate emotions." It means "Don't beat yourself up!" and it relates to Western psychological virtues such as self-esteem and positive regard.

"Being nonjudgmental" can also mean making an *accurate* judgment. A psychologist recently explained to me that the injunction to be "nonjudgmental" only applies to "bad," self-destructive judgments. The good judgments we make are quite okay. When I asked her whether an appropriate judgment was still a judgment, she smiled and said, "No. That would be an evaluation." She was trying to draw a line in a bucket of water and she knew it. And how can you decide which is a good or bad judgment without judging them?

The word "acceptance," on the other hand, is the positive side of "nonjudgmental," and it is a useful concept when we meditate. Hardly anyone has a "perfect" meditation. Most of us have some physical discomforts or unwanted thoughts or emotions, however minor, when we sit. Moreover our lives are often a mess. Because it is so easy to live in denial, fantasy, distraction, and hope, it can take a lot of mindful effort and courage to see where we actually are. "Being present" is not just about smelling the roses. It is also about smelling the shit. Persuading people to sit still for a long time trains them to be more comfortable within their less-than-perfect, present-moment experience as it occurs during the meditation. Psychologists call this "negative affect tolerance." It is similar to older Stoic virtues such as patience and endurance.

"Nonjudgmental" is often promoted as a self-evident universal virtue on a par with compassion and tolerance. It seems to imply that making any kind of judgment, at least when we meditate, is wrong and is likely to increase our suffering. Psychologists and popular writers would of course say, "I don't mean it that way," but this is a persistent problem with the term. In practice the word "nonjudgmental" *always* has to be qualified.

Writers often tie themselves up in knots trying to explain it. In *The Mindful Brain*, Daniel Siegel somewhat apologetically says that "this nonjudgmental view in many ways can be interpreted to mean something like 'not grasping onto judgments,'" but "being able to note those judgments and disengage from them may be what nonjudgmental behavior feels like in practice."[2] And the clinician Ruth Baer says that if you label a negative judgment as "aversion," then it ceases to be a judgment: "Disliking peanut butter is not a judgment. Rather an aversion to peanut butter can be mindfully observed and accepted without judgment."[3]

"Nonjudgmental" can work as a general mood-setter in meditation. It can also work to suggest a more sympathetic attitude toward yourself. As a technical term, it lacks precision. Many Modern Mindfulness writers see its practical shortcomings in that respect and prefer to use other terms. Fortunately, there are some excellent alternatives.

"Nonreactive" is a better technical term than "nonjudgmental" because it more accurately describes what happens. We can't avoid making judgments, but we can choose not to react. We may quite correctly judge a chronic pain or a depressive state as "bad," but we can reduce our usual response to them. Many writers and researchers are now dropping "nonjudgmental" as unworkable and are using "nonreactive" instead. This small shift alone is helping to make the language of Modern Mindfulness more compatible with our actual experience.

Another good replacement term in relation to thought is "nonelaborative." This term describes the mental action of noticing an emerging thought but not entering into an open-ended conversation with it. It involves responding to a thought but in a way that quickly closes it down. Non-elaboration is an essential part of attention as a cognitive skill. We have to be able to shut down any thought in order to switch to another or to maintain focus on a more important one. In meditation language, this is called "noticing without reacting."

An even more accurate term is "no secondary processing." To notice anything at all, however slight or subliminal, including thoughts, involves what cognitive psychology calls "processing." Within milliseconds the brain assesses it: "What is this? (Perception.) Is it good or bad, useful or useless?

(Evaluation.) Does it deserve any more attention or some action? (Response)."

This "primary processing" occurs with every momentary change in our inner and outer environments, and it can't be avoided. It is mostly automatic or unconscious, and the most common response is a nonresponse. When meditating, however, we can make sure that this primary processing doesn't spill over into elaborative, goal-directed secondary processing.

Despite all the above, the word "nonjudgmental" can still be awkward to use. Paradoxically, the main function of mindfulness in vernacular English is to *improve* our judgments, not to abandon them. For at least six centuries, "to be mindful" has meant "to pay attention in order to avoid mistakes or improve performance." The modern understanding of "mindfulness" as meaning "nonjudgmental and accepting," on the other hand, has only been around for forty years.

This raises an obvious point. There is surely nothing wrong with making judgments. We do this thousands of times each day. Good judgments really are good. Only faulty, self-destructive judgments are bad. Aristotle regarded an ability for this type of discernment as the first of the social virtues. He said that being able to make good judgments in situations of uncertainty is essential for a well-directed, satisfying life.

To summarize, mindfulness in the sense of "nonjudgmental" can be a useful rule-of-thumb term in therapy or meditation instruction. It is an umbrella term for a wide range of loosely related concepts, but it tends to crumble at the first level of scrutiny. Anyone who works in the field of mindfulness should recognize the limitations of this iconic word, and use it carefully.

NOTES

Introduction

1 The *Satipatthana Sutta* is the tenth in an important collection of 152 *sutta* (texts of the Buddha's sermons) called *The Middle Length Discourses of the Buddha*. All of these texts are part of the Pali Canon, a collection of original discourses and monastic rules set out by the Buddha and recorded in Pali (the liturgical language of early Buddhism)—which is why we discuss them using the Pali word *sutta* rather than the more familiar Sanskrit word, *sutra*.

2 David R. Vago and David A. Silbersweig, "Self-Awareness, Self-Regulation, and Self-Transcendence (S-ART): A Framework for Understanding the Neurobiological Mechanisms of Mindfulness," *Frontiers in Human Neuroscience* 6 (October 2012), introduction.

Chapter 7: Why Focus on the Body?

1 Bhikkhu Bodhi and Bhikkhu Nanamoli, *The Middle Length Discourses of the Buddha* (Boston: Wisdom, 1995), 949.

2 Bodhi and Nanamoli, *The Middle Length Discourses*, 949.

3 Bodhi and Nanamoli, *The Middle Length Discourses*, 953.

Chapter 8: To Sit or Not to Sit

1 This is my own translation, which resembles other translations except that I have added the exclamation mark to the phrase "By not thinking!" If you want a direct taste of Dogen's style, you can find various translations of "Fukanzazengi" on the internet. It is only three pages long. If you also examine his *Bendowa* (twenty pages, also easy to find on the internet), you will have almost all you need to understand Soto Zen.

2 Dogen, "Fukanzazengi: Universal Recommendations for Zazen," trans. Norman Waddell and Abe Masao, in *The Art of Just Sitting*, ed. John Daido Loori (Boston: Wisdom, 2002), 23.

3 Dogen, *Shobogenzo Zuimonki: A Primer of Soto Zen*, trans. Reiho Masunaga (Honolulu: University Press of Hawaii, 1975), 44.

4 Dogen, "Fukanzazengi: Universal Recommendations for Zazen," 21.

5 Sheng Yen, *Attaining the Way: A Guide to the Practice of Chan Buddhism* (Boston: Shambhala Publications, 2006), 163.

6 Jon Kabat-Zinn, *Coming to Our Senses* (New York: Hyperion, 2003), 65.

Chapter 14: *Sati:* The Analysis of a Word

1 Nyanaponika Thera, *The Heart of Buddhist Meditation: Satipatthana* (London: Century Hutchinson, 1962), 24.

2 Thanissaro Bhikkhu, "Mindfulness Defined," accesstoinsight.org/lib/authors/thanissaro/mindfulnessdefined.html (2008).

3 U Pandita, *In This Very Life* (Boston: Wisdom, 1992), 100.

4 Soma Thera, *The Way of Mindfulness* (Colombo, Ceylon: Vajrarama, 1949), xii.

5 Buddhaghosa, *The Path of Purification*, trans. Nanamoli Bhikkhu (Kandy, Sri Lanka: Buddhist Publication Society, 1991), 467.

6 Buddhaghosa, *The Path of Purification*, 262.

7 U Pandita, *In This Very Life*, 100.

8 Soma Thera, *The Way of Mindfulness*, xiii.

9 Buddhaghosa, *The Path of Purification*, 658.

10 Joseph Goldstein, *Mindfulness: A Practical Guide to Awakening* (Boulder, CO: Sounds True, 2013), 11.

11 Analayo, *Satipatthana: The Direct Path to Realization* (Cambridge, MA: Windhorse, 2003), 41.

12 Soma Thera, *The Way of Mindfulness*, xiii.

13 B. Alan Wallace and Bhikkhu Bodhi, "The Nature of Mindfulness and Its Role in Buddhist Meditation: A Correspondence between B. Alan Wallace and the Venerable Bhikkhu Bodhi" (unpublished manuscript held at the Santa Barbara Institute for Consciousness Studies, Santa Barbara, CA, winter 2006). Bodhi cared for Nyanaponika in his declining years.

14 Nyanaponika Thera, *The Heart of Buddhist Meditation*, 39.

15 Soma Thera, *The Way of Mindfulness*, xiii.

16 Buddhaghosa, *The Path of Purification*, 24.

17 U Pandita, *In This Very Life*, 99. Notice that U Pandita also dislikes the term "mindfulness" as a translation of *sati*, as do all the Buddhist commentators in the chapter.

18 Kabat-Zinn, *Coming to Our Senses*, 65.

19 Dogen, *Shobogenzo Zuimonki: A Primer of Soto Zen*, 44.

20 Robert H. Sharf, "Is Mindfulness Buddhist? (and Why It Matters)," *Transcultural Psychiatry* 52, no. 4 (2015): 478.

21 Sharf, "Is Mindfulness Buddhist? (and Why It Matters)," 476.

Chapter 16: Emotion at the Atomic Level

1 Bodhi and Nanamoli, *The Middle Length Discourses*, 217.

2 Buddhaghosa, *The Path of Purification*, 337.

Chapter 17: Painful Emotion

1 People often refuse to believe me when I say the Buddha was an extreme ascetic. It is so alien to the popular view of him that I've even been accused of lying. So here are some further quotes from

the Buddha to illustrate his views, from Bhikku Bodhi and Bhikku Nanamoli's *The Middle Length Discourses of the Buddha*: "This body should be regarded as impermanent, as suffering, as a disease, as a tumour, as a dart, as a calamity, as an affliction, as alien, as disintegrating, as void, as not-self" (605). "Sensory pleasures are impermanent, hollow, false, deceptive, illusory. Sorrow, lamentation, pain, grief and despair are born from those who are dear to you" (718). "The pursuit of sensual desires—low, vulgar, coarse, ignoble and unbeneficial—is a state beset by suffering, vexation, despair, and fever" (1080).

Satipatthana Sutta itself has meditations on the nine stages of the decomposition of a corpse and a contemplation of the thirty-two parts of the body as repulsive. The Buddha felt that the deliberate cultivation of disgust was a good antidote to the snares of sensuality.

Chapter 18: States of Mind

1 Because the Pali Canon is addressed almost entirely to monks, Buddhism lacks the sophisticated social prescriptions that we find in other religions. It can't draw on the national histories and dramatic stories of human interactions that serve as guides for behavior in the Western religions or in Hinduism. Even its myths tend to be confined to moral homilies and stories of heroic monks. Buddhism has little to say about familial or societal norms other than recommending that laypeople try to behave like monks as much as possible.

2 U Pandita, *In This Very Life*, 110.

3 Buddhaghosa, *The Path of Purification*, 658.

4 B. Alan Wallace, *The Attention Revolution* (Somerville, MA: Wisdom, 2006), 101.

5 I can't find the exact quote, but there is a similar metaphor in another original Pali text, the Anguttara Nikaya 3:32.

Chapter 19: Optimizing Emotion

1 If you suspect that your diagnosis for anxiety or depression isn't right, and the medication isn't helping, I recommend this book by Edward Shorter (Oxford: Oxford University Press, 2013). I can also recommend *Anatomy of an Epidemic: Magic Bullets, Psychiatric Drugs, and the*

Astonishing Rise of Mental Illness in America by Robert Whitaker (New York: Crown, 2010).

2 Allen Frances, *Saving Normal* (New York: Harper Collins, 2013), xiv.

3 Frances, *Saving Normal*, xvii.

4 Antonio Damasio, *Descartes' Error* (New York: Penguin, 1994), 34–39.

5 Damasio, *Descartes' Error*, 41.

Chapter 20: Embodied Thought

1 Paul R. Fulton and Ronald D. Siegel, "Buddhist and Western Psychology: Seeking Common Ground," in *Mindfulness and Psychotherapy*, 2nd ed., ed. Christopher K. Germer, Ronald D. Siegel, and Paul R. Fulton (New York: Guilford, 2013), 44–45.

2 Mark Williams and Danny Penman, *Mindfulness: An Eight-Week Plan for Finding Peace in a Frantic World* (New York: Rodale, 2011), 11.

3 Paul R. Fulton, "Mindfulness as Clinical Training," in *Mindfulness and Psychotherapy*, ed. Germer, Siegel, and Fulton, 70.

4 Jon Kabat-Zinn, *Arriving at Your Own Door* (New York: Hyperion, 2007), 49.

5 Jon Kabat-Zinn, *Full Catastrophe Living*, 2nd ed. (London: Piatkus, 2013), 65.

6 Dogen, "Fukanzazengi: Universal Recommendations for Zazen," 22.

7 Dogen, "Fukanzazengi: Universal Recommendations for Zazen," 21.

8 John Daido Loori, "Yaoshan's Non-Thinking," in *The Art of Just Sitting*, ed. Loori (Boston: Wisdom, 2002), 140. Dogen's baroque and hyperbolic masterpiece, nearly one thousand pages long, is the *Shobogenzo*, which elaborates at great length on the themes presented here. Fortunately, Dogen's key ideas on practice are found in the three-page "Fukanzazengi," which is readily available in various translations on Google. His other major text is *Bendowa*.

9 Hakuun Yasutani, "Shikantaza," in *The Art of Just Sitting*, ed. Loori, 51–52.

10 Bodhi and Nanamoli, *The Middle Length Discourses*, 941.

11 Bodhi and Nanamoli, *The Middle Length Discourses*, 949.

Chapter 21: Attention

1 Joaquin M. Fuster, *The Prefrontal Cortex*, 5th ed. (London: Academic Press, 2015), 3.

Chapter 22: Good Judgment

1 Analayo, *Satipatthana*, 41.

2 Bodhi and Nanamoli, *The Middle Length Discourses*, 451.

Chapter 23: The Scientific Evidence

1 Linda Heuman, "Meditation Nation," tricycle.com/blog/meditation-nation (April 25, 2014).

2 Scott R. Bishop et al., "Mindfulness: A Proposed Operational Definition," *Clinical Psychology: Science and Practice* 11, no. 3 (2004): 231.

3 Madhav Goyal et al., "Meditation Programs for Psychological Stress and Well-Being: A Systematic Review and Meta-Analysis," *JAMA Internal Medicine* 174, no. 3 (March 2014): 357.

4 Sedlmeier et al., "The Psychological Effects of Meditation: A Meta-Analysis," *Psychological Bulletin* 138, no. 6 (November 2012): 1139.

Chapter 24: The Story of Modern Mindfulness

1 Taigen Dan Leighton, *Cultivating the Empty Field: The Silent Illumination of Zen Master Hongzhi* (Tokyo: Tuttle, 2000), introduction, second paragraph.

2 Daniel J. Siegel, *The Mindful Brain* (New York: W. W. Norton, 2007), 19.

3 Loori, "Yaoshan's Non-Thinking," 138.

Chapter 25: The Modern Definition

1 Vago and Silbersweig, "Self-Awareness, Self-Regulation, and Self-Transcendence (S-ART)," introduction.

2 Jon Kabat-Zinn, *Wherever You Go, There You Are: Mindfulness Meditation in Everyday Life* (New York: Hyperion, 1994), 4.

3 Jon Kabat-Zinn, "Mindfulness-Based Interventions in Context: Past, Present, and Future," *Clinical Psychology: Science and Practice* 10, no. 2 (2003): 145.

4 Kabat-Zinn, "Mindfulness-Based Interventions," 145.

5 Bishop et al., "Mindfulness: A Proposed Operational Definition," 230.

6 Wallace, *The Attention Revolution*, 62.

7 Wallace, *The Attention Revolution*, 61.

8 Wallace, *The Attention Revolution*, 61.

9 Thanissaro, "Mindfulness Defined."

10 Thanissaro, "Mindfulness Defined."

11 Thanissaro, "Mindfulness Defined."

12 Thanissaro, "Mindfulness Defined."

13 Nyanaponika, *The Heart of Buddhist Meditation*, 35–42.

Chapter 26: Using the Language

1 Kabat-Zinn, *Full Catastrophe Living*, 22.

2 Siegel, *The Mindful Brain*, 10.

3 Ruth A. Baer, *Mindfulness-Based Treatment Approaches: A Clinician's Guide* (San Diego, CA: Elsevier, 2006), 21.

REFERENCES

Analayo. *Satipatthana: The Direct Path to Realization*. Cambridge, MA: Windhorse, 2003.

Baer, Ruth A. *Mindfulness-Based Treatment Approaches: A Clinician's Guide*. San Diego, CA: Elsevier, 2006.

Bishop, Scott R., et al. "Mindfulness: A Proposed Operational Definition." *Clinical Psychology: Science and Practice* 11, no. 3 (2004): 230–41.

Bodhi, Bhikkhu, and Bhikkhu Nanamoli. *The Middle Length Discourses of the Buddha*. Boston: Wisdom, 1995.

Buddhaghosa. *The Path of Purification*. Translated by Nanamoli Bhikkhu. Kandy, Sri Lanka: Buddhist Publication Society, 1991.

Damasio, Antonio. *Descartes' Error*. New York: Penguin, 1994.

Dogen. *Shobogenzo Zuimonki: A Primer of Soto Zen*. Translated by Reiho Masunaga. Honolulu: University Press of Hawaii, 1975.

Dogen. *Moon in a Dewdrop*. Edited by Kazuaki Tanahashi. New York: North Point Press, 1985.

Dogen. "Fukanzazengi: Universal Recommendations for Zazen." Translated by Norman Waddell and Abe Masao. In *The Art of Just Sitting*, edited by John Daido Loori. Boston: Wisdom, 2002.

Dogen. *Shobogenzo*. Edited by Kazuaki Tanahashi. Boston: Shambala Publications, 2012.

Frances, Allen. *Saving Normal*. New York: HarperCollins, 2013.

Fuster, Joaquin M. *The Prefrontal Cortex*. 5th ed. London: Academic Press, 2015.

Germer, Christopher K., Ronald D. Siegel, and Paul R. Fulton, eds. *Mindfulness and Psychotherapy*. 2nd ed. New York: Guilford, 2013.

Goldstein, Joseph. *Mindfulness: A Practical Guide to Awakening*. Boulder, CO: Sounds True, 2013.

Goyal, Madhav, et al. "Meditation Programs for Psychological Stress and Well-Being: A Systematic Review and Meta-Analysis." *JAMA Internal Medicine* 174, no. 3 (March 2014): 357–68.

Grossman, Paul, and Nicholas T. Van Dam. "Mindfulness, by Any Other Name . . . Trials and Tribulations of Sati in Western Psychology and Science." *Contemporary Buddhism* 12, no. 1 (2011): 219–39.

Heuman, Linda. "Meditation Nation." tricycle.com/blog/meditation-nation, April 25, 2014.

Kabat-Zinn, Jon. *Wherever You Go, There You Are: Mindfulness Meditation in Everyday Life*. New York: Hyperion, 1994.

Kabat-Zinn, Jon. *Coming to Our Senses*. New York: Hyperion, 2003.

Kabat-Zinn, Jon. "Mindfulness-Based Interventions in Context: Past, Present, and Future." *Clinical Psychology: Science and Practice* 10, no. 2 (2003): 144–56.

Kabat-Zinn, Jon. *Arriving at Your Own Door*. New York: Hyperion, 2007.

Kabat-Zinn, Jon. "Some Reflections on the Origins of MBSR, Skillful Means, and the Trouble with Maps." *Contemporary Buddhism* 12, no. 1 (2011): 281–306.

Kabat-Zinn, Jon. *Full Catastrophe Living*. 2nd ed. London: Piatkus, 2013.

Leighton, Taigen Dan. *Cultivating the Empty Field: The Silent Illumination of Zen Master Hongzhi*. Tokyo: Tuttle, 2000.

Loori, John Daido, ed. *The Art of Just Sitting*. Boston: Wisdom, 2002.

Nyanaponika Thera. *The Heart of Buddhist Meditation: Satipatthana*. London: Century Hutchinson, 1962.

Rhys Davids, Thomas William, ed. and trans. *Buddhist Suttas*. Oxford: Clarendon Press, 1881.

Sedlmeier, Eberth, et al. "The Psychological Effects of Meditation: A Meta-Analysis." *Psychological Bulletin* 138, no. 6 (November 2012): 1139–71.

Sharf, Robert H. "Is Mindfulness Buddhist? (and Why It Matters)." *Transcultural Psychiatry* 52, no. 4 (2015): 470–84. (This paper closely follows Sharf's 2013 YouTube lecture: "Mindfulness or Mindlessness: Traditional and Modern Buddhist Critiques of 'Bare Awareness.'" youtube.com/watch?v=c6Avs5iwACs.)

Sheng Yen. *Attaining the Way: A Guide to the Practice of Chan Buddhism.* Boston: Shambhala Publications, 2006.

Shorter, Edward. *How Everyone Became Depressed: The Rise and Fall of the Nervous Breakdown.* Oxford: Oxford University Press, 2013.

Siegel, Daniel J. *The Mindful Brain.* New York: W. W. Norton, 2007.

Siegel, Ronald D. *The Mindfulness Solution.* New York: Guildford, 2010.

Soma Thera. *The Way of Mindfulness.* Colombo, Ceylon: Vajrarama, 1949.

Thanissaro Bhikkhu. "Mindfulness Defined." accesstoinsight.org/lib/authors/thanissaro/mindfulnessdefined.html, 2008.

Wallace, B. Alan. *The Attention Revolution.* Somerville, MA: Wisdom, 2006.

Whitaker, Robert. *Anatomy of an Epidemic: Magic Bullets, Psychiatric Drugs, and the Astonishing Rise of Mental Illness in America.* New York: Crown, 2010.

Williams, J. Mark, John Teasdale, Zindel Segal, and Jon Kabat-Zinn. *The Mindful Way through Depression.* New York: Guildford, 2007.

Williams, Mark, and Danny Penman. *Mindfulness: An Eight-Week Plan for Finding Peace in a Frantic World.* New York: Rodale, 2011.

Williams, J. Mark G., and Jon Kabat-Zinn, eds. *Mindfulness: Diverse Perspectives on Its Meaning, Origins, and Applications.* New York: Routledge, 2013.

U Pandita. *In This Very Life.* Boston: Wisdom, 1992.

Vago, David R., and David A. Silbersweig. "Self-Awareness, Self-Regulation, and Self-Transcendence (S-ART): A Framework for Understanding the Neurobiological Mechanisms of Mindfulness." *Frontiers in Human Neuroscience* 6 (October 2012): 1–30.

INDEX

ABOUT THE AUTHOR

ERIC HARRISON was born in Wellington, New Zealand, in 1949. He graduated from Victoria University with a BA in English literature and music, and started his working life as a schoolteacher and journalist. Between 1974 and 1985 he spent a total of 18 months doing retreats in the Burmese, Tibetan, Zen, and yoga traditions. While he appreciated the opportunities to do long retreats, he found he had no appetite for Buddhism itself.

When Eric opened the Perth Meditation Centre in 1987, he chose to use secular, rational, and science-based language to explain meditation. He later supplemented his knowledge with five years' study in biology, cognitive science, and Western philosophy. This approach made his work acceptable to the many doctors and psychologists who referred clients to him, and to corporations that have employed him since. He has now taught 30,000 people how to meditate, and his previous six books, including *Teach Yourself to Meditate* and *The 5-Minute Meditator*, have been translated into 14 languages.